OP

6 ⁵⁰

FROM *DESIRE* TO *GODOT*

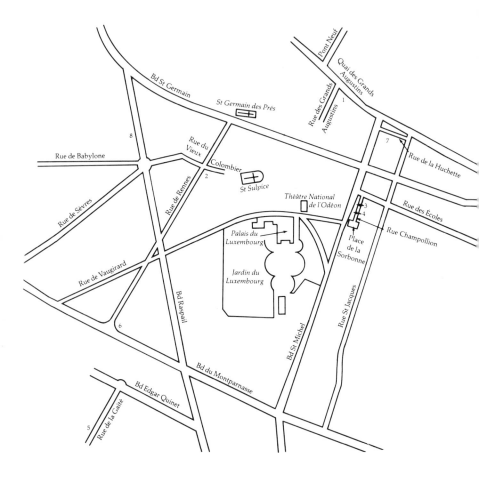

1 53 bis Quai des Grands Augustins
2 Théâtre du Vieux Colombier
3 Théâtre du Noctambules
4 Théâtre du Quartier Latin
5 Théâtre de la Gaîté Montparnasse
6 Théâtre de Poche
7 Théâtre de la Huchette
8 Théâtre de Babylone

FROM *DESIRE* TO *GODOT*

POCKET THEATER OF
POSTWAR PARIS

RUBY COHN

University of California Press
Berkeley · Los Angeles · London

University of California Press
Berkeley and Los Angeles, California

University of California Press, Ltd.
London, England

© 1987 by
The Regents of the University of California

Library of Congress Cataloging-in-Publication Data
Cohn, Ruby.
From Desire to Godot.

Includes index.
1. Experimental theater—France—Paris.
2. Theaters—France—Paris.   3. Theater—France—
Paris—History—20th century.   4. Drama—20th
century—History and criticism.   I. Title.
PN2636.P3C53   1987   792'.022   86–16156
ISBN 0–520–05825–9 (alk. paper)

Printed in the United States of America

1   2   3   4   5   6   7   8   9

I am grateful for research funds awarded by the University of
California, Davis, which encouraged this humanistic research, despite the school's bias in favor of science. To Geneviève Latour and Dorothy Knowles I offer sincere thanks for
sharing their research on Paris pocket theater. For scrupulous
care of this manuscript, I warmly thank Stephanie Fay, Doris
Kretschmer, Marilyn Schwartz. I am most grateful to Denise
Helmer for battling French press agencies to obtain some of
the pictures in this book.

To John Russell Brown for the inception
Bernard Dort for the conception
Martin Esslin and Leonard Pronko for inspection

On n'écrit pas la véritable histoire du théâtre
qu'avec des succès.

—Charles Dullin

Contents

List of Illustrations

Preface

> If you are lucky enough to have lived in Paris as a young man, then wherever you go for the rest of your life, it stays with you, for Paris is a moveable feast.
>
> Ernest Hemingway to a friend in 1950

At that time—1944 to 1953—a student would savor the myth of Paris, while witnessing how the actual city inched toward full palette: geometric mounds of fresh fruit seasonally enriched, bursts of cloth to be clipped to fashion, a graceful gleam of bicycles not yet outnumbered by automobiles, uncut pages of uncensored and unbound books, an immediacy of theater in small, close houses. At that time—1944 to 1953—romantic fantasy wafted students to the Latin Quarter of Paris, a privileged domain since the year 1200. Young people abandoned old provinces and slipped through new frontiers. In those years before plebeians flew, they came by ship or rail. Or even on foot. They spent more time in cafés than in classrooms. With meager and inconstant funds, they nevertheless bought books on the quais, peered at art in dark galleries, shivered in the dim intimacy of pocket theaters.

Those theaters are the subject of this book—by one of those students. Although no other book limits itself to the theater of that decade, several of its plays have been reviewed, discussed, dissected. In France these performances of my youth are still called New Theater. A few of the plays, taught in classrooms, are hallowed as classics; many more of them are forgotten. My book seeks to recapture performances in their time, while noting that we are now in another time. Through the years, these plays have been grouped under several rubrics—antitheater, theater of the absurd, blasphemous thea-

ter, metatheater, theater of protest and paradox, compression-
ist theater, theater of derision, metaphysical theater, theater
of misfits, theater of rupture, shocking theater. Whatever the
label, that theater was born in a heady climate of war-end.
Beginning with a manifold *Desire* that was performed during the intermittently dark Occupation of Paris, I end on the
bright moon of *Waiting for Godot*. From the dozens of new
plays produced during the decade 1944–1953 I have made a
deliberately eclectic selection that seems to me to reflect the
energetic disorganization of the arts at that time. For the Anglophone reader the selection may seem arcane as well as arbitrary, since I describe several plays that have not been translated. By this focus I hope to convey a sense of the climate of
French little theater before a surprising number of the plays
entered the international theater repertory. Although I offer
some information not previously published, I address this
book to any readers who are beguiled by at least one of "my"
plays and who may wish to trace the dramas to their origin.

Plays are not conceived in a vacuum, and avant-garde theater was already a Paris tradition by the mid–twentieth century.
My first chapter sketches a review of that tradition, but the
body of the book is devoted to an account of remarkably varied performances during a decade of pocket theater. As modern criticism has taught us, description is itself interpretation,
but the many ramifications of *Waiting for Godot* demand a view
in wider perspective. That tragicomedy's last words are "Yes,
let's go." Although Vladimir and Estragon do not move, it is
time to obey what they say rather than what they (do not) do.

1

Paris and Theater

Françoise: We love Paris, its streets, its cafés.
Xavière: How can one love sordid places, ugly things,
and all those nasty people?

I was formed by the past, continued Labrousse. The Bal-
lets Russes, the Vieux-Colombier, Picasso, Surrealism; I
would be nothing without all that. And of course, I want to
make an original contribution to the art of the future, but it
has to be the future of that tradition. One can't work in a
void; that leads nowhere.

Simone de Beauvoir, *L'Invitée*

A POCKET HISTORY

Paris offered an early home to theater. At the turn of the first
century the Romans built a theater in what was then Lutetia
Parisiorum. Buried for centuries, the Lutèce Arena was un-
covered in the nineteenth century, and in 1921 it inspired the
directorial prowess of Firmin Gémier, who had earlier enacted
the original King Ubu; in 1961 Ariane Mnouchkine, who later
founded the Théâtre du Soleil, conceived a mammoth spectacle for the arena. Between these two dates—in 1939, to be
exact—Samuel Beckett titled a French poem for this amphi-
theater; in "Arènes de Lutèce" Beckett's persona is at once
actor and audience of his own acting, and the poem implies
an irretrievable past resonating from the entrance on the Rue
des Arènes and an inscrutable present hovering at the entrance on the Rue Monge.[1] However it may attract poets, the
arena has left no trace of what was performed before the original audience of Romans and Gauls, an early ethnic mix of
some seventeen thousand spectators. The basic structure of

the arena stands triumphant over war and weather, but performance fades into evanescent memories—even recent performance.

In Paris Roman lettering on concrete rectangles commemorates places and events capriciously culled from the past, but few plaques name theaters, which proliferated only in the eighteenth century. Yet theater as activity rather than building is uninterrupted in Paris after the fifteenth century. Jugglers, minstrels, farceurs, both amateurs and professionals, beckoned seductively to students and tourists, whose descendants were enticed by strident Romantic playwrights in 1830, by André Antoine's Naturalists in 1887, Paul Fort's Idealists in 1890, Aurélien Lugné-Poe's Symbolists in 1893. Turn-of-the-century artistic effervescence has been vividly evoked by Roger Shattuck in his *Banquet Years*, and it is against such artistic banquets that Jacques Copeau, the critic, inveighed before Jacques Copeau as a director created his own Spartan performances for an elite audience to which he frankly appealed when he founded the Vieux-Colombier Theater: "The public that we first intend to reach is a minority public composed partly of people who no longer want to encourage the banalities and falsities of the commercial theater, and partly of a new contingent of humanity. We hope to recruit the first section of this public in our neighborhood among a cultivated elite, students, writers, artists, foreign intellectuals who live in the old Latin Quarter."[2]

The Latin Quarter, that den of instruction, held no monopoly on cultural experimentation. Nor were official theaters always located on the Right Bank of the Seine. However, the earliest durable Paris theater company, the Confraternity of the Passion, did cling to the Right Bank during its long history.[3] As early as 1402 the company performed Passion plays in the Hospital of the Trinity on Rue St. Denis, today specializing in sex for sale. The Confraternity performed both outdoors and inside; in 1548 it built a theater on land once owned by the dukes of Burgundy—the Hôtel de Bourgogne—near today's Rue Etienne-Marcel. No sooner was the theater completed than the guild was forbidden to perform its mixture of sacred and profane plays. By the end of the sixteenth century the Confraternity was renting its theater profitably.

Early in the seventeenth century Cardinal Richelieu equipped a theater in his Palais-Royal so as to present the tragedy he had penned, and by 1634 the Marais theater opened in an indoor tennis court. In 1660 Louis XIV gave Richelieu's theater to Molière's company, whose main competitor was lodged in the Marais theater. After Molière's death in 1673, his troupe absorbed the Marais group, and the enlarged company played in another converted tennis court, Hôtel Guénégaud on the Left Bank on Rue Mazarine.

In 1680 Louis XIV created the Comédie-Française by merging the Guénégaud company with its competitor at the Hôtel de Bourgogne (wrested from the Confraternity in 1677), but the new national company did not acquire its own theater until 1689, after clerical opposition barred it successively from Hôtel de Sourdis, Nemours, and Lussan. The national company was then authorized to buy the indoor tennis court at today's 14 Rue de l'Ancienne Comédie, and they hired the architect François d'Orblay to design a sumptuous building with seats in what the French continue to call the *parterre*, "on the ground." The section of seats was ringed by three tiers of boxes, each holding eight chairs. This building served the national company from 1689 to 1770, offering the public 576 new plays as well as the classical dramas of Corneille, Racine, Molière. In 1759 three rows of onstage seats were removed, and for the first time the actors took possession of the entire performance space. In 1700 the Comédie-Française building and the old Hôtel de Bourgogne (rented exclusively by Italian actors) were the only active theaters in Paris. By 1754 there were five theaters, by 1774 ten, and by 1791 fifty-one theaters, or one less than in 1940.[4]

In 1782 the Comédie-Française inaugurated a new building at the Odéon, seating over two thousand spectators; its prestige was such that a street was paved to facilitate access—the first paved street in Paris, with gutters at the sides. By 1799 the Comédie acquired its present home on the Right Bank, the Salle Richelieu in the Palais-Royal, also seating about two thousand spectators. In 1980 the three hundredth anniversary of the Comédie-Française was marked by a gigantic exhibition at the National Library, but there were no commemorative performances at the Salle Richelieu because it was undergoing extensive renovation, which left its seating hierarchy intact and its seating capacity at about nine hundred.

These dry facts and figures reflect the orthodoxy of a continuous French theater tradition, but rebellion erupted in the eighteenth century when the Comédie actors alone were awarded the privilege of speaking dialogue. Around and against this voluble royal favor other theaters mushroomed, sometimes in tents at the fairs of Left Bank St. Germain or Right Bank St. Laurent. By the middle of the eighteenth century unused Right Bank forts were appropriated by enterprising showmen, notably Jean-Baptiste Nicolet on the Boulevard du Temple, near what was later to be the Place de la République.[5] The energy of Nicolet's motto—"De plus en plus fort"—imbued melodrama a century later, and its spirit endures in the work of such twentieth-century directors as Georges Lavelli, Jacques Lebel, Antoine Vitez. Eighteenth-century entrepreneurs followed Nicolet into construction, and febrile theater activity also energized schools and homes. The *Journal des Spectacles* for July 16, 1793, announced: "If this goes on, Paris will have a theater in every street, an actor in every house, a musician in every basement, and an author in every garret." (Note the hierarchy!)[6]

One might add: "And a café near every theater." Legend has it that a Sicilian nobleman came to Paris in 1685 and opened the first establishment to serve a new aromatic brew—café. He gave the enterprise his own name—Procope, today a restaurant. When the Comédie alighted across the street in 1689, his fortune soared. Through the years, and then the centuries, cafés proliferated in Paris, and at the three hundredth anniversary of that Sicilian transplant, Paris had some seven thousand cafés in its twenty *arrondissements*.

If Francesco Procopio dei Coltelli (or his analogue) had not invented the café, theater workers would lead more arduous lives in Paris. Often dwelling far from their theaters, always working long and late hours while most of the world sleeps, theater people in Paris depend on cafés for sustenance, sometimes even for artistic sustenance. Bar, bistrot, and brasserie are varieties of the ubiquitous café, and the café as stage set has entered twentieth-century drama, as the public square was often the setting for classical French comedy.

At the turn of the twentieth century, painters congregated in the cafés of Montmartre. After World War I painters moved to the cafés of Montparnasse, especially the Dôme and the Select. Even Copeau's ascetic companions availed themselves of short-lived cafés near their whitewashed Vieux-Colombier theater before World War I. Surrealists of the 1920s met in Right Bank cafés near the newspapers where several of them worked when not surrealizing, but they also had a tributary at the Left Bank Deux Magots. For the Surrealists the café was at once an icon and an observation post: "The passersby, the clients, the list of prices, the arrangement of the curtains, everything was precious; everything there meant a possible meeting with a woman, a play on words, an object."[7]

Although Montparnasse was the artists' domain before World War II, cafés also burgeoned in St. Germain-des-Prés, and one of their denizens paid them homage: "The place lives, breathes, palpitates, and sleeps by virtue of three cafés that are as famous today as government buildings: the Deux Magots, Café de Flore, and Brasserie Lipp; each one has its high officials, heads of department, and paper-scratchers who may be novelists translated into twenty-six languages, painters without a studio, critics without a column, or ministers without portfolio. Art and politics shake hands there; the upstart and the upper crust rub shoulders; master and disciple duel in courtesies to see who will pay."[8]

By and large, these cafés remained French during the Nazi Occupation of Paris, and after the Liberation each was a joyous nucleus of a busy little atom. With the Liberation, too, came café-theaters, where a show entertained imbibers. Although my account will cleave to dramatic theater, the spontaneous informality of café-theaters spilled over to more ambitious stages.

The history of twentieth-century dramatic theater in France sounds almost like a royal lineage—André Antoine, Aurélien Lugné-Poe, Jacques Copeau, the Cartel, Jean-Louis Barrault, Jean Vilar. At mid-century some fifty theaters of Paris fell into three quite distinct groups: (1) two spacious subsidized houses for the classics; (2) boulevard or commercial theaters (near the city's boulevards, or main arteries) for problem plays and/or adultery comedies; (3) small, more adventurous places that I group as pocket theaters.

MODERN POCKET THEATER

The phrase "pocket theater" denotes small size, but it connotes experiment for a discriminating audience.[9] During the eighteenth century Paris aristocrats might perform in a salon converted to a small theater, but small experimental theaters trickled into existence only in the last decades of the nineteenth century, in vehement opposition to Boulevard melodrama and vaudeville as well as to the state-subsidized Comédie-Française. Most modern pocket theaters barely lasted through a theater season; actors performed bravely in ill-equipped rooms that accommodated fifty to three hundred spectators, whereas the usual Paris commercial theater starts at about five hundred.

The father of Paris pocket theater in our modern sense is the father of modern French theater, André Antoine (1858–1943). As enthusiastic about new theater architecture (which he was never able to initiate) as about an eclectic repertory (which was not limited to the Realism often associated with his name), Antoine played here and there in Paris. His Théâtre Libre occupied three inadequate sites. To performances in a meeting room of Le Cercle Gaulois in Montmartre (37 Passage de l'Elysée-des-Beaux-Arts, today Rue André-Antoine), Antoine delivered invitations on foot so as to save postage. For his first naturalistic set he wheeled his mother's furniture through the Paris streets to his makeshift theater. After scraping through one frugal season of performances, he managed in 1888 to rent an actual theater in Montparnasse. By 1893 he moved again to the Right Bank and soon afterwards to the newly built but inadequate Théâtre des Champs-Elysées. When the Théâtre Libre closed in 1896, it had produced nearly two hundred plays. Antoine was famous but still practically penniless. Only as head of the state-subsidized Odéon from 1906 to 1914 did he compensate for his early penury by directing a *Julius Caesar* with 45 actors, 250 extras, 60 musicians, 70 stagehands, and 100 miscellaneous workers.[10] It is not the Odéon, however, but the avant-garde Théâtre Libre that heralds modern theater, with Antoine demanding four main reforms: new plays, new sight lines, cheap seats, ensemble acting. And these remain watchwords in today's theater.

A student of Antoine's, Aurélien Lugné-Poe (1869–1940), is often cited as his Symbolist opponent (he added the name Poe in admiration of the American poet). Lugné-Poe desired a permanent theater even more fervently than Antoine, and he was even less successful in achieving it. Lugné's Théâtre de l'Oeuvre opened in 1894 in Les Bouffes du Nord, an old vaudeville house that Peter Brook was to refurbish in the 1970s. Of twenty-six productions of the Oeuvre in its first seven years, nineteen took place at the Nouveau Théâtre—*nouveau* indeed, but not quite a theater since it had been built in 1891 as an annex to the Casino de Paris on Rue Clichy, and nightclub noises were a discordant background for atmospheric Symbolist staging, although such sounds enhanced Alfred Jarry's *Ubu roi*, produced in 1896. A sympathetic critic wrote proudly of the Nouveau: "There is only one place in the world, Paris, that could gather such an audience full of intelligence, attention, clairvoyance, and daring."[11] Hardly a pocket theater, the Nouveau could contain a thousand spectators, of whom on a typical evening a hundred might pay.

The first sustained avant-garde theater of Paris was the Vieux-Colombier of Jacques Copeau (1879-1949).[12] This intrepid director entered the theater by sheer willpower. After collaborating with André Gide to found the still prestigious *Nouvelle Revue Française* in 1909, Copeau wielded an acid pen against the theater of his time, where the clichés of *La Belle Epoque* anachronistically lingered on into the early twentieth century, in spite of Antoine and Lugné. In 1913, at age thirty-four, without formal training in the theater but with the support of such literati as Léon-Paul Fargue, Georges Duhamel, Henri Ghéon, André Gide, Jules Romains, and Roger Martin du Gard, Copeau founded a company to renovate French theater. At his mother's home, some fifty miles from Paris, Copeau spent a summer training his company physically and metaphysically. Although Konstantin Stanislavsky had charted the way, Copeau was the first Frenchman—there would be others—who demanded not only a professional but a total commitment to an ideal of theater. He in turn committed his theater to the actors, virtually eliminating the scenery and costumes whose flamboyance had seduced the nineteenth-century spectator.

Renting one of the many unused old theaters of melodrama available in pre–World War I Paris, Copeau renamed it for the street of its location, Vieux-Colombier, "old dovecote" (with its felicitous resonance of purity), and he chose two doves as the theater's emblem. Copeau stripped away the many decorations that usurped the old theater's stage space—chandeliers, pictures, mirrors, sculpted garlands. Although the proscenium arch remained, it was denuded of ornament and painted black. Boxes, those focal points for reciprocal ogling, were removed so as to preclude an offstage spectacle in the theater. The stage itself, thrust forward, was ascetically bare, giving rise to Copeau's clarion call: "Pour l'oeuvre nouvelle, qu'on nous laisse le tréteau nu"(For new works, give us the bare boards). Although classics rather than new works were the spine of Copeau's repertory, his bare-boards approach inspired such later theater artists as Jean Vilar, Jerzy Grotowski, Eugenio Barba, and Ariane Mnouchkine.

Copeau's radical reforms became talismanic in the avant-garde: "The willful sobriety of the auditorium, the unvarying scene structure, the refusal to take on any actor 'corrupted by success,' the ban on tips to program sellers, the Wagnerian bolting of the doors as soon as the houselights went down—

all this added up to 'les Folies-Calvin' in the eyes of some of Copeau's contemporaries."[13] With nearly five hundred seats, the Vieux-Colombier opened to provocative comment in October 1913. It attracted four thousand season subscribers before World War I closed it. When Copeau's company returned from New York after the war, he imposed an even stricter geometry on the structure of the theater, reducing the seating capacity to 360. Through Copeau's rigorous hands passed the actor-directors Charles Dullin and Louis Jouvet, and in 1920 Copeau founded a theater school that has served as a model for many others.

It is a commonplace of theater history that French theater was dominated by directors between World War I and World War II and by playwrights after World War II. Antoine, Lugné-Poe, and Copeau, still active during the first period, were joined in their chorus against commerce by four younger men—Charles Dullin and Louis Jouvet, who were trained by Copeau; the Russian Georges Pitoëff, who had assembled an international company during seven years in Switzerland; and Gaston Baty, the only nonactor, who had, however, worked with the actor Firmin Gémier. These four directors began in pocket theaters but were in time able to play in larger houses.

The so-called Cartel (of these four younger men) had an accidental birth in 1927.[14] As Voltaire in the eighteenth century had objected to the privileged aristocrats who sat on the stage, Dullin objected to the admission of latecomers once the performance had begun. When the curtain rose on his production of Aristophanes' *Birds*, Dullin ordered the theater doors closed, and a well-known reviewer (Fortunat Strowski) was refused admission. Vanity wounded, several of his colleagues persuaded their journals to refuse advertisements for Dullin's Atelier. The director reacted by summoning an aviator friend to drop publicity leaflets from his plane, but Jouvet suggested a more practical response. He invited the support of Baty and Pitoëff in boycotting the publications that boycotted Dullin. Faced with this rebellion, the journalists surrendered, and the cartel of four directors continued to cooperate when it was to their mutual advantage, sharing subscription lists, buying joint advertisements, and coordinating publicity, but each went his own aesthetic way. Celebrated today, all four were often in perilous financial straits in their several theaters, which were commercial in ambition since their seating capacity was about five hundred.

Copeau endowed his most-favored heir Louis Jouvet (1887–1951) with the Vieux-Colombier actors and subscription lists. Jouvet spent a dozen years in the middle-sized theater of the Champs-Elysées complex on the Right Bank, on Avenue Montaigne. More to his taste were his dozen years (six before World War II and six after) at the Right Bank Athénée (today named after Jouvet) before whose 450 seats he directed Molière and Giraudoux to acclaim. During the German Occupation of Paris, faced with playing Schiller and Goethe rather than French classics, Jouvet took his company first to Switzerland, then to South America, returning to the Athénée only in 1945.

His colleague from the Vieux-Colombier, Charles Dullin (1885–1949), founded a theater school before he established a theater, hence the name of the eventual theater—Atelier, "studio." For several years critics dismissed Dullin's theater as a "student theater." Dullin's first production was staged in his apartment in the northern part of Paris (177 Boulevard Péreire). After an out-of-town stint, he moved from a store on the Left Bank (7 Rue Honoré Chevalier) to an old theater on Rue des Ursulines and then back to the Vieux-Colombier before he rented a century-old theater in northern Paris in 1922. Gradually he remodeled it to his needs, and by the time he left it in 1940, Place Dancourt (today Place Charles Dullin) was a picturesque legend with its 580-seat theater, well-manicured trees, small police station, and outdoor urinal (for men only). Dullin's disciples filled the prewar and postwar Paris stage: Antonin Artaud, Tanya Balachova, Jean-Louis Barrault, Marguerite Jamois, Jean Marais, Madeleine Robinson, Raymond Rouleau, Jean-Marie Serreau, Jean Vilar, Michel Vitold.

The nonactor Gaston Baty (1885–1952) was seduced by what we would today call high tech, and he equipped his several theaters accordingly. In contrast to Copeau, Dullin, and Jouvet, who valued words highly, he in 1921 scorned "Sire le mot." After a stint at the middle-sized Comédie des Champs-Elysées, Baty built what he called a *baraque* (shanty) in a garage at 143 Boulevard St. Germain, where Hôtel Madison now stands. Though the *baraque* lasted only forty-seven days, its reforms made an impression—the elimination of boxes and balcony, the enlargement of the stage to four different playing areas, the limitation of props to geometric objects, and the installation of a sophisticated (for 1922) lighting system. In less than a year Baty was bankrupt, retreating to the newly built Studio des Champs-Elysées with its 240 seats. In 1928 he rented the large Théâtre de l'Avenue, but by 1930 he was back on the Left Bank at the small Théâtre Montparnasse, which now bears his name. Baty remained there until 1947, when he shifted from live actors to marionettes. Nevertheless, his hundredth stage production was celebrated with actors at the subsidized Odéon on January 11, 1949. Illness forced him south to Aix, where he died in 1952.

The fourth member of the Cartel, Russian-born Georges Pitoëff (1884–1939), was something of a poor relation, even though (or perhaps because) he directed the most impressive repertory—Chekhov, Pirandello, Ibsen, O'Neill, Cocteau, Gide, Lenormand, and above all Shakespeare. After seven years in Geneva (1915–1922), Pitoëff moved his company to Paris, where he wandered impecuniously from theater to theater, mainly on the Right Bank—Théâtre des Arts, Comédie des Champs-Elysées, Théâtre des Mathurins, Théâtre de l'Oeuvre, Théâtre de l'Avenue, Vieux-Colombier. No Paris theater now bears his name. In 1936, under the Popular Front government, when the playwright Edouard Bourdet as head of the Comédie-Française appointed Baty, Copeau, Dullin, and Jouvet to direct there—Pitoëff did not receive official recognition, although he was the favorite of such powerful critics as Robert Brasillach (who translated Seneca's *Medea* for him).

The path of these directors led from avant-garde pocket theaters to larger, well-publicized, sometimes subsidized houses. But Antonin Artaud (1896–1948) was destined for a permanent avant-garde. Acting for Dullin and Lugné, wishing to act for the others, he became the major influence on directors of the second half of the twentieth century. The first of his many manifestos dates from 1924, and in 1926 he persuaded two friends to join him in founding the Théâtre Alfred Jarry, which could find resources for only four productions in eight evenings over a period of eighteen months. Discouraged by the lack of funds, the hostility of the Surrealists, and poor critical reception, Artaud allowed the Théâtre Alfred Jarry to die, but he crystallized his vision of theater after seeing the Balinese dancers in the Colonial Exposition of Paris in 1931. Letters, manifestos, and articles almost blistered the pages as he penned plans for a Theater of Cruelty. In a large boulevard theater, he directed and acted in *Les Cenci*, which ran for seventeen indifferently greeted performances. Before fleeing to Mexico, Artaud gathered what he had written about the theater between 1931 and 1935 and entitled the collection *The Theater and Its Double* (*Le Théâtre et son double*)—one of the most influential books on the theater ever published.[15] But not in 1938, when the four hundred copies printed went virtually unnoticed.

World War II had little effect on Paris theater. By the beginning of the war Artaud was in an asylum. Pitoëff died in 1939, Jouvet went to South America, and Baty was relatively inactive, but Dullin became head of the Théâtre de la Cité. Theater flourished during the Occupation since it was encouraged by the Nazis and often subsidized by Vichy.[16] After the Germans were gone, a new generation of theater workers seized the opportunity to break uncensored theater ground. In contrast to members of the generously funded Comédie-Française, which had two houses after 1946, these young men sought new plays, their enthusiasm compensating for frugal resources. Dingy pocket theaters first housed unusual works that excited the imagination. Rather than following a common style, each director shaped what he loved.

Pierre-Aimé Touchard headed the Comédie-Française between 1947 and 1959 when pocket theater peppered Paris, but only after his retirement did he recognize the abyss between his official formulations and the avant-garde: "Our betrayal was to banish the irrational from the theater. It was to banish madness from the theater; it was to close our eyes to the fact that we are living in a world of madness, in an absurd world, and that we have to use all sonic means, all vocal means, all lighting effects to explode what might be called the aesthetic comfort within which we lived without noticing that we were lying to ourselves. For our young generation, we the older one are hypocrites."[17]

After World War II Jean-Louis Barrault and Madeleine Renaud left the Comédie-Française, not because of its hypocrisy but because as *sociétaires* (lifetime voting members) they were not permitted to act outside of the Comédie. (This rule no longer holds.) They formed their own company and rented the Théâtre Marigny near the American Embassy and the Champs-Elysées, where they remained from 1946 to 1959. After directors less famous than Barrault had risked playing in pocket theaters, he built the Petit Marigny in 1954. Similarly, he initiated a Petit Odéon of one hundred seats four years after the company moved to the subsidized Odéon in 1959. (In 1984 the Petit Odéon became the Salle Roger Blin.) Pocket theaters were also attached to the larger Renaud-Barrault Theaters at the Quai d'Orsay and at the Rond-Point des Champs-Elysées.

The post–World War II pocket-theater directors managed deviously to survive, though not always as directors. A distinction should be made between theater directors, or managers (*directeurs* in French), and directors of plays, or artists (*animateurs* in French), but both lived precariously. The *animateurs*—Tanya Balachova, Nicholas Bataille, Roger Blin, Marcel Cuvelier, Sylvain Dhomme, Jacques Mauclair, André Reybaz, Jean-Marie Serreau, Georges Vitaly—played musical theaters (on analogy with musical chairs) in low-rent houses almost always managed by others. The Russian-born director Vitaly describes the climate: "Post-Liberation Paris was a fine place for performance so long as you could get along with almost nothing! There was a double force: on the one hand, modern playwrights who hadn't been played and on the other hand, *animateurs* like Reybaz, Serreau, Mauclair, Blin, or myself who wanted to stir things up. . . . So we began to look for different places, sometimes ratholes where we had to do everything ourselves."[18]

Among the "different places" were three Right Bank theaters: (1) The Oeuvre at 55 Rue de Clichy was managed by André Barsacq, who rented it cheaply on Tuesday, its dark night; (2) The Lancry at 10 Rue de Lancry, an unused cinema, was not far from the nineteenth-century Boulevard of Crime, so called after the most popular kind of melodrama; (3) In contrast, the Studio des Champs-Elysées was located in a fashionable building of a fashionable quarter of Paris, easily reached from the Left Bank by bus, less easily by subway and foot. Yet the Studio was second only to the Vieux-Colombier in its continuous avant-garde tradition, that oxymoron. Under instructions from Jacques Hébertot, the manager of the Champs-Elysées complex of theaters on the Avenue Montaigne, Louis Jouvet drew up plans for a small experimental theater on the third floor. It opened in 1923 with Theodore Komisarjevsky as artistic director. In 1924 Baty became the artistic director for four years; then other directors came and went until the theater closed before World War II. After the Occupation the Studio was remodeled by a Copeau alumnus, Maurice Jacquemont, but Copeau would have hated the red plush seats if not the two banks of five-seat rows stretching back for fourteen rows from the narrow proscenium stage. As manager Jacquemont welcomed musical comedies in the American style as well as the plays of Lorca and the mime work of Marcel Marceau. Relinquishing artistic control only in 1972, Jacquemont balanced the needs of two audiences— that of appreciators of the avant-garde for art theater and that of a bourgeois clientele for an entertainment house. During his tenure the Studio was the only theater willing to present the French premiere of Beckett's *Endgame* (*Fin de partie*), occasioning a letter from the author to his American director Alan Schneider: "The Royal Court is not big, but 'Fin de Partie' gains unquestionably in the greater smallness of the Studio." And: "In the little Studio des Champs-Elysées the hooks [of *Fin de partie*] went in."[19]

Unlike these scattered Right Bank pocket theaters, those on the Left Bank could be contained in a circle with a three-mile diameter. The oldest theater, the Noctambules, dates from 1894, when it opened as a nightclub on the Rue Champollion, a few steps from the Rue des Ecoles. Now a cinema, the Noctambules has no plaque to inform us that Racine and Balzac once lived there—in different centuries, to be sure. In 1939 two Belgians, Pierre Leuris and Jean-Claude, converted the Noctambules from a nightclub to a 240-seat theater. They survived the Occupation on the strength of a single play, *End of the Road* (*Le Bout de la route*) by Jean Giono. Vichy and the Nazis both sang the praises of nature as opposed to the decadent city, and Giono painted the tragic nobility of a man at home in stark natural surroundings. After the Occupation, the Belgian owners welcomed less pastoral spectacles. In 1952 the Noctambules was bought by Fernand Voiturin, who wanted to encourage new theater and therefore appointed André Reybaz as artistic director. The latter produced his favorite playwrights, whom he saw as Dionysian—Ugo Betti, Michel de Ghelderode, Jacques Vauthier. As a result of allowing Reybaz a free hand, Voiturin was bankrupt by 1957, and Reybaz thereupon limited himself to acting and directing.

Next door to the Noctambules another nightclub became the Latin Quarter Theater, hospitable at first to skits and then to short plays. Director Michel de Ré welcomed sketches by Roland Dubillard, Jacques Prévert, and Jean Tardieu and then graduated to the full-length plays of Guillaume Hanoteau and Armand Salacrou. In 1954 the director Jacques Mauclair rented the theater for Ionesco's *Victims of Duty* (*Victimes du devoir*), shortly before debts dictated the conversion of the Latin Quarter Theater to still another cinema.

Another nightclub-turned-theater was managed by the actor-director Roger Blin. Because his Greek friends the actress Christine Tsingos and her husband, a painter, were not legally eligible to manage a theater in France, Blin signed the lease for the Gaité Montparnasse on the aptly named Rue de la Gaité. Assuming control in May 1949, Blin produced Denis Johnston's *Moon on the Yellow River*, which failed critically and commercially. In the fall Blin directed Strindberg's *Ghost Sonata*, but he could not lure an audience to this street of nightclubs. Or if he did, they expected other entertainment. On Christmas Eve at *Ghost Sonata* an impatient drunk called out: "Alors? et les petites femmes, ça vient?"[20] Realizing what he had suspected—that managing a profitable theater was not his forte—Blin resigned in 1951. But extricating himself did not prove so simple. As manager, he was responsible for the pocket theater's debts, and during the following thirty years a fraction of his earnings was deducted toward their payment. He might even have gone to debtor's prison were it not for de Gaulle's pardon—of this inveterate leftist. Blin died January 20, 1984, having received few subsidies and little recognition from French governments of diverse political complexions.

Two Left Bank pocket theaters were constructed by obsessive tenacity. The smaller of the two is appropriately named Théâtre de Poche, "Pocket Theater." It was the brainchild of Marcel Oger, who had degrees in law and letters. Responding in 1942 to the widely proclaimed encouragement of youth by both Vichy and Occupation authorities, Oger decided to open a theater for young unknowns. He leased an empty storeroom on the ground floor of 75 Boulevard du Montparnasse, near the corner of the Rue de Rennes. He then financed and supervised the slow conversion of the empty space to a small theater, which opened as soon as the stage was built—6.9 meters wide, a scant 2.75 meters deep, and only 2.6 meters high. Sixty mismatched seats were acquired from cafés, apartments, movie houses. Three rheostats controlled the few lights.

Although Oger was forty years old in 1942, he sought out theater enthusiasts half his age. The theater opened insignificantly enough during the Occupation, but by 1943 it housed Jean Vilar's second production—Strindberg's *Storm* (on a double bill with *Césaire* by NRF author Jean Schlumberger). Acting Strindberg's Gentleman as well as directing, Vilar began to gather a company that would eventually become the National Popular Theater. In 1943, however, Vilar had to borrow thirty thousand francs (about eighty dollars) to rent the Poche for the legal minimum of thirty performances. Soon after Vilar came another remarkable beginner—Marcel Marceau with his mute Bip.

Oger managed the Poche off and on until 1949. The theater then fell to a series of short-term renters relatively well known in France—Pierre Valde, France Guy, Marcel Cuvelier, and finally André Cellier, who briefly opened a Right Bank Poche. In 1956 the directors Etienne Berry and Renée Delmas took possession of the theater and renovated it to its present dimensions, a stage still 6.9 meters wide but double the original depth at 4.5 meters. The theater has a modern light panel and one hundred comfortable seats, still separated by an aisle. (A smaller theater was constructed next door.) During the 1960s the renovated Poche was distinguished by actor-authors who are unknown outside of France—Roland Dubillard, Romain Bouteille, Claude Cyriaque, Victor Haïm, Romain Weingarten. The Poche has remained a "literary" theater specializing in nonrealistic plays that demand a subtle nuance not easy to obtain from French actors. After forty years it is the longest lived of the Left Bank pocket theaters, but the unfamiliar names in these paragraphs testify to the rapid turnover of pocket-theater dreamers.

One such dreamer was attracted to the Rue de la Huchette after World War II. The street was already a favorite of Rabelais's in the sixteenth century, and it was also rumored that Abbé Prévost wrote *Manon Lescaut* on that short street. In the twentieth century Rue de la Huchette acquired notoriety as the protagonist of Elliot Paul's *Last Time I Saw Paris*. Paul devotes little space to 23 Rue de la Huchette, which had once belonged to an alchemist but was merely a flower shop before World War II. After the war, the shop was bought by Marcel Pinard, who owned his own cleaning establishment (not on that street). With no experience of theater, Pinard had happened upon a volume of Stanislavsky (in French) and became an instant convert. He taught himself to act by following the precepts of the Russian master, but no Paris director wanted to hire him. Undaunted, he decided to found his own theater, but the cost of renting a theater was prohibitive, so he bought the shop space at 23 Rue de la Huchette. Hiring cheap labor to construct the rudiments of a theater, he decided to take a few formal acting lessons, and in his class was Georges Vitaly, whom he chose as his artistic director. Vitaly in turn chose André Reybaz to direct the first play at what turned out to be a ramshackle eighty-seat house. With a few box-office failures behind him, Reybaz chose an Italian play to be translated by Jacques Audiberti, a writer he admired. *Albertina* by Valentino Bompiani, a romantic tale of passion and adultery during wartime, opened in April 1948. Bompiani invited to the opening Paris Italians who lived a dolce vita, but he did not contribute money to the production.

Vitaly's tenure at the Huchette lasted from April 1948 to December 1951, and he left in triumph. He directed *La Belle Rombière* by Guillaume Hanoteau and André Wiener, a miniature musical so popular that crowds came down to queue for tickets on the narrow street. All traffic—vehicular and foot—was impeded, and the police chief of the area (far less amiable than the one described by Elliot Paul) ordered Vitaly to transfer to a larger theater, so he did.

Another young director, Nicholas Bataille, thereupon moved into the Huchette with a production of Eugène Ionesco's *Bald Soprano* (*Cantatrice chauve*). In 1952 for the first time there was a double bill of *The Bald Soprano* and *The Lesson* (*La Leçon*) at the Huchette, and afterward a series of performances lumbered in and out until the same double bill returned in 1957, to remain for the next quarter century and beyond. At the death in 1975 of Marcel Pinard, who had conceived and constructed the theater, the Ionesco actors formed a corporation to control the Huchette.

Like the Poche and the Huchette, the Babylone was converted to a theater because of the vision of one man—Jean-Marie Serreau (1915–1973). Since Serreau had been trained as an architect before he became an actor-director, he wanted to build a new theater for new plays. (Later he would rebel against all formal theaters.) At 38 Boulevard Raspail, near the subway stop Sèvres-Babylone, he bought the lease for space used by Sillon, a left-wing Christian organization. With the help of the architect Pierre Dufau, Serreau drew plans for a theater with a movable proscenium and a rake in the auditorium; the engineer Pierre Sonrel designed a lighting system with twelve five-hundred-watt projectors, but the lack of funds caused a considerable stripping down, and the hero of the project was a mason who contributed his labor, only to have his name forgotten. The Club des Amis du Babylone was more generous with friendship than funds. Unlike the Huchette, which Pinard ran as an autocracy, the Babylone was incorporated as a workers' cooperative by a group of ten since they did not belong to the proper theater unions. Aside from Serreau, there were three actors, two directors, two composers, an accountant, and an administrator, Max Barrault, the brother of Jean-Louis. Before the cooperative members exercised their special skills, they cooperated on the physical construction of the theater—plastering, painting, doing carpentry, and installing lights and seats, 223 of them, removed one by one from an unused cinema. Their zest was infectious, and other members of what would be known as the New Theater contributed odd hours of hard work. Administrative chaos thrives on minimal funds, and as tempers frayed, the group coined its own comic condemnation: "It's a Babylone tale." Nevertheless, the newspaper *Combat* boasted on April 24, 1952, that the new construction would be a blend of gallery, garden, theater school, and theater "where one sees from every seat."

In May 1952, before the theater itself opened, the gallery displayed an exhibition of the School of Paris, that name of the 1920s for foreign painters in Paris, which had made the city the art center of the world between the two wars. Serreau hoped that the Babylone would be a home for avant-garde artists in music, painting, and film as well as theater. Convenient to bus and subway, the Babylone was located at the end of a cobblestoned courtyard. To the right slumbered two stone lions that looked as though they had been sculpted by

Douanier Rousseau. Before the door of the theater arched four acacia trees, as though patterned after the set of O'Neill's *Desire under the Elms*. The interior of the theater was red and pale gray. Long, narrow, and relatively bare, the Babylone clearly belonged to the same family as the Vieux-Colombier, but the red seats were a departure. The stage was six meters wide and five deep; despite Serreau's ambitious plans, there was no money for curtain or lights.

From the first, playwrights gravitated to the Babylone. The actress Eléanore Hirt was in charge of scripts, and she recalls receiving Husson's *Cuisine des anges*, Ionesco's *Rhinocéros*, Vauthier's *Personnage combattant*—plays that were successfully performed elsewhere after the rats had gnawed at them in the Babylone attic. For the Babylone opening, the cooperative chose Max Aldebert's *Spartacus*, whose theme of rebellion attracted the young artists. They may have been swayed by the hope of a subsidy for production of a first play—that farsighted fund that would support the first production of *Waiting for Godot*. Unlike *Godot*, however, *Spartacus* was a disaster. The usually encouraging Georges Neveux, himself a playwright, reviewed it: "The author, whose first play it is, and the director, whose first production it is (I believe) offer us an exercise in a style that is majestic and thoroughly boring."[21]

Serreau's enthusiasm never flagged. Instead of retrenching in an effort to balance the books, he continually launched new projects. Inspired by the state-subsidized Festival of Nations, which invited famous foreign companies to Boulevard theaters in Paris, he founded a festival of Left Bank theaters, to which he invited productions of Blin and Mauclair as well as the Babylone Cooperative directors Maurice Cazeneuve and Frank Sundstrom. Warned by government officials that he would be sued if he stole the word *festival*, Serreau named his enterprise Estival of Nations.

The Babylone was often full to capacity, but the number of tickets sold was limited. At no time did anyone suggest choosing a play to make money. *Spartacus* was followed by Strindberg's *Miss Julie*, then by Boris Vian's adaptation of George Kaiser's *Fire at the Opera*. During less than three years of existence the Babylone presented Pirandello, Beckett, Adamov, Jarry, Kafka, Brecht, Ionesco, and Dubillard, sometimes in repertory. When it was forced into bankruptcy (by the city's demand for an emergency exit), Strindberg's *Miss Julie*, Brecht's *Exception and the Rule*, and Ionesco's *Victims of Duty* were playing in rep. If ever a theater deserved to succeed, it was the Babylone.

During the 1950s other pocket theaters came and went—the Lutèce, the Alliance Française—but none was able to muster the verve of these early houses. Little did audiences dream that some of these performances would inform the culture of many countries. Lacking the specific aims of a Brecht or the sporadic madnesses of an Artaud, most of those theater dreamers floated on the fantasy of sheer effervescence.

Actors, directors, dramatists, and, less often, designers of that postwar period wanted theater to be at once meaningful and theatrical. They were thus severed from the two main sources of funds—the subsidies of houses that played mainly classics and the box office receipts of Boulevard houses that played mainly trivia. So they turned to pocket theater in order to have any theater at all. Except for Tuesday evenings at the Oeuvre, these theaters rented for a minimum of thirty performances, and it is under these minimal rental contracts that audiences first saw *Waiting for Godot*, *The Blacks*, and *The Chairs* as well as plays that have never been translated into English. As early as 1948 one of these untranslated playwrights, Jacques Audiberti, praised these pocket theaters: "Everybody shares the work in these little theaters, and the personal benefits are all the more concrete. Should one encourage a little theater with about a hundred seats, which combines the qualities of an explosive atom and the latest vogue? . . . [The actors] of these little theaters move in place, like cyclists in vaudeville. They pedal without advancing. Their strides measure three centimeters. But they refrain from showing the chains that impede them."[22]

2

Pocket Theater Performance
of Postwar Paris

Ionesco: (*At a Left Bank café table, spying Beckett and Genet strolling past in animated conversation*) Hey! Sam! Jean!

Genet: Hey, it's Eugene! Sam, it's Eugene!

Beckett: Well, I'll be damned. Hi there, Eugene boy.

Ionesco: Sit down, kids.

Genet: Sure thing.

Ionesco: (*Rubbing his hands together*) Well, what's new in The Theater of the Absurd?

Beckett: Oh, less than a lot of people think. (*They all laugh.*)

Edward Albee, "Which Theatre
Is the Absurd One?"

And we laugh too, at this 1962 sketch by Edward Albee, who does not wax nostalgic at the Paris Left Bank setting and who seems unaware of that paradox, a tradition of the avant-garde. Many avant-gardes have passed into the rear guard, and at this distance Albee's sketch does not seem so improbable. Although Beckett and Genet were not given to "animated conversation," they were inveterate strollers, and Ionesco could be convivial. "I'll be damned" has served Beckett as subtext, and his late plays imply that "less" is more.

The Albee sketch seems less improbable today than yesterday because the names of Beckett, Genet, and Ionesco are familiar throughout the "civilized" world. Unlike the famous Jean-Paul Sartre and Simone de Beauvoir or the less famous Arthur Adamov and Audiberti, they did not write in cafés. Albee's playwrights did not know one another at the beginning of their careers, but they soon knew *of* one another, and Albee captures in these few lines the feeling of an intimate clique in postwar Paris theater. More than the playwrights, actors and directors tended to form such cliques—of necessity, since they depended more immediately on one another. An analogous sketch might be composed about the actor-directors Roger Blin, Jean-Marie Serreau, and André Reybaz, but these names would not be familiar to Anglophone readers. Or, reverting to dramatists, one might substitute the names of Arthur Adamov, Jacques Audiberti, and Jean Vauthier, which are also unfamiliar to the English speaker. Publication, translation, and foreign performance ensured the durability of the Paris-based troika of Beckett, Genet, and Ionesco.

Reaching around them, I want to reset Beckett and Ionesco in the scrubby theaters where their works (unlike those of Genet) were first performed. Their familiar names will thus jostle strange ones. Their radical themes and techniques will be juxtaposed with a three-hundred-year-old French theater tradition, which has been summarized by the English critic James Agate: "The essence of French acting is pace. The mark of French enunciation is clarity. Of gesture, elegance. Of miming, appositeness."[1] Innovative postwar plays taint these essences, and even though some dozen performances may be woven into a continuous narrative, the continuity is largely fictional. The individual performances are inscribed in theater history, but few of the plays respond directly to the larger frame of history. During the Nazi Occupation of Paris, such a direct response would not have passed the censors; after the Occupation, such a response tended to take the weary old form of the realistic play. Since I seek innovation, Realism will be absent from my narrative, as it was from most of these small, poorly equipped theaters.

In June 1940, at the very beginning of the Nazi Occupation of Paris, Hitler announced: "It is our responsibility at several levels to preserve undamaged this wonder of Western civilization. We have succeeded."[2] They did indeed. At one level of civilization, music halls opened right after Paris was occupied in June 1940; at another level, the national theaters opened in August of that same year. By 1941 Parisians had at their disposal thirty-four theaters, fourteen music halls, two circuses, six cabarets, and about thirty cinemas.[3] Performance thrived in spite of censorship, in spite of transportation difficulties, in spite of economic stringency, in spite of the proscription of Jewish artists.

Theater was an easy escape from the everyday reality of the Occupation. Audiences might suffer air-raid alerts; they armed themselves with flashlights as they stumbled through dark streets between subway and theater; to obey the curfew that extended from midnight to 5 A.M., they rushed for the 11 P.M. subway, the last one, which prompted the title of François Truffaut's film, set in the Occupation. While in one of the thirty-four theaters, Parisians were in French surroundings into which a Nazi uniform rarely intruded. Although electric power might fail, there was power in the French language that resounded in the fashion honored through the centuries—long speeches in stentorian tones pitched at the audience. Costume rather than posture distinguished Boulevard acting from that of the Comédie-Française. The Popular Front government had attempted to reform the Comédie under the leadership of the playwright Edouard Bourdet, who had invited Gaston Baty, Jacques Copeau, Charles Dullin, and Louis Jouvet to direct, but these directors made no inroads on the acting.

Early in the Occupation Edouard Bourdet was injured in an air-raid blackout, and he appointed Jacques Copeau as a temporary replacement. The latter usurped the office, only to be dismissed by the Occupiers. Dullin accepted the management of the large Théâtre Sarah Bernhardt, also accepting the racially motivated change of name to Théâtre de la Cité. On temperamentally disorganized Paris the Nazis imposed a series of organizations under the umbrella of the Comité d'organization des entreprises de spectacle, in which membership was compulsory for all theater managers, who communicated with the Occupiers through a triumvirate of Baty, Dullin, and Pierre Renoir. Materials were rationed, but nonetheless sets and costumes were ingeniously concocted; paper was rationed, but posters and tickets could be scanted. Theater reviews appeared regularly in the collaborationist weeklies, and the prewar theater weekly *Comoedia* continued to publish. The anti-Vichy collaborationist weekly *La Gerbe* printed lively debates about censorship, as if there were any possibility of escaping its shackles. In contrast to book publishers, who voluntarily purged their lists, theater managers exercised quixotic caution in selecting plays for the Vichy-controlled government theaters and Nazi-controlled private theaters. No list survives of censored plays, but not surprisingly, German classics were forced into the Comédie repertory. Plays on Joan of Arc were encouraged, since she had fought the English. Jean Cocteau and François Mauriac were unpopular with the Germans, yet some of their plays passed the censors. During the Occupation there were productions of plays by Jean Anouilh, Albert Camus, Paul Claudel, Jean Giono, Jean Giraudoux, Henri de Montherlant, and Jean-Paul Sartre. Outside of prison camps there was no theater of the Resistance, although this distinction was later claimed for *The Flies* (*Les Mouches*) by Sartre (1943) and *Antigone* by Anouilh (1944). After examining the evidence, Patrick Marsh concludes: "There was no real interruption or change of direction in theater development between 1940 and 1944."[4] That direction was heavily verbal. On thirty-four stages from the former cabaret Noctambules to the rebaptized Théâtre de la Cité, actors framed by a proscenium and romanticized by footlights spoke with clarity, resonance, and the security of a long tradition.

DESIRE CAUGHT BY THE TAIL
(LE DÉSIR ATTRAPÉ PAR LA QUEUE)
Pablo Picasso

It was partly in revulsion at this business-as-usual attitude of Paris theater under the Occupation that on March 19, 1944, some hundred people gathered in a large living room that provided as much space as a pocket theater. That living room, on Quai des Grands-Augustins facing the Seine, belonged to Michel and Louise Leiris, who had bought the apartment in 1942. (Not only theater but also business went on much as usual during the Occupation.) Michel was a former Surrealist, an ethnologist, and a founder (with Georges Bataille and Roger Caillois) of the School of Sociology; he would attain literary acclaim as an autobiographer. His wife Louise—"Zette" to her friends—had purchased the gallery of her Jewish brother-in-law, Daniel-Henry Kahnweiler, to protect its treasures from the Nazis.

As a former Surrealist, Michel Leiris might have attended the first performance at the Théâtre Alfred Jarry in 1927, with its triple bill of short plays by founders Raymond Aron, Antonin Artaud, and Roger Vitrac. Accounts of that brief run are sparse, but Vitrac's play is still extant. Only three of the five scenes of his *Mysteries of Love* (*Les Mystères de l'amour*) were performed, with Raymond Rouleau in the lead. In the second scene, set in a small house on the Quai des Grands-Augustins, erotic rivals take unusual forms; moreover, the desired woman's parents are played by actors of opposite sexes—a man for the mother and a woman for the father; dismembered heads and arms assume an integrity of their own. Although the Leiris apartment on that same quai was far more lavishly furnished than the one on the Alfred Jarry stage, its visitors may have expected a comparable theatricalization of the Marvelous.

The Leiris's fourth-floor apartment at 53 bis Quai des Grands-Augustins, despite its five rooms facing the Seine, sometimes harbored Jews and Resistants during the Occupation, but they must have been safely absent on the evening of March 19, 1944. The Leiris home, rich in books and paintings, was a short walk away from Picasso's studio at 7 Rue des Grands-Augustins. Today no plaque marks the Leiris home, but golden letters honor Picasso. On the outside wall of 7 Rue des Grands-Augustins we can read: "Pablo Picasso lived in this building from 1936 to 1955. It is in this studio that he painted 'Guernica' in 1937. It is also here that BALZAC situated the action of his story 'The Unknown Masterpiece.'"

Unmentioned is Jean-Louis Barrault, who inhabited the studio after Balzac's fictional painter and before the real Picasso and who rehearsed there *Around a Mother* (*Autour d'une mère*), a performance piece based on Faulkner's *As I Lay Dying*. Although the piece was performed only four times, it was praised by Antonin Artaud, the self-proclaimed prophet of a new theater. In March 1944 Artaud suffered almost forgotten at Rodez Asylum while Barrault was an admired member of the Comédie-Française, where he triumphantly directed Paul Claudel's *Satin Slipper* (*Le Soulier de satin*).

Picasso is the most flagrant example of artistic liberty during the Occupation of Paris. An anti-Franco Spaniard, a friend of Jews and Communists, a sexual libertine, he was never harassed. A month before the presentation of *Desire*, Picasso's apolitical friend the Surrealist Robert Desnos was arrested; he would die within the year in Czechoslovakia. Two weeks before the presentation, Picasso's friend the poet Max Jacob died of pneumonia at Drancy, the French concentration camp for Jews. But Picasso was celebrated wherever he went.

Picasso composed *Desire* during the first winter of the Occupation, when many Parisians were eating turnips in dark cold rooms, and their ill-shod feet were the main means of transportation. In January 1941 the snow was so thick that Parisians went skiing at Porte de St. Cloud. The writer Colette, determinedly cheerful, describes the queues for milk, rutabagas, mayonnaise made without oil or eggs, and shoes made without leather, but she valiantly offers recipes to her readers.[5]

Picasso, the grand old master of new painting at age sixty, was not French, and he could have fled almost anywhere in the Old or New World, but he chose to remain in Paris. Although he was not a Surrealist, he had been idolized by André Breton, and *Desire* is sometimes viewed as Surrealistic automatic writing, since Picasso had earlier penned poems by indulgence of the unconscious. However, his biographer Roland Penrose describes a process of composition less spontaneous than Surrealist decorum would allow.[6]

On January 14, 1941, after a day of painting in his unheated

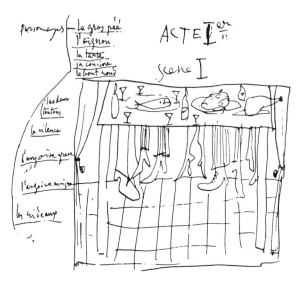

1.   Picasso drawing for *Desire Caught by the Tail*

studio, Picasso sat down at his round table and wrote a title in an old exercise book. He then drew a sketch of himself with pen in hand, as though viewed from above; he labeled this drawing "Portrait of the Author." Next he drew a rectangular banquet table from which dangled nine legs, like Christmas stockings. On the table are three bottles, six wine glasses, and three large platters on which lie, respectively, a fish, a roast, a ham. (The drawing line is strangely unsure—perhaps because of the cold, perhaps because of this venture into a new genre, drama.) The whole banquet is framed by open curtains. At the top left of this drawing are five names: Big Foot, Onion, Tart, her Cousin, Round End.[7] Down the left side of the drawing Picasso listed other characters: two Bow-Wows, Silence, Fat Anguish, Skinny Anguish, Curtains. (In the original French, Picasso's spelling is idiosyncratic.) A third drawing shows a nondescript room with stove and packages. A fourth is labeled Sordid's Hotel, and bare feet (rather than the customary shoes) perch outside five Roman-numbered doors. Finally, Picasso drew a lottery wheel and only then proceeded to supply a text for these scenes. The whole was completed between January 14 and 17, 1941.

The six acts of Picasso's *Desire* flout the classical five-act form, but Picasso's play still accommodates the towering protagonist of classical drama. This protagonist bears the farcical name Big Foot, which can easily be decoded as a different large member. Big Foot is a self-centered writer who is erotically involved with Tart. (In the original French *Tarte* is a foolish rather than a loose woman.) Discontinuously, the play traces the erotic affinity—desire—between Big Foot and Tart, who also interact with eight other characters. Three of Picasso's ten characters are named for food in this period of privation—Tart, Onion, Round End (of a sausage); two names recall the theater—the Curtains common in traditional theater, which laugh and fart to create a storm in this play, and the Silence that is proper conduct for the audience. Three other characters mock number: a single actress plays two Bow-Wows, and, conversely, Anguish bifurcates into two people, Fat and Skinny. Only Cousin is a conventional, if nameless, character.

Almost plotless, the play is nevertheless full of events. Act 1 ends in a sudden storm. A picnic in act 2 dissolves in universal burial. In act 3 Big Foot's four female admirers cut off his hair and are in turn covered with blood. In act 4 all the characters win a fortune in a lottery. Act 5 is a love scene between Big Foot and Tart. Act 6 closes with the whole cast blinded by a man-sized golden ball, labeled "Nobody."

In 1945, a year after playing Onion, the writer Raymond Queneau pointed out the relevance of Picasso's 1941 play to desires unfulfilled under the Occupation—cold, hunger, love (his word for sex).[8] In the play itself Big Foot prophesies: "I no longer see the end of this winter without our being greeted by a bigger famine." Round End in turn evokes the vanishing amenities of cafés: "I'm going to the corner bistrot to claw off the bit of chocolate colour which is still prowling around in the black of its coffee." It is such desires that in Picasso's witty title are caught by the tail, or not quite fulfilled.

Picasso often expresses sexual desire with images of food. Thus Big Foot rhapsodizes about Tart: "your buttocks a dish of baked beans, and your arms a shark-fin soup, and your . . . and your nest of swallows still the fire of swallow's-nest soup." Such synesthesia about woman's charms is at least as old as the Song of Songs, but a Picasso woman also voices *her* appetite for masculine delectation when Skinny Anguish draws a verbal portrait of Big Foot: "His hands are of transparent peach and pistachio ice-cream. The oysters of his eyes enclose the hanging gardens their mouths wide open to the gaze of his words and the colour of garlic-flavoured mayonnaise . . . encircles him."

Despite such succulent words and the drawing of a banquet, Picasso shows few foods in his scenic directions, but he does transfer to the stage his drawing of cold, since the bare feet rub each other for warmth while they chant the total dialogue of act 2, scene 1: "My chilblains," repeated by five pairs of feet. The various characters occasionally mention coal and central heating. On the other hand, at this time when soap was as rare as coal in Paris, the whole cast bathes together in a giant tub. Tart alone is nude, except for stockings. Once out of the tub, the characters busy themselves with preparations for a *déjeuner sur l'herbe*, but unlike Manet's picnickers, they succumb in coffins before they are resurrected in the next act.

Although the play is rich in verbal imagery, it makes few specific references to the visual arts. Big Foot nevertheless recalls two of his creator's paintings, the first obliquely and the second explicitly. The horrors of *Guernica* are suggested by "The guts which Pegasus drags behind him after the fight draw her portrait on the whiteness and hardness of the gleaming marble of her sorrow." Big Foot accurately announces the number of years that have elapsed since the creation of a famous Picasso painting: "The maidens of Avignon already have thirty-three long years of their annuity." More often than images, Picasso juggles words in untranslatable sound play: nuit câline, une nuit de Chine; derrière le derrière de l'histoire; il sent bon ce savon; esclave slave; charme chamarré, amarré à son corsage; la gloire noire; d'humeur de l'amour; ses manières si maniérées.

Raymond Queneau perceptively pointed to Picasso's desire

for warmth, food, and love, and he reveled in the play's farcical tone. Desire for warmth, for example, takes the form of
the hot sudsy bath of act 2. Desire for food becomes in act 4
the pot of frying potatoes whose odor should engulf the theater. In act 5 the two Anguishes dip their bread in a sauce
whose thinness belies the gourmet menu they recite.

It is, however, sexual desire that most often bobs up in the
six acts, as in the long fertile life of their author. In the very
first speech of the play Big Foot speaks to Round End of "our
adulterous marriage." Big Foot woos Tart in act 2 and elo-
quently praises an unnamed love in act 3, scene 1. In act 3,
scene 3 the sleeping Big Foot is assaulted by four lecherous
ladies—the two Anguishes, the Cousin, and Tart. Only in act
5 is love reciprocated: "Big Foot takes [Tart] in his arms and
they fall to the floor." Far from signaling romance, however,
the embrace of Big Foot triggers Tart's defecation. Later Tart
declares her love for Big Foot, but she soon leaves him. In act
6 she describes her meeting with Love, a beggar who returns
kindness with malice. In that act, too, Tart vaunts her charms,
and she dances with Big Foot only when ordered to do so by
Skinny Anguish.

Although love—or rather, lust—is the most sustained desire of the play, it disappears before the end, which returns
obliquely to the immediacies of the Occupation. Instead of
closing in the traditional way of comedy, on a stageful of danc-
ing couples, Picasso prolongs the play with Big Foot's last
speech, followed by the startling appearance of a man-sized
golden ball. Implicitly, Big Foot pits a desire for peace against
an unnamed war. In a time of blackouts he commands: "Let's
light all the lanterns. Let's throw the flights of doves against
the bullets with all our might and let's close the houses that
have been demolished by the bombs, with a double lock." In
eight years Picasso would produce his famous dove of peace,
but already his Big Foot calls for flights of doves. Instead of
lanterns, however, a huge golden ball lights the stage and
blinds its occupants. The ball is at once a threat and a promise.
Its brightness causes the characters to don blindfolds and
point accusatory fingers at one another, their "You! You! You!"

prophetic of the accusations that were to come when the Resistance began in 1942. Picasso's golden ball sprouts the label "Nobody." Everybody wins the national lottery of act 4, but nobody is illuminated by the golden globe of act 6.

A decade after that first performance of *Desire* during the Occupation, Michel Leiris wrote an introduction to a collection of 180 drawings by his friend, which he entitled "Picasso and the Human Comedy or the Avatars of Big Foot."[9] Pointing to his friend's humor and variety, Leiris also insists on his thematic unity: "art envisaged as a whole with many facets (painting, literature, choreography, the circus, and so forth) and all the vicissitudes of human love." Occasionally quarrying *Desire* for analogies to the drawings, Leiris quotes the scenic directions for the blindfolded accusatory characters before the golden ball labeled "Nobody." He then interprets the image:

> The lights go on, we show ourselves, each gazing at his neighbor in the hope that discovering him will help us to find ourselves. But the light blinds him and we, too, are blinded. Between the anonymity of indiscriminate desire and the comedy of the observed-observers—blind men who are (or are not) seen and cause (or do not cause) others to see—lies the wasteland of Time, of Time which inexorably wears us down, and whenever we try to lay hold of Somebody we find—NOBODY!
>
> Nobody, not even ourselves; and so perfect is the void that we cannot even speak of solitude. For nothing survives except, so long as we remain alive, that human tension shared by all the living and binding us to them. And may it not be that those two terms "nobody" and "all" stand for two complementaries, not opposites, the poles between which has evolved, to the rhythm of a dramma gioccoso ruling out optimism and despair alike, the amazing art of Pablo Picasso, by common consent the greatest artist of our age?
>
> (Stuart Gilbert translation)

Even if not the greatest playwright!

Despite Picasso's fame and seeming invulnerability under the Occupation, no theater apparently desired his play. Perhaps fear of censorship discouraged potential directors, or the requirement of expensive properties. Unproduced, Picasso's play was lavishly published in 1943; the editor Jean Lescure slipped it past the Vichy censor by designating the author as Robert Brasillach, a writer who had welcomed fascism.[10] By 1944, however, Brasillach had fallen from Nazi favor, and Allied partisans were confident of Nazi defeat.

In this anticipatory climate Michel Leiris offered his home for the staged reading of his friend Picasso's play.[11] Leiris not only conceived the whole festive evening but also played the main role and chose the rest of the remarkable cast—remarkable but not professional. Zanie Campan was the only trained actress to perform. Married to the publisher Jean Auber, she played Tart, the female lead. Otherwise, the cast reads like a who's who of Aryan Paris literati:

Big Foot	Michel Leiris
The two Bow-Wows	Louise Leiris
Round End	Jean-Paul Sartre
[Tart's] Cousin	Simone de Beauvoir
Onion	Raymond Queneau
The Curtains	Jean Auber
Skinny Anguish	Dora Maar
Fat Anguish	Germaine Hugnet
Silence	Jacques-Laurent Bost

The poet Georges Hugnet was in charge of music; the writers Valentine Hugo and Pierre Reverdy helped with rehearsals. The performance was directed by a left-wing intellectual with experience in amateur theater—Albert Camus, a newcomer to Paris.

The performance took place at seven on the evening of March 19, 1944, so as to end well before the midnight curfew. Although several rows of chairs were prepared for the invited audience, word had spread through the Latin Quarter, and some hundred spectators were present in this makeshift theater. Among them were the actor-director Barrault, the writer Georges Bataille, the painter Georges Braque, the photographer Brassaï, the actress Maria Casarès, the poet Paul Eluard, the psychiatrist Jacques Lacan, the poet Georges Limbour, and the playwright Armand Salacrou. Camus as director made no attempt to comply with Picasso's freewheeling scenic directions; from stage right he merely read them aloud, punctuating with a cane. Before the large curtained windows, framed by paintings by Picasso and Juan Gris, the performers sat in an arc, each rising to speak his or her lines. Rather than costumes, they wore their best clothes, and Beauvoir records how pleased she was that Picasso admired the red sweater and pearls she had borrowed for the role of the prim cousin. The quality of the acting was probably low, since the actress Maria Casarès does not even mention it in her autobiography. In high spirits, the readers lunged through the six acts and then basked in praise and applause, later mingling with the audience. Afterward Picasso invited a few friends to his home-studio around the corner, where he favored them with a glimpse of the manuscript of Jarry's *Ubu*, a cherished possession. Some few guests may have recalled Barrault's tenancy of that same studio, where he was visited in the 1930s by Antonin Artaud, Roger Blin, André Breton, Jean Dasté, Robert Desnos, Sylvain Itkine, Jacques Prévert, Roger Vitrac—dispersed by the Occupation. Most of the cast celebrated the performance in the Leiris apartment, restored from pocket theater to mere domicile. Since the curfew during the Occupation lasted from midnight to five A.M., the festivities lasted all night. Rare foods were at once a recollection of prewar insouciance and a prediction of post-Liberation amenities. For Simone de Beauvoir that evening was the first of what she calls *fêtes* of St. Germain-des-Prés, which gave that quarter of Paris notoriety after the Liberation. The performance of *Desire* was not reviewed.

Picasso's biographers testify to his delight at the Leiris project. This major visual artist was apparently willing to forgo the staging of his elaborate images—the whole cast in a giant tub, potatoes frying in a huge pot, a man-sized golden ball—for the pleasure of hearing his words spoken by acquaintances dressed up for the occasion. Simone de Beauvoir claims that she, Sartre, and Camus were merely having fun at the event, whereas others took very seriously "tous les faits et gestes de Picasso."[12]

Desire Caught by the Tail need not be taken very seriously, but that staged reading nevertheless predicts a segment of subsequent theater. Beauvoir dismisses *Desire* as a Surrealist piece redolent of the 1920s, linking it to Apollinaire's *Breasts of Tiresias* (*Les Mamelles de Tirésias*). Ideologically, however, the plays are poles apart. Apollinaire, who volunteered to serve in World War I, joyously espoused fornication for repopulation. Rather than the Vietnam War slogan—Make love not war—Apollinaire implies: Make love because we are at war. During the Occupation Picasso could not have published an antiwar piece, but *Desire* obliquely stages the physical privations of the period. The end of the play hints at a desire for peace camouflaged under the sexual desire that propels the play.

If the play was indeed taken seriously in Picasso's milieu, Raymond Queneau alone has left a record of it, and he makes Occupation sense out of the seeming nonsense. What the cast did not, apparently, appreciate is what was usually unappreciated in Surrealist plays—the dominance of scenic images over characterological dialogue. Beauvoir, Camus, and Sartre wrote plays after they participated in the performance of *Desire*, but in their drama specific problems were dialogically posed and resolved. In a collection of some four hundred pages of writing on the theater, Sartre does not even mention Picasso. As one of Picasso's biographers points out, however, "Pablo is a fore-runner of today's avant-garde theater, in which words signify much less than action, which is intended to decondition the spectator, wrest him out of his passiveness and fixedness, and allow him to make his own montage of events as he does in daily life, itself a sort of permanent collage of successive and/or simultaneous visions."[13] On the one hand, then, *Desire* is a throwback to the Surrealism of the 1920s and its inundation of images, and on the other, it is a prophecy of the Happening and its preoccupation with process. (The Happener Jean-Jacques Lebel produced *Desire* in 1970—with extravagance.) The three playwrights acting in

Desire did not suspect that vivid imagery and disjunctive dialogue would usher in a new theater idiom that dramatized their worldview. Soon after the March 19, 1944, performance of *Desire* Camus composed *The Misunderstanding* (*Le Malentendu*) and Beauvoir *Useless Mouths* (*Les Bouches inutiles*), both of them conventional realistic dramas, for all their geographic and/or chronological estrangement. But Jean-Paul Sartre's role as Round End hints at the circular structure of his *No Exit* (*Huis clos*).

NO EXIT
(HUIS CLOS)
Jean-Paul Sartre

The actress Gaby Sylvia thought that the setting linked Picasso's *Desire* with Sartre's third play:

> Albert Camus, Jean-Paul Sartre, and two of their friends had a very good time during the Occupation, playing Picasso's *Desire Caught by the Tail* in a living room. Camus asked Sartre to write a short play for four characters, without set or costumes, which they could play in the home of friends. What do you find in any living room? A sofa, a small table, armchairs, a mantelpiece and sometimes a Barbedienne bronze sculpture. So much for the set. There would be no intermission, because of the curfew. Next necessity. There had to be a reason that these four characters are together in a living room and unable to leave it. "Let's shove them into hell," Sartre said to himself. And in two weeks at a table at the [Café] Flore he wrote *No Exit*, a play from which metaphysical background was completely absent.[14]

Sartre's account of the genesis of *No Exit* diverges slightly:

> When one writes a play, there are always chance circumstances and deep needs. The chance circumstance when I wrote *No Exit* in 1943 or the beginning of 1944 was the fact that I had three friends for whom I wanted to write a play, without giving any one of them a larger part than the others. In other words, I wanted them to be together on the stage all the time, because

I said to myself: "If one of them leaves the stage, he'll think that the other two have better parts in his absence." So I wanted to keep them together, and I said to myself: "How can one put three characters together without an exit, and keep them there on stage to the end of the play, as though eternally?" That's when the idea came to me to put them in hell and make each one of them the torturer of the other two. That's the circumstantial cause.[15]

Simone de Beauvoir amplifies this account, informing us that a play was requested from Sartre by the Lyon publisher Marc Barbezat for two would-be actresses, his wife Olga Barbezat and her sister Wanda Kosakiewicz.[16] Sartre first thought of characters trapped in a cellar during a bombardment, but he soon moved them to hell. He wrote the play rapidly at the Café Flore, which was like home to him.

Backed by Barbezat and the theater critic Marc Beigbeder, *No Exit* was intended to tour unoccupied France (about one-third of its territory). At first Sartre thought of Sylvain Itkine as director, but then he shifted to Camus, whom he had met a few months earlier at the premiere of his *Flies*. Since Itkine was Jewish, he was forbidden to work in the theater in Paris, and perhaps Sartre thought it would be just as dangerous for Itkine in unoccupied France. It was not like Sartre to drop an old acquaintance for a newer one, but the change is not explained by the many commentators on *No Exit*, and everyone seemed pleased that Camus, who had dabbled in theater in his native Algiers, consented to direct and play Garcin. René-Jacques Chauffard, a former student of Sartre's who had played bit parts for Dullin, was cast as the Valet. Rehearsals began in the round room of Beauvoir's hotel—La Louisiane at 60 Rue de Seine. But rehearsals collapsed when during Olga Barbezat's visit with friends active in the Resistance the Nazis raided the home and arrested everyone present. (Olga Barbezat was released unharmed in time to attend the premiere of *No Exit*.)

Early in 1944 the Vieux-Colombier Theater acquired a new manager in the businessman Annet Badel. Introduced to

2.   The damned trio of *No Exit*

Sartre by his son's tutor Robert Kanters, Badel immediately requested a play, and Sartre offered him *No Exit*. They signed the contract at the Café Flore, where the play had been written a few months earlier.

The Vieux-Colombier, seating about 335, was larger than most pocket theaters, but it still retained an experimental aura, suitable to a play set in hell. As director for *No Exit* Badel chose Raymond Rouleau, a professional with avant-garde credentials: he had been trained by Dullin, had acted in Artaud's Théâtre Alfred Jarry, and had directed Vitrac's *Werewolf* (*Loup-Garou*). Rouleau proceeded to choose a professional, if virtually unknown, cast. For Garcin, he called on Michel Vitold, a fellow alumnus of Dullin's Atelier. The shocking role of the Lesbian Inez went to Tanya Balachova, another Dullin graduate. Estelle was the problem role, coveted by Badel for his actress wife, Gaby Sylvia, but claimed by Sartre for Wanda Kosakiewicz, for whom he had written it.[17] Of the original hotel-room cast only Chauffard, as Valet, retained his part. Busy with writing, impressed by professionals, Sartre attended few rehearsals and did not revise his text.

Sartre's characters act through speech; three people lacerate one another verbally during the course of the play, but earlier events, slowly unveiled in delayed exposition, are so intricate that reviewers would summarize them inaccurately. In order of entrance (but not of revelation) a Brazilian journalist, Garcin, has abused his wife and fled from his country in time of war; a Lesbian postal clerk, Inez, has seduced her cousin's wife, who is then goaded to kill them both; a beautiful society matron, Estelle, has drowned her unwanted baby, driving the father to suicide. After such violent lives, the deaths of the infernal trio were maudlin: Inez was asphyxiated when her lover turned on the gas; Estelle succumbed to pneumonia; most striking, Garcin was executed for desertion.

Sartre was an omnivorous reader, and he learned from such dramatists as Racine, Ibsen, and Strindberg, but the details of the long exposition come from the Paris scandal sheets. Melodramatic, the material is sexually bolder than theater melodrama would have countenanced.[18] Even after Edouard Bourdet's *Captive* (*La Prisonnière*), a 1936 play about a Lesbian, a homosexual seduction onstage was shocking. What is forgotten in our sexually permissive time is Sartre's original shock impact. *Nausea* is today his most highly valued fiction, but in its own day *The Age of Reason* struck readers, opening as it did on the search for someone to perform an abortion. Comparably, Sartre's *Flies* was produced in a large theater, but the shocking *No Exit* established him as a celebrity.

Eric Bentley early recognized the stuff of melodrama in the infernal living room of *No Exit*: "adultery, infanticide, Lesbianism, a traffic accident, double suicide in bed, refusal to fight for France, death before a firing squad."[19] Aside from the understandable errors (one of the bedded deaths is not suicide, and the deserter is not French), Bentley saw that the quantity of Sartre's violence overflows any single melodrama, but he fails to mention that Sartre confines all that violence to exposition. Moreover, Sartre whittles away superfluities, as Bentley appreciated: "A man is . . . placed in the center; two women are peripheral. A neat, old-fashioned Parisian pattern."

What did not conform to pattern, however, was the man's sexual indifference to both women for much of the play. Sartre sounds a new moral note in the "neat, old-fashioned Parisian pattern": the Lesbian Inez desires Estelle, who desires Garcin, who desires the *moral* approval of Inez. Desire is not caught and not fulfilled in this version of hell.

Sartre's deep concerns were neatly captured by the accidental causes of *No Exit*. For the play's stifling atmosphere Sartre must have recalled his own experience as a prisoner of the Germans. In performance, however, the closed space of the set became a metaphor for the enclosed self to whom hell is other people, as in the most frequently quoted line of the play. Misinterpreted, Sartre later clarified his intention: "Relations with other people, encrustation, and freedom . . . are the three themes of the play. I should like you to remember this when you hear that hell is other people" (Frank Jellinek translation).[20] But Sartre's explanation belittles his accomplishment, even if it did provoke T. S. Eliot to a rebuttal: "Hell is oneself."[21]

Sartre dramatizes a hell in which three people *interact*, and the set compresses the interaction. Not only is the furniture ugly and the props—bronze Barbedienne sculpture and paper cutter—useless, but the studied sparseness of the set forces attention on behavior rather than atmosphere, as in the very different plays of Brecht. In spite of the bright light, full awareness seeps only gradually into the minds of the trio—first Inez, then Garcin, and not until the very end Estelle, when she realizes that the paper cutter can kill no one because they are already dead. Dead—the word she has avoided throughout the play.

In 1946, in a widely reprinted essay translated as "Forgers of Myths," Sartre issued a manifesto for postwar French drama. Although he barely mentions *No Exit*, it most closely fits his prescription for "brief, violent dramas sometimes reduced to a single long act . . . written in a clear and extremely taut style, containing few characters, who are not presented as individuals, but who are plunged into a situation that forces them to make a choice."[22]

The characters of *No Exit* are not psychologically nuanced but stereotyped: a womanizing journalist, a society playgirl, a sadistic Lesbian—yet Sartre does individualize them, mainly through the extreme situation in which he places them. Estelle is a narcissist, Inez a sadist, and Garcin both a sadist and a narcissist. In their respective lives on earth, all three have treated other people as objects. The characters are thus adequate to their task of mutual torture—until the door opens. This peripeteia is theatrically exciting, but it weakens Sartre's philosophical point that choice is possible only for the living, who define themselves by their acts. Since the characters of *No Exit* are dead, their opportunity for choice is behind them, yet they seem to choose to remain in their fetid Second Empire room. They affirm their damnation.

Before the door opens, Sartre wastes no words; the verbal economy of his "taut style" heightens the tension in this frequently performed play. Once the choice is made to remain in a familiar hell, the play limps to its end. Sartre lapses into pseudo-philosophy; or rather he endows Garcin with too rich a rhetoric and Inez with too elaborate a riposte. But Sartre's dramatic skill returns for the conclusion, as the play circles back to its opening details. Only at the end can Garcin appreciate the suitability of the ugly bronze he noticed at the play's start. Only at the end, after Estelle's ineffectual thrusts with the paper cutter, can she utter the word "dead." Only at the end do the three characters laugh, even as Garcin and the Valet laughed in the opening moments. But laughter dies when Garcin rises front and center to close the play: "Well, let's continue." They are locked into an eternal continuation under two sets of eyes—those on stage, which can never close, and those of the audience offstage.

The infernal atmosphere grows oppressive through the repetitions of the unrealistic common language of the three roommates. Garcin is Brazilian, but he speaks French. Inez and Estelle are of different social classes, but their speech ignores that. Even the Valet adopts the same conversational mode. In the opening scene particularly, Garcin and the Valet hiss their *ça*'s through the sultry air. Garcin takes note—aloud—of the spare surroundings and the absence of window, mirror, and bed. He is so vivid in evoking the lost ability to sleep that the Valet calls him *romanesque*, "romantic," but the French word carries the sense of "one who invents fictions." By the play's end we realize that Garcin is *romanesque* in his fiction about his basic bravery. Earlier, when Garcin utters the word "live," the Valet retorts ironically: "Live?" And Garcin mutters: "You're not going to quibble about a matter of vocabulary." But Garcin himself will spend eternity quibbling about "a matter of vocabulary," which reflects character. Should he be called a coward?

Inez reacts less volubly to her surroundings; stoic, she objects to the nervous tics of Garcin's fear. She names Garcin a coward even before we know that his most obsessive fear is precisely being named a coward. Estelle, in contrast, notes the color combinations in hell. Beneath her initial good manners, her syntax and vocabulary do not differ from those of the others, except that she will not pronounce the word "dead."

In the second of four rounds of earth watching, all three are surprised to find that it is already night. When they return to the present of their inferno, Inez starts her technique of insidious repetition with the withering word *hasard*, implying that there is no chance; they are together by design. But whose design? All three begin to refer to the mysterious "they" who have apparently pronounced their damnation. The repetition of the word "damned" serves Inez as another weapon against the two hypocrites. Before the play is half over, Inez articulates the infernal principle: "Each of us is the torturer of the other two."

The three agree to an armistice, but soon Inez tries to seduce Estelle—more pointedly in French, since she shifts to the familiar *tu* form. When Garcin has the advantage, he too *tutoyers* Estelle, but in contempt. Jockeying for sexual supremacy, both Garcin and Inez keep repeating the word "traps," and that indeed is what their words are. After Estelle spits in Inez's face, the latter taunts the heterosexual couple, and Garcin flings vicious insults at Estelle, calling her octopus and swamp. Just before the door opens, Garcin's anguish reaches a climax; he calls for a whole lexicon of traditional tortures as more bearable than his abiding uncertainty whether he is a coward. The rising rhythm of that speech is punctuated by the door opening. That speech should be minimally separated from Estelle's paper-cutter "murder" and the play's end. Familiar as the play is today, *No Exit* was shocking in its own time, and it is still open to conflicting interpretations, although it has also been dismissed as a thesis play "for children who are very advanced philosophically."[23]

Sartre has expressed pleasure at the first production of *No Exit*: "The roles were played by the three actors and also by Chauffard, the majordomo of hell, who has invariably acted him ever since, so extremely well that I have never afterwards been able to imagine my own creations save as Vitold, Gaby Sylvia, Tanya Balachova, and Chauffard" (Frank Jellinek translation).[24] Conceived for one cast, the play was for its author indelibly incarnated by other actors at the Vieux-Colombier.

The director Rouleau imposed a proscenium on the theater's open stage, within which Max Douy designed a Second Empire drawing room in swamp green.[25] The single door opened at stage left, and one of the wall panels at stage right was bricked over. Upstage center on a mantel was a false bronze sculpture (not a Barbedienne) of a nude woman sitting astride a nude man. Behind the sculpture was an empty frame devoid of reflecting glass. High ceilings dwarfed the infernal inmates, and a chandelier hung low, all bulbs sporadically lit. The three sofas were uncomfortable as well as mismatched— dark green, bordeaux red, and blue in clashing styles.

Although the sets and costumes of subsidized theaters were lavish during the Occupation, *No Exit* was spare. Chauffard as the Valet wore the white apron and striped jacket habitual in French hotels; he smoked a pipe and gave sulky service. Sylvia as Estelle, her blonde hair piled high on her head, wore a sleeveless white evening gown. Balachova as Inez, her hair hidden under her turban, wore a long-sleeved black dress and incongruous high-heeled patent-leather sandals. Vitold as Garcin in a dark suit and dark shirt, his hat far back on his head, loosened his tie in the heat of self-laceration; he resembled a Humphrey Bogart of the avant-garde.

Although Sartre's characters have never seen each other before they are condemned to spend eternity together, the first Paris actors knew one another. The producer Annet Badel was married to the actress Gaby Sylvia, who played Estelle as a disarmingly naive blonde. (In a revival four years later she was more mature and ruthless. Some two decades later she directed the play in Tokyo.) After they both had taught at the Vieux-Colombier, the director Raymond Rouleau was divorced in 1940 from the Russian-born actress Tanya Balachova, who played Inez. Rouleau was to survive on an eclectic repertory in both small and large theaters, but Balachova confined her post–*No Exit* career to acting in pocket theaters and to coaching other actors. Vitold was to continue acting in or directing Sartre's plays as well as those of a spate of foreign playwrights—Ugo Betti, William Saroyan, Robert Sherwood, Michel de Ghelderode, Fernand Crommelynck. Chauffard also continued to act in several Sartre plays, but he alone of the cast launched into the New Theater, playing Schéhadé's M. Bob'le in 1951, Ionesco's Choubert in 1953, Adamov's Arthur in 1955, Duras's Salesman in 1956, Beckett's Krapp in 1960.

In 1944 *No Exit* ran without intermission for an hour and twenty minutes, and even during the Occupation no theater manager dared ask his audience to pay for so short an evening, so Badel coupled the tense drama with a frothy farce. The plays went into rehearsal without any guarantee of opening, since the Occupiers granted permission, then withdrew it, and then relented—all without explanation. The exact date of the opening is uncertain. The Gallimard edition says May 1944. Simone de Beauvoir mentions June 10. The Sartre scholar Michel Rybalka graciously informed me that "the official date is May 27, 1944, but the first accounts in the press are dated June 3, 1944. It is quite possible that the play had a first showing on May 27, and then, because of a holiday or for some other reason, the second showing was in June." It is also possible that the Allied invasion of France on June 6, 1944, made for general confusion in the capital.

Instead of wooing the good will of the Parisians, the Nazis increased their arrests and their censorship. André Castelot, the vicious and powerful reviewer for *La Gerbe*, wished to censor *No Exit* "not only because of its mediocrity, but because of its evil ugliness and disgusting garbage."[26] Even more powerful, Alain Laubréaux, the reviewer for *Je suis partout*, objected: "The play censors itself because it is so boring." He thought it would be an error to endow the play with notoriety by censoring it.[27] Other reviewers used adjectives like "scandalous," "rotten," "venereal," "lugubriously unhealthy." But the drama was also admired. The playwright Henri Lenormand praised the "nervous interdependence" of the infernal trio, and he described a performance in which enthusiastic young spectators threw their cigarette rations to the stage. Friends and foes agreed that both the play and its performance were "intelligent"—the adjective that often recurred.[28]

The most favorable review was surprising—that of the French fascist Robert Brasillach in the penultimate issue of his *Chronique de Paris*. After excoriating the performance of Racine's *Andromaque*, which had just been censored, Brasillach surveys Sartre's works, then accurately recapitulates the action of *No Exit*. He concludes:

> Everything blends to make of this rigorous act the most frightful confession of an age lacking faith. . . . I don't presume to offer a final judgment on the play. Jean-Paul Sartre is certainly at the opposite pole from what I love and still believe. His play may be the symbol of a lucid and rotten art that was the unsuccessful result of the last war, but I don't think I'm risking much when I say that by its dark cold structure, by its rigor, by its demonstrative *purity* opposed to its fundamental impurity, it is a masterpiece.[29]

The last (July) issue of Brasillach's *Chronique de Paris* laments the Allied invasion of Normandy but nevertheless reviews the 1943–1944 theater season as brilliant. After praising Barrault's staging of Claudel's *Satin Slipper* and the recent plays of Giraudoux and Montherlant, he awards highest honors to Anouilh's *Antigone* and Sartre's *No Exit*. "Yes, it smells of sulphur, and the poison of this intellectualist hell has never been distilled with such implacable rigor. *No Exit* will remain as a bizarre monument of an agonizing world where the future will undoubtedly seek evidence of the most lucid negation." He was not far off the mark.

As any tourist knows who has visited Paris in August, the natives leave the capital during that month. Not, however, in August 1944. The Nazis retained control of the capital, and no one knew how they might devastate the city before the arrival of Allied armies from the north. Hitler did order the destruction of Paris, which was not obeyed only because the German commander thought him insane.[30] Rationing grew more stringent, and only national theaters were allowed to play a full program; others were limited to one or two performances a week. The audience in what had long been called the City of Light laughed at the Valet's line in *No Exit*: "We have all the electricity we want."

Returning to the capital after a brief vacation, Robert Brasillach saw *No Exit* again on August 17, 1944.[31] It was the last theater he was to see.

Paris was liberated on August 25, 1944, a day of unparalleled élan in spite of casualties. Sartre in the Resistance was among those ordered to occupy the Comédie-Française, and at one point he refused entrance to Barrault.[32]

Unlike several of his colleagues, Brasillach did not attempt to flee the country, although he did go into hiding. When his mother was arrested, however, he surrendered on September 14. *No Exit* reopened the Vieux-Colombier on September 20 and celebrated its one hundredth performance on September 30. The curtain raiser was replaced by an André Roussin farce, *The Tomb of Achilles* (*Le Tombeau d'Achille*), which had been forbidden as indecent by the Vichy censor. On October 5, in the Liberation euphoria, French women at last gained the right to vote.

No Exit signaled at once French Resistance and French culture. Rouleau was a stretcher-bearer for the Resistance. Sartre and Vitold had spoken on Resistance radio; the Badels said they had hidden arms for the Resistance. After the Liberation, collaborationist reviewers went abroad or to prison. Alain Laubréaux, for example, fled to fascist Spain, where he became a reviewer of bullfights, living comfortably until his death in 1968, a fitting year for him to die. In 1980 Truffaut based his character Daxiat in *The Last Subway* on Laubréaux.

Robert Brasillach was tried early in 1945 and, unlike most collaborators, was condemned to death. Led by François Mauriac, fifty-nine French intellectuals—among them Jean Anouilh, Marcel Aymé, Jean-Louis Barrault, Paul Claudel, Jean Cocteau, Colette, Paul Valéry—petitioned General de Gaulle to commute the sentence. Apolitical Anouilh, who had met Brasillach only once but was horrified at the post-Liberation purges, collected seven signatures in twelve attempts, and he later recalled that experience: "The young man Anouilh that I had remained until 1945 set out one morning . . . to collect signatures for Brasillach among his colleagues. For a week he went from door to door, and he returned home old— as in a tale by Grimm."[33]

Except for Camus, Sartre's circle was not inclined to ask for mercy, recalling that Brasillach had never asked mercy for

Jews or Resistants. De Gaulle denied the plea. "The evidence is contradictory, but the most reasonable version . . . is that de Gaulle was particularly angered by Brasillach's journey to Germany to encourage French volunteers who fought along-side German troops against the Soviet Union; when Brasillach went on trial, the war against Germany was still raging on both the eastern and western fronts."[34]

Like Sartre's Garcin, Brasillach faced a firing squad—on February 6, 1945. Unlike Garcin, he died courageously—according to his attorney's eyewitness report. *No Exit* was no longer playing at the Vieux-Colombier, having been replaced by the other play that Brasillach admired, Anouilh's *Antigone*. Anouilh was shattered by the execution of the only writer to suffer the postwar death penalty: "In reflecting on it since, calm, skeptical, distressed (in the strong sense of the word) and strangely relieved by my age, I perceived that the young man that I was and the young man Brasillach died the same day and—making all due allowances—from the same cause."[35]

While *No Exit* was in rehearsal, Robert Brasillach published his own play in his *Chronique de Paris*, which was rather a chronicle of Brasillach's reactions to events in Paris. That play, later entitled *Caesar's Queen* (*La Reine de Césarée*), was written in 1940 when Brasillach was a German prisoner, as was Sartre. Before Sartre twisted *The Oresteia* into *The Flies*, before Anouilh twisted Sophocles' *Antigone* to his own ends, Brasillach twisted Racine to his. Racine bases his *Bérénice* on moral nobility; Titus and Bérénice renounce consummation of their love, acceding to the demands of Rome. Antiochus, who also loves Bérénice, closes Racine's play with a tragic "Alas." Brasillach follows Racine's plot, except that his Titus foists Bérénice upon Antiochus before the queen leaves Rome. In her desire for Titus, Bérénice is outmaneuvered by the Roman racist, Paulin, who is invented by Brasillach. The Jewish queen departs reluctantly, but she leaves behind her in Rome a young niece. In the play's last line Brasillach implies that that niece will taint the racial purity of Rome. Speaking of the fourteen-year-old girl, Antiochus closes Brasillach's tragedy: "That was the age of Cleopatra when she met Caesar."[36]

When published in April 1944, shortly before the premiere of *No Exit*, Brasillach's play received little attention. Ten years later, Brasillach's friends arranged for republication and opened negotiations for production. A well-known Paris director, Raymond Hermantier, directed a well-known actress, Alice Cocéa, as Bérénice; the play opened in July 1957 in the provinces but moved on November 15 to Paris, to the newly renamed and lavishly refurbished Théâtre des Arts. Although Brasillach was dead, there were protests at every performance so that the play was forbidden to all but invited audiences. At the same time, Peter Brook's production of Jean Genet's *Balcony* was forbidden to any audience at all, even before the play went into rehearsal. Sartre leaped into the fray, denouncing "right-wing Scapins." He acknowledged that the death sentence for Brasillach was "too severe," but fulminated against the anti-Semitic forces that had revived the collaborationist play. Sartre concluded a long article in ringing polemics: "To fight for the liberty of the theater means to struggle against the monopoly of the Right and for plays of the Left, for *The Balcony* and against *Caesar's Queen*. And it is also and above all to struggle for the liberty of the spectator."[37] He did not argue that the spectator is not free if he or she cannot see both plays.

By 1957 the debate was not between equals, any more than it would have been during the Occupation when Brasillach was in power. By 1957 Brasillach was dead and nearly forgotten, whereas Sartre was a world celebrity. Both writers had dramatized their views with Racinian economy, but only Sartre had structured his play in a vicious circle in which speech furthered action even while repetition implied eternity.

No Exit became a symbol of the Liberation of Paris, which was accomplished largely by the political Left. It was not clear at the time that *No Exit* was also a step in the theater's path away from the reasonable, talkative French tradition. To be

sure, the Romantics of 1830 had already rebelled against reason, as did melodrama and vaudeville. In the twentieth century, Surrealist playwrights were the illegitimate children of
the melodramatists, gnawing at the same old erotic triangle.
After World War I, both Boulevard and experimental theaters
wallowed in a plethora of words, despite Jean-Jacques Bernard's so-called Theater of Silence. The loquacious Giraudoux
was the interwar darling of drama, and in *The Flies* Sartre im-
itates his garrulity, but *No Exit* thrives on a new verbal economy and the feeling of circular rather than linear action. It is
a parody of the well-made play. What earlier drama limits
properties to a bronze sculpture and a paper cutter? What
other play rises to a climax of a door opening, without entrance or exit?

Strindberg's chamber plays first dramatized a few characters in an inferno—what has been called compressionism or
the cycle of sequestration. Vivian Mercier believes that Beckett's major plays stem from *No Exit*, and Thomas Whitaker
traces Beckett's *Play*, Genet's *Screens*, and Pinter's *No Man's
Land* to that root. Pinter played Garcin in a telecast of *No Exit*,
and his *Old Times* may also be described as the sexual power
struggle of three characters in a stripped-down setting.[38]

Influential both at home and abroad, *No Exit* was revived
in larger Paris theaters in 1946, 1948, 1953, 1956, 1961, and
1965. It has also played in a theater literally underground in
Paris. Sartre's play has been filmed twice and televised twice,
and has been widely translated. Although the English translation (*In Camera*) was censored by the Lord Chamberlain, *No
Exit* was voted the Best Foreign Play of 1946 in New York. Back
in Paris, *No Exit* helped seed the myth of St. Germain-des-
Prés, and Sartre's photograph was ubiquitous so that he could
no longer write undisturbed at a café table. Become a father
figure to the youth of St. Germain-des-Prés, he was described
by the writer Boris Vian, who contributed to the myth and
lampooned him affectionately as Jean-Sol Partre, as a "writer,
playwright, and philosopher whose activity has strictly nothing to do with checked shirts, cellars, and long hair, and who
deserves to be left in peace, because he's a good guy."[39]

"Peace" doesn't seem quite right for Sartre, enthusiastic polemicist and committed commentator on culture. A volume of nearly four hundred pages of occasional writing on the theater testifies also to his enduring preoccupation with that art, including approaches wholly alien to him, like Artaud's *Theater and Its Double*.

TÊTE-À-TÊTE
Antonin Artaud

After the Liberation, Badel continued his management of the Vieux-Colombier, opening it to such avant-garde ventures as Michel de Ré's production of Jarry's *King Ubu*. De Ré's effervescence, like that of many others who worked in the postwar theater, soon bubbled away. Artaud, in contrast, gave to the theater decades of unrewarded dedication. To his 1946 production of Vitrac's *Victor*, de Ré invited Antonin Artaud, newly released from the asylum of Rodez. The 1927 premiere of *Victor*, directed by Artaud, had had only three performances, and de Ré's production was its first revival. Artaud was sure that de Ré's *Victor* would fail because its director was not chaste, and he therefore accorded it small attention. Throughout the performance he scribbled away. Afterward Artaud voiced his disapproval to his friend the poet Jacques Prevel.[40]

Born in Marseilles, Antonin Artaud (1896–1948) came to Paris in 1920.[41] A man of talent and energy, he not only acted on stage and screen, designed sets, and drew self-portraits but also wrote poems, fiction, scenarios, theater history, and a tempest of letters. Prey to illnesses for which he took drugs as early as 1919, Artaud was declared legally insane in 1937. When Gallimard published *The Theater and Its Double* in 1938 (in an edition of four hundred copies), Artaud was in an asylum, and the book went almost unnoticed in the shadow of an imminent war. During the brief war ("le Drôle de Guerre" for the French) and the long Occupation, severe rationing aggravated the condition of the alienated, particularly in the region around Paris. The poet Robert Desnos (who was to die after incarceration in a concentration camp) arranged for Artaud to be transferred to the care of a psychiatrist friend, Dr. Gaston Ferdière at Rodez in the unoccupied zone.

Soon after the Liberation Artaud's friends obtained his personal liberation—release from Rodez Asylum. The handsome young actor of the 1920s had metamorphosed shockingly into an ailing, toothless, and emaciated old man by age fifty. But his energy was unabated, and in the twenty months between his release and his death, Artaud wrote compulsively, as though he knew there would not be time to verbalize his incandescent passions.

Spurred by the nearly penniless Arthur Adamov, Artaud's friends formed a corporation to collect funds for him; Michel Leiris became president of the Friends of Artaud. On June 7, 1946, the large Théâtre Sarah Bernhardt (its name restored) was the site for readings from Artaud's works, with tickets ranging from ten to fifteen hundred francs. Although Artaud himself did not attend, posters beckoned with well-known names of the Paris theater scene—Adamov, Barrault, Blin, Bogaert, Casarès, Cuny, Dullin, Jouvet, Renaud, Rouleau, Colette Thomas, Vilar. A week later, an auction of manuscripts and art works yielded another sum toward Artaud's sustenance in Paris, still largely unheated and subject to food shortages. (Ironically, the newspaper *Combat* published daily bulletins on "Le Ravitaillement" on its *Spectacles* page.)

Housed in Ivry, a Southern suburb of Paris, Artaud often took the subway to the cafés of St. Germain-des-Prés, especially le Bar Vert, writing frenetically wherever he was—in subway, bus, café, bed, or even in the street, standing and propping his notebook against the nearest wall. In August 1946 Gallimard undertook to publish his complete works, a project that is still in progress forty years and twenty-one volumes later.

Immersed in his difficult post-Liberation poems, Artaud was not so free of the theater as he sometimes claimed. He toyed in 1946 with the idea of directing *The Bacchae* at the Vieux-Colombier, and he considered his late poems to be pieces for performance. Roger Blin offered his own services as well as those of the actor Alain Cuny, both to recite under Artaud's direction, but Artaud wanted no surrogate reciters for these poems wrested from his entrails. Blin later described Artaud's attitude toward theater at this time:

> At the end of his life he believed that theater was solely an outlet for a pile of words. It was a means of struggling against the spells which victimized him and which he thought victimized his friends. Earlier the theater had been his laboratory for aesthetic research. Whether or not he used a text, all his productions were interspersed with cries, dances, music, and projections. His was a "total theater." But finally, for Artaud, the theater became his only means of struggling against what haunted him.[42]

Desiring to be heard at the Vieux-Colombier, Artaud wrote to the manager, Badel, but received no answer. He then asked his friend Yves Benot whether Badel was a *salaud* but was told there were worse men in the world than those who, like Badel, made money in business only to lose it in theater. When Benot realized that Artaud wanted a single night at the Vieux-Colombier, he made arrangements with the critic Robert Kanters, who was in charge of special programs on Monday nights, when the theater was dark. Benot describes the meeting between Artaud and Kanters:

> Artaud asked about the price of tickets, and Kanters replied: "The usual thing for Monday nights, one hundred francs and fifty francs for students."
>
> "Fifty francs is too dear. Everyone should be able to come; I want tickets at thirty francs."
>
> I must have signaled to the startled Kanters to accept. As a result, it wasn't a full house that evening but doubly full, with bodies piled up, overwhelmed and fascinated. The next day (or the day after) Artaud told me that Kanters had given him ten thousand francs and he asked me what I had received. I told him that there was never any question of money for me.
>
> "You're wrong; you should never work for nothing."[43]

On the evening of January 13, 1947, Artaud ignored the inventive visual effects and sonorities of his theater theory to focus on a man and a manuscript. He prepared carefully for his single performance at the Vieux-Colombier on its dark night. Posters read "Lived History of Artaud-Mômo" in large letters above "Tête-à-tête by Antonin Artaud with three poems recited by the author, The Return of Artaud-the-Mômo, Center-Mother and Boss-Darling, Indian Culture." The posters gave no hint of what Artaud planned from the start—an accusatory account of his nine years' suffering in asylums.

By New Year's Day, 1947, French consumers were impatient with continued privation, and a wave of strikes would punctuate the year. For French consumers of culture, Artaud was almost a ghost. Although *The Theater and Its Double* had been reprinted in 1944 (in an edition of 1525 copies), many people thought Artaud himself was dead, so the many curiosity seekers joined his friends on January 13, 1947. In the first row sat André Gide, wearing a bonnet against the cold. Not far from him were the writers Arthur Adamov and Albert Camus, and the artists' patron Adrienne Monnier. The Surrealist leader André Breton vociferously protested that the whole evening was an exploitation of a sick man. Artaud's old friend Barrault did not attend, but most of his other friends did—the publisher Jean Paulhan, the actor Roger Blin, the poets Henri Pichette and Jacques Prevel. Artaud's biographer Thomas Maeder claims to have received twenty different accounts of that evening from the twenty spectators he interviewed. Artaud's hagiographer Alain Virmaux claims that most printed accounts were influenced by that of André Gide, published fifteen months after the event. Some ten published reports that I consulted describe the emotional effect of the performance rather than its textual content. The newspaper *Le Monde* was on strike between January 9 and 16 so that its usually objective account is lacking. Only on January 24 did the daily *Combat* carry a pseudonymous report by one of Artaud's friends. It affirms that Artaud had desired this confrontation ever since his return to Paris.

The Vieux-Colombier was filled far beyond its capacity of about 350 seats. After some laughter at the outset, the audience was extraordinarily quiet and attentive. For the first time since the disastrous production of *The Cenci* in 1935 Artaud took the stage in Paris. It was to be the last time. The *Combat* article reports:

> When he came onstage, with his thin, ravaged face that evokes both Baudelaire and Poe; when his raging hands flew around his face like two birds, restlessly raking that face; when he began in his hoarse voice, punctuated with sobs and tragic stuttering, to recite his beautiful, scarcely audible poems—we felt ourselves carried into a dangerous zone, as though reflected by this black sun, overcome by this "generalized combustion" of a body that was prey to the flames of the spirit.[44]

A sketch by the artist Victor Vasarely conveys the emotional climate of Artaud's performance at the Vieux-Colombier. Seated at the table where his manuscript lay, Artaud inspired the artist to draw two pairs of hands with long tapering fingers, one pair supporting Artaud's massive head and the other gesturing below his face. Between the lower hands and the manuscript is a spinning top that may designate Artaud's heart. The contrast is striking between the stillness of the lower body, blended into the table, and the dynamism above that table, a representation that reverses Artaud's own obsession with the maleficent but energetic lower body and its devouring of the mind.

Most (but not all) accounts have Artaud begin his performance with the reading of his recent, still unpublished, poems, which shocked his audience by naked autobiography, obsession with sexuality, renunciation of logical sequence, neologisms, and irregular rhythms. The first two poems Artaud read were selected from a group of five entitled "Artaud the Mômo," written between July and September 1946. (Bordas agreed to publish them with five etchings by Picasso, and Artaud made several trips to Picasso's studio on the Rue des Grands-Augustins but never managed to see the painter. The poems were published with eight drawings by Artaud himself.) A note in Susan Sontag's edition of Artaud's *Selected Writings* explains: "Mômo is Marseilles patois; it means simpleton, village idiot. . . . In Latin and in several modern languages, the name came to mean—more generally—any

3. Sketch of Vasarely drawing of Artaud, by Ralph Fetterly

captious or irascible critic, someone impossible to please."[45] The entire group of poems is vitriolic in its attack on materiality and especially sexuality. Vivid in carnal imagery, strong in incantatory rhythm, the poems rave around the pain that drives them.

Even when he was not onstage, Artaud attached enormous importance to the voice. He chanted his poems aloud as he wrote them, and his whole body seemed to participate in the activity. Onstage his vocal range and idiosyncratic breathing often obscured the sense of the words, but their theatricality was intense. Artaud probably began his performance with the first poem of the group to be written, "Center-Mother and Boss-Darling," which has also been translated (by Clayton Eshleman) as "Mother Center and Kitty Owner." The poem immerses us at once in Artaud's elliptical density:

> I speak the walled totem
> for the mural totem is such
> that the viscous formations
> of being
> can no longer mount close by.

Punning and resonant, Artaud inveighs against sexuality that seeks to strangle a totem that is in a sense himself. Seated, nervous, violating French tonic accent, interrupting himself or repeating himself, the poet was scarcely understood even by those who knew him.

With the second (and far more difficult) poem that he read, however, Artaud seemed to gain expressive control. After a moment of hiccups, he enunciated more distinctly. Not only is "The Return of Artaud the Mômo" the longest poem of the group of five, but it is also more ostentatiously personal, more virulent in its denunciation of the flesh, and it breaks into three incantatory groups of neologisms that his editor, Paule Thévenin, calls glossolalia. For Artaud the body is meat, with the tongue and the sexual organs its excrescences. Malignant enchanters suck and devour him, and the most malignant of all is God. Fearful of nonbeing, Artaud is haunted by the hole, which becomes a dominant image in the last French lines of the impassioned text:

> He is this unframed hole
> which life wanted to frame.
> Because it's not a hole
>   but a nose
> that always knew too well how to sniff
> the wind of the apocalyptic
>   head
> which they suck on his tight ass,
> and how good Artaud's ass is
> for the pimps in penitence.
>
> And you too have the gum,
> and right gum buried,
>   god,
>
> your gum has been cold too
> for an infinity of years
> since you sent me your innate ass
> to see if I was going to be born
>   in the end
> since the time you waited for me
>   scraping
>   my absentee's belly.
>   (Weaver translation)

The poem, instead of indicting society, belches revulsion for man's mortality.

The third poem, "Indian Culture," despite its title, burns with Artaud's own hatred of sexuality and procreation, screamed in elongated vowels. (Reading it publicly later in 1947, Roger Blin nearly broke down as he imitated his friend.)

After a brief intermission, during which no one reports going backstage to see him, Artaud returned to his table and in a conversational tone (at least at first) began either to read or to improvise an account of his trip to Mexico, his arrest in Dublin, his extradition to France, and his electric shock treatments while imprisoned in an asylum. He was virulent against the Dublin police, French sailors, miscellaneous enchanters, and, above all, those who had sentenced him to electric shock treatments. At some point he described his soul detaching itself from his body as from the ceiling he watched hospital attendants torture that body with electric shocks. At another point he read another poem from the "Artaud the Mômo" sequence—"Insult to the Unconditioned," whose opening lines reveal the division within him that he saw as cosmic:

> It is by bad meat
> filthy bad meat
> that one expresses
>   The
> That one doesn't know
>   That
>   To place oneself outside
>   In order to be without. . . .

For all the fragmentation of the evening—poems out of context, snatches of an autobiography—it was a whole in passionately condemning "civilized" society, including its metaphysical basis. As the journalist André Delmas later realized, Artaud was a man who "by his poems, that is to say, by words, pronounced a judgment against everything that protects the human race (in order to perpetuate it) from life and death, from good and evil, from sex, from language, and from the accomplishments of art."[46]

For some three hours—the length of an ordinary evening in the theater, but how extraordinary the performance—Artaud literalized the advertised tête-à-tête as his mind assaulted the minds in the crowded theater. At some point in the evening his agitated hands swept a few pages of his manuscript to the stage floor. When he knelt to pick them up, his glasses fell off. On hands and knees, with impaired sight, he reached around uncertainly. Seventy-eight-year-old André Gide in the front row pointed to the pages, but Artaud, supporting himself on the table, rose to his feet and then sank into his chair, from which he addressed the audience directly: "I put myself in your place, and I can see that what I tell you isn't at all interesting. It's still theater. What can one do to be truly sincere?"[47] That question has preoccupied many subsequent theater artists, but a gestural reply on January 13, 1947, came from the old humanist André Gide.

When Artaud ceased speaking in the silent theater, the dean of French letters was helped to the stage by his neighbor Adamov. The old man embraced the ill man and guided him offstage. Afterward two writers published polar reactions to a scene reminiscent of Lear and Gloucester. The Surrealist poet Sarane Alexandrian, nineteen years old and seated on the floor, was overcome with emotion: "I had just had the revelation of a great poet in rebellion against all the invisible powers of the Cosmos, and I hardly slept that night." The novelist Marcel Jouhandeau understood Artaud's condemnation of God, but not his obsession with sexuality. He thought Artaud had purchased freedom at the price of his sanity: "Gide alone then had the courage to stride across the footlights and get on the stage, so as to mask by a little greatness and humanity the atrocious bad taste in the exhibition of such misery."[48]

Artaud's friend Roger Blin was so stirred by the experience that he projected his feeling to the rest of the audience:

> [Artaud] was seated, a blackboard before him and a pile of papers, because he had written a text specially for that evening. The whole room was in an extraordinary state of emotion. And then, gradually, at a certain moment, he made a clumsy gesture, I don't know . . . his papers flew around . . . he lost his glasses. . . . He got down on his knees to gather his papers . . . but naturally there wasn't a laugh in the room. . . . We were all in extreme anguish . . . and suddenly he was afraid . . . he felt . . . he told us afterwards that the void in the room made him afraid.[49]

The writer Jacques Audiberti interpreted the silences less sympathetically:

> In his lectures Artaud plays nothing, does nothing. Before everyone he is the man imprisoned in the man, who is fed up, who wants to get out, and who howls. At the Vieux-Colombier Artaud (auto-actor) interrupted his discourse with outrageous silences. Each of his silences thundered like the prelude to the end of man and of the world. Partial panic convulsed the au-

dience. . . . The silhouette of the lucid madman gesturing around his table created immense shadows that shaped the monsters that will succeed us. Suddenly, without looking at his watch, Artaud stopped torturing himself and assaulting us. At the very moment planned for the intermission. At once, from all sides, hawkers came into view, crying: "Eskimo pies! Chocolates!"[50]

After Artaud's death fifteen months later, Gide published his own impression of that performance:

In the back of the auditorium—of that dear old auditorium of the Vieux Colombier that could seat about three hundred persons—there were a half dozen rowdies come to the meeting in the hope of having some fun. Oh! I believe they would have gotten themselves locked up by Artaud's warm friends scattered about the auditorium. But no; after one very timid attempt at rowdyism, there was no call to interfere. . . . We were present at a stupendous spectacle; Artaud triumphed, turning mockery and insolent nonsense into respect; he dominated. . . .

I had known Artaud for a long time, both his anguish and his genius. Never before had he seemed so admirable to me. Nothing remained of his material being except expression. His long ungainly form, his face consumed by internal fire, his hands like those of a drowning man, either extended toward assistance beyond reach, or twisted in agony, or most often tightly clasped over his face, hiding and revealing it turn and turn about, everything about him disclosed the abominable human anguish, a kind of damnation without succor, without possible escape except into a wild lyricism which reached the public only in ribald, imprecatory and blasphemous outbursts. And without a doubt here was the marvelous actor that this artist could become. But it was his own person he was offering to the public, with a sort of shameless third-rate acting, through which penetrated a total authenticity. Reason beat a retreat; not only his, but that of the whole audience, of all of us, spectators at that atrocious drama, reduced to the roles of ill-willed supernumeraries, jackasses and mere nobodies. Oh, no, no one in the audience had any more desire to laugh, and Artaud had even taken away from us, for a long time, the desire to laugh. He had forced us into his tragic game of revolt against everything that, admitted by us, remained for him, purer, inadmissible . . . [my ellipsis].

On leaving that memorable performance, the audience remained silent. What could they say? They had just seen an
unhappy man, fearfully shaken by a god, as on the threshold
of a deep grotto, secret cave of the Sibyl where nothing profane
is tolerated, where, as on a poetic Carmel a *vates* exposed, offers to the thunderbolt, to the devouring vultures, at the same
time both priest and victim. . . . We felt ashamed to go back
to our places in a world where comfort consists of compro-
mises.

(Elsie Pell translation; except where
noted, dots are Gide's punctuation
and do not indicate ellipses)[51]

Gide waited some fifteen months to record his reaction to
Artaud's performance on the evening of January 13, 1947, but
others felt its impact well over fifteen years later—even when
they were not among the throng of spectators in the Vieux-
Colombier. For Michel Foucault, Artaud is among the inspired
madmen—Hölderlin, Nietzsche, Roussel—whose discourse
he exalts. For Jacques Derrida, Artaud is a prophet of the de-
construction of texts to celebrate their indeterminacy or, in his
popular neologism, their *différance*. Artaud serves Derrida as
the springboard for two essays of *Writing and Difference*. Although he makes almost no reference to "Artaud the Mômo,"
the main text of Artaud's performance at the Vieux-Colombier, Derrida's consecration of Artaud as the key figure in the
closure of representation—the representation hallowed by
twenty-five hundred years of Western philosophy and art—
may be juxtaposed with Artaud's own last appearance in a
theater, an art about which Artaud himself came to be ambivalent.

Artaud often wrote of two different kinds of theater: the
theater of his time, which he despised, and an ideal theater
elevated to the mystical; so he seemed to waver in his attitude
toward his *Tête-à-tête* of January 13, 1947. To his friend Blin,
he had insisted on a solo performance, implying a role. And
yet to his friend Breton he denied the charge of playing a role
when he found himself on a stage: "Yes, I appeared on the
stage once again A LAST TIME at the Vieux-Colombier, with

the clear intention of exploding the frame, and exploding it from inside. I don't think that the spectacle of a man who bellows and howls in such fury as to vomit his intestines is a very theatrical spectacle."[52]

Prophet of the theater though he became, Artaud was wrong about the performance of January 13, 1947. Not only was his presence sufficiently moving to captivate an overflow crowd in the most distinguished avant-garde theater of Paris, but the evening itself has become legendary, and it has been dramatized in several performances based on Artaud's life. Perhaps inspired by that evening, Arthur Adamov published an article on Artaud in April 1947, urging readers not to limit their acquaintance with him to *The Theater and Its Double* but to immerse themselves in the late visionary poems. For the critics Georges Charbonnier and Alain Virmaux, Artaud's performance on January 13, 1947, is the only example of his Theater of Cruelty.

Fifteen months after his Vieux-Colombier performance, Artaud died of cancer. He wrote vehemently during that period, and legend has it that dead, he was sitting up, as though overtaken at work. At unfriendly journalist, however, describes a visit in February 1948 to a madman with knife and axe, who died lying in his own excrement.[53] Although that report does not enhance the portrait of an enchanted enchanter, it is not inconsistent with Artaud's mortal hatred of corporeality as an excrescence.

EVIL IS RUNNING OUT
(LE MAL COURT)
Jacques Audiberti

André Gide viewed Artaud's final performance through his own humanistic aesthetic. Through his homemade humanism, Jacques Audiberti viewed that same performance, feeling it was all the stronger because Artaud spurned set, costumes, and technical apparatus. Artaud is a household god of anyone who appreciates theater; for example, there is an Artaud Company in London, a Project Artaud in San Francisco. In contrast, Jacques Audiberti (1899–1965) is virtually unknown outside his native France. Yet there are a few striking similarities between the two men. Born three years apart in southern France, they both came to Paris in their early twenties. Autodidacts, neither was punctilious about intellectual rigor, but both expressed themselves voluminously in highly charged emotional works of uncertain genre. Both contrast sharply with Sartre, university trained and so adept at national examinations that he took first place (on second try) in philosophy, whereas Artaud and Audiberti crafted their own less erudite philosophies—Cruelty and Abhumanism. During the 1930s Artaud erupted in a series of manifestos of a Theater of Cruelty that rejected Western civilization, and during the 1940s Audiberti developed his philosophy of Abhumanism to ground his diffusion of literary efforts; he saw man as part of nature, without privileged status. Like Artaud, Audiberti did much of his writing at café tables. He married a West Indian teacher and had two daughters, but he lived alone in Paris hotels. In 1940 he and Arthur Adamov were neighbors in the still-functioning, much-refurbished Hôtel Taranne at St. Germain-des-Prés; Adamov transferred the name Taranne to a professor who appeared to him in a dream, and Audiberti used its setting in his novel *Talent*. Audiberti has recorded his witness of Artaud's Vieux-Colombier performance, but there is no evidence that the two writers met in more private circumstances. Although Audiberti viewed Artaud as a prophet of Abhumanism, there is no evidence that he read *The Theater and Its Double*. The Audiberti scholar Jeanyves Guérin has succinctly listed what the two writers shared:

> contacts with surrealism, admiration for Jarry, admiring interest in the primitive tribes of Mexico, an undeniable fascination with the Orient—Bali in the one case, India in the other—affinities with the gnostic tradition, passion for film, indifference to politics, a will to go beyond ideology, disdain for construction. . . . Artaud and [Audiberti] are similarly incapable of a rationally planned discourse, and they both declare them-

selves fervent readers of the Kabbala which is devoted to the
sonic value of words and not their semantic quality.[54]

For all these resemblances, however, the two men had distinctly separate visions of theater. Artaud's unsystematic the-
ories, imperfectly realized in his few productions, became the
inspiration of many directors in our shrinking world—the
Becks, Brook, Grotowski, Serban, and many amateurs in
American universities. Audiberti, in contrast, accommodated
himself comfortably to the rhetorical tradition of French theater. Although he wrote a play, *Ampelour*, as early as 1937 and
even though he was rumored to speak theatrical dialogue
spontaneously, he never came to the attention of such word-
loving directors as Copeau, Dullin, or Jouvet. Nor did he attend the theater before the Liberation, harried as he was with
free-lance journalism and the rejection of masses of his
poems. But friends were attracted when he recited his poems
in cafés—among them the young actor André Reybaz, who
begged him to write a play. In 1945 Audiberti offered him
Quoat-Quoat, subtitled "*poem* in dialogue" (my emphasis).

With Audiberti's warm but ineffectual support, André Reybaz founded a theater company in 1946. Still bruised by the
recent war and continued deprivation, Paris left-wing intellectuals were suspicious of those who had continued in their
professions during the Occupation, especially actors who had
acted, painters who had exhibited, writers who had published. Audiberti, as the film critic of the weekly *Comoedia*,
which had continued to appear during the Occupation, was
non grata on the Left, whose members warned Reybaz not to
direct *Quoat-Quoat*, but the young director ignored them. He
named his new company the Myrmidon, after the ship that
represented the world in *Quoat-Quoat*, which in turn was
named for the mighty army of classical Achilles. Typically, Audiberti blends that classical residue into the titular Aztec god,
a spirit of evil. At the mundane level of theater, an evil spirit
hovered over the young Myrmidon company that rented the
pre-Blin Gaité-Montparnasse for their maiden voyage, only to
be run aground by cursory reviews and sparse attendance.

Undaunted, Audiberti continued to write plays and even a hint of theater theory: "The theater is a Tribunal. Fear and plea and mime of the Last Judgment. For a man who has always trembled, it is serious and risky, but it's great to seek to communicate with open heart, facing the arrows."[55] This is not quite Artaud's martyr signaling from his pyre, but Audiberti's stance too calls for courage.

By Audiberti's own (somewhat dubious) account, his most popular play was a hit-and-miss affair: "I wrote *Evil Is Running Out* at one sitting of two or three hours, on graph paper, as though these three short acts awaited me somewhere in space. They existed before existing. Three times in *Evil Is Running Out* someone knocks at the door of the young princess, and each time she asks: 'Who's there?' and someone on the other side of the door answers: 'The king.' Well, I myself never knew who was actually behind the door. I learned it only by continuing to write rapidly."[56] And *we* learn how Audiberti's words gush out and eventually englobe a plot.

As Audiberti poured out his plays—twenty-eight of them, including adaptations—his stage fills with people and props; plots and prose grow more intricate. But his first few plays, notably *Evil Is Running Out*, are almost classical, each with a single set, continuous action, and few characters. Only the language is baroque, brimming with archaisms, neologisms, and regionalisms, often woven into long, Germanic sentences. Like most of his subsequent plays, *Evil is Running Out* (subtitled "philosophical operetta") is set in the past—the eighteenth century. Like *No Exit* it traces a growing awareness that hell is other people, but hell in Audiberti's play is called evil, and the awareness is limited to Alarica, Princess of Courteland.

In contrast to Sartre's tight triangle of people who make one another's hell, Audiberti's "other people" are more diffuse—an engaging scoundrel who poses as a king, the actual and marriageable King Parfait, his foreign minister the Cardinal, the Governess of the Princess, her father the King of Courteland, his Marshall. The innocent Princess Alarica, on her way to marry King Parfait, is betrayed by one character

4. *Evil Is Running Out*

after another; the handsome poseur intrudes on the privacy of the Princess; the King breaks his engagement to her; the Cardinal plunges her into political exigencies; her Governess and the seductive scoundrel prove to be agents of King Parfait; and finally her own royal but penurious father is bribed to sever the alliance. Evil runs rife, and finally it catches Alarica with its lure of power. She rejects the King, sleeps with her seducer, and dominates the other characters with her acquired knowledge of how to manipulate evil.

Although eight characters may not seem like a great increase over the three of *No Exit*, diffusion dilutes intensity.

Alarica high-handedly takes command of her own destiny, but her only evil deed in the play is to sleep with the attractive stranger, and this is evil only in the context of an outworn sexual morality. Nevertheless, punning on the meanings of *court* in French, "runs" and "short," Audiberti claims: "Alarica's cry at the end of the play—evil is running out—bears witness to this fact that evil spreads rapidly [runs], but it also expresses the wish that this evil be of short duration [is running out], and that love and goodness will displace it." Or, in a critic's pithy and untranslatable summary: "Il faut que le mal coure pour que le mal soit court."[57]

Despite a bold conclusion for 1947—a lusty princess seizes absolute power—*Evil Is Running Out* relies on two staples of French Boulevard theater, sexual titillation and mannered speeches. When the dissembling seducer woos the princess, he waxes eloquent: "But you, Alarica, you, flesh of my life, thought of my flesh, you whom I know, you whom I feel listening to me through all your apertures, who seize me in all your curls, you whose heart leaps with love and sorrow, how will you dare to look at me when, this very day, this evening, not far from the river, before the cathedral, we meet in the presence of our ministers and our recording officials?" Preciosity suffuses Alarica's political lesson to her former fiancé, King Parfait: "The error, the only error would have been your Majesty's risking the luster of so many battles and great men, the whole Roman Occident, the iris and the cross, in an alliance with a princess, myself, whose father not so long ago gave lessons in salad making." Having failed to win the King, Alarica snuggles up loquaciously to her lover: "But since the King could not—and his reasons are neither suspicious nor petty—since he could not climb all the steps to the altar, I judge it equitable to have given you the joy of my body, you who first, not without courage, came to take my lips." Although Audiberti's characters all speak alike, they all speak with verve and variety. The language shifts without warning from the courtly to the parodic, from the witty to the pathetic.

It seemed as though Audiberti was blending the prewar preciosity of Giraudoux with the contemporary colloquialism of Anouilh. Rather than exploit well-known myths as they did, however, Audiberti dredges up familiar motifs—the fair innocent maiden, a weak old father, conniving courtiers—to serve them with a modern twist.

Evil Is Running Out was Audiberti's first play to be written with the theater in mind, but after the failure of *Quoat-Quoat* the neophyte playwright hesitated to approach Reybaz again. Providentially, Audiberti met the Russian-born actor-director Georges Vitaly, for whom 1947 began propitiously. On January 15, two days after Artaud's performance at the Vieux-Colombier (which he did not attend), Vitaly turned thirty and, considering himself a Parisian, became a French citizen. He had spent five years training as an actor, memorizing hundreds of scenes, but he first appeared professionally as a mute in a prewar production of his fellow countryman Pitoëff. During the Occupation Vitaly played bit parts here and there, but he returned to Paris at the Liberation, anxious to direct new plays. After meeting Audiberti at a café and listening to his verbal onrush, Vitaly requested a play and promptly received *Evil Is Running Out*. The neophyte director, having directed a double bill of Chekhov and Courteline at the Théâtre de Poche, again rented that small theater for the play of the unknown Audiberti.

Vitaly decided to set Audiberti's baroque language against a flat background, envisioning the spectacle as a game of cards.[58] He cast the play in open auditions and then called the cast members the Georges Vitaly Company—"une distribution d'illustres inconnus." With their help, he built the set for the shallow stage, insouciantly obstructing the entrance to 75 Boulevard Montparnasse. Onstage he had to block with care, so that the eight actors would not bump into one another or knock down the fragile flats. He taught the actors to navigate around the main set pieces, a bed and a screen. Not only were the flats and costumes of bright hue, but the actors also wore heavy makeup that was all too visible in the tiny theater. Audiberti's flamboyant prose in their resonant voices almost exploded the Théâtre de Poche on the warm June evenings.

The reviews were brief and modest, in spite of the vibrant

performance of Suzanne Flon as Alarica. A friend of Edith Piaf, Flon had acted small parts during the Occupation, mainly Ismene in Anouilh's *Antigone*. André Roussin, soon to be a successful Boulevard playwright, was so captivated by her (although she did not appear nude, as specified at one point in the text) that he cast her in his new comedy *The Little Shack* (*La Petite Hutte*), which yielded them both years of profit. During her long successful career on the Paris stage Flon zigzagged between the Boulevard and the avant-garde, sought by both. Finally, she turned to modern classics—such as Pirandello's *To Each His Truth* in 1984.

When *Evil Is Running Out* opened, however, Flon's rich and varied career seemed improbable, and the play would have closed after the mandatory thirty performances were it not for the Contest for New Theater Companies inaugurated in 1946. Some sixty groups competed, and Vitaly's very new company took first place, enabling him to pay his debts and to lease the larger Comédie des Champs-Elysées for a summer's *good* run (as opposed to the evil run of his title). That summer the last American soldiers left France, and tobacco became available without ration cards. For his company, Vitaly enlisted actors who later became well known in Paris—Chauffard (the bellboy of *No Exit*), Jacques Fabbri, Guy Retoré. In 1953 Vitaly was doing so well that he rented a theater of respectable size—the Right Bank La Bruyère, which still proudly displays the posters of his eclectic repertory during seventeen years' tenancy.

In 1955 Vitaly revived *Evil Is Running Out* with the original cast in his larger theater, which was better suited to Audiberti's panache. In 1963, again at La Bruyère, Vitaly directed another successful revival of *Evil Is Running Out*, with Sylvia Montfort as Alarica. Flon's innocent princess awoke only slowly to evil, but once alert, she determinedly used her sexual wiles to gain power. Montfort was more carnal and canny from the start, in keeping with Vitaly's new view of the play as a Voltairian fable. Léonor Fini designed delicate sets and costumes, so that evil ran out as gracefully as Montfort waved her evil whip. Stage flats were white, gold, and red in a setting for Montfort's final assumption of dominance as a *mise à mort*.

Nearly twenty years later, in 1982, Vitaly introduced a new generation to Audiberti's play at the small Théâtre Tourtour near the Beaubourg Museum. In this pocket theater, carved out of a seventeenth-century cellar, Vitaly carried over the golden beige of the old walls to his set and costumes, using strong black lines for contrast. On the shallow vaulted stage, the action looked like a moving fresco. The years had passed, and Vitaly, who had played King Parfait in 1947, played a grayed, rheumatic, partially deaf Marshall in 1982. His energy was nevertheless undiminished, and Audiberti's wordy text was swiftly delivered by the mainly young cast. The role of Alarica went to Anne-Marie Philipe, daughter of the beloved French actor who died in 1959.

Through the decades Vitaly justified the vitality of his name by directing seven Audiberti plays in twelve different productions, but the critic Jeanyves Guérin has accused the faithful director of being insufficiently outrageous for Audiberti. Vitaly believes that his productions of Audiberti were Dionysian, and he looks back on them nostalgically after directing everything from Greek tragedy to musical comedy, with a specialty in Grand Guignol that demands its own kind of outrage.

Audiberti, who died in 1965, has been revived in the 1970s under the bright, boisterous direction of Marcel Maréchal in the large theaters of Lyon and Marseilles, whereas Vitaly returned to his beginnings in pocket theater. After the run the production was televised in 1982, but *Evil Is Running Out* still has not been translated into English.

EPIPHANIES
Henri Pichette

When Vitaly introduced himself to Audiberti at Café des Deux Magots, the neophyte director was seeking new material, even coaxing poets and novelists to write plays. One of these poets was Henri Pichette.[59] Son of an American father and a French mother, Pichette led a chaotic childhood, buffeted as he was between parents and adoptive parents; he attended schools sporadically in several parts of France. As a teenager, influenced by Rimbaud and Lautréamont, Pichette began to write prose poems. After leaving the lycée, he worked desultorily. Drafted as a farm laborer during the Occupation, he deserted to take part in the liberation of Marseilles—at age twenty. In 1945, on his twenty-first birthday, he married and subsequently went to Germany as a journalist. In 1946 he came to Paris with a sheaf of poems, arriving at about the same time as Artaud—already one of his heroes. When poems by both Pichette and Artaud were rejected for publication in one of the post-Liberation periodicals, Pichette undertook to publish them privately in a small edition (fifty-three copies) with a long title: *Xylophonie contre la grande presse et son petit public* (Xylophony against the mainstream press and its petty public).

Vitaly admired Pichette's *apoèmes* and urged him to consider writing a lyrical play, dangling before him the bait of actor Gérard Philipe, the soft-spoken, handsome southerner who had been acclaimed in Paris in 1945 when he enacted the mad emperor in Camus's *Caligula*. Vitaly played the philosopher Helicon in that tragedy, and the two actors became friends. Philipe also admired Pichette's poems and tried to lure Pichette to the theater. No sooner did Pichette begin the "profane mystery" that evolved into *Epiphanies* than Philipe left for Italy to make the movie *The Charterhouse of Parma*, but Pichette sent him segment after segment in bold red ink. Immediately enthusiastic about the exuberant lyricism of *Epiphanies*, Philipe showed the pages to Maria Casarès, his colleague in the film, who agreed to play opposite him on the stage when they returned to Paris.

In the winter of 1947, when many buildings still lacked fuel, Philipe personally rented the warm Right Bank Théâtre Edouard VII for *Epiphanies*, and Vitaly cast the supporting roles, notably Roger Blin as the Devil. Before rehearsals began, Philipe would listen for hours as Pichette read aloud

5. Stars of *Epiphanies*, with Vitaly (*left*) and Pichette (*standing*)

from his play, but finally he imposed his own reading on the central role of the Poet. As Pichette later described the effect: "One morning, like a painter who distributes his colors, [Philipe] controlled the palette of his voice, and, sure of his tone, he launched out, and my ear thought it was seeing the nuances of love, the joyous sunny outbursts, a monochrome of nocturnal sadness, the reason of the poem resting on a depth of madness."[60] To enhance Pichette's lyricism, Vitaly persuaded the Chilean Surrealist Roberto Matta, just returned from New York, to paint five background canvases, one for each act. Concrete music was composed by the musician Maurice Roche.

After two weeks of activity, the manager of the Théâtre Edouard VII attended a rehearsal and then forbade the cast to continue. Jean Marais's production of Racine's *Andromaque* had been censored during the Occupation in that very theater, and the manager, Béteille, wished no invidious comparisons, so he wrote to Vitaly: "I'm a nice guy. Here is my proposition. I'll bring a few normal people to one of your rehearsals. If they are not too outraged, I'll allow you to perform a few matinees from 6 to 8 P.M. And if these matinees do not cause a scandal, I'll continue the performances of *Epiphanies* in the evening."[61]

Unabashed and undiscouraged, Philipe rented the Left Bank Noctambules, but Pichette, furious, stormed into print in the hospitable pages of *Combat*. Pichette charged that Béteille had accepted a play he had not read only to exploit the stellar names of Philipe and Casarès. Condemning sordid commercial motives, Pichette sounded a clarion call for a new theater whose only scandal would be to fight for free respiration against strangulation and for luminous rocks against garbage, in the imagery that poured out from his play to his manifesto.

In a time of general strikes in postwar Paris, when the Communists staged an all-night sit-in at the Chamber of Deputies, Vitaly at the Noctambules launched a revolt in the theater with the declaration that his group was committed to a theater of rupture: "How fine it is, in these joyless days, that a group of young people come together, animated by an unshakable faith, challenging bad taste, base behavior, and despair, in opposition to a Paris that is almost always lulled by digestive, toothless, and inert theater." *Epiphanies* seemed to Vitaly the perfect vehicle for a theater of rupture: "Rupture with normal dialogue, with a normal sequence of scenes, also rupture with audience contact, for we no longer appeal to their reason and critical sense, but to their sensitivity, to their emotional capacity, and their ability to be impressed. Also rupture in the set, for the background is abstract, synthesizing the mood of each act. Finally, rupture in the musical accompaniment."[62]

When the high-spirited young cast opened on a cold night during the Cold War—December 3, 1947—they seared Paris with their ardor, although critics professed some confusion about the play's subject. Pichette claimed that his play was literally a series of appearances; Philipe thought that as the Poet, he performed man's inner life; and Vitaly agreed that the play was the externalization of a long interior monologue. No one associated the performance with Christian epiphany, despite the title.

Epiphanies, a profane mystery in free verse, is divided into five movements: (1) Genesis, (2) Love, (3) War, (4) Delirium, (5) Accession, State, or Accomplishment (in different revisions). All five acts center on the Poet protagonist, a Herculean role for an actor. Only two other characters emerge with any amplitude—the Beloved of the Poet (played by Casarès) and the Devil (played by Blin). In "Genesis" the protagonist is born as a poet: "I am an adult." The Poet learns about nature and culture, country and city, individual and society, and the plenitude of life on earth. The Poet is rhapsodic about the dawn of his sensitivity and sensuality. Occasionally, he is aware of his mediating function: "And things have dramatic eyes." "Actors drill into the continent of the public. . . . The stage is no longer separate from the rest of the world." The words of the Poet are rhythmic rather than vivid, tumultuous rather than precise. Like Whitman, Pichette's Poet thrives on contradictions; he hymns and claims to be the dawn.

The second act opens on short lyrical lines by a number of minor characters, who are accompanied by music and nonverbal sounds. When the Poet arrives, he utters a long epithalamium to his Beloved, whom he has fashioned to his need: "I manufacture my lover to order." At first monosyllabic, she soon raises her voice in response: "By day and night you reveal me. By night and day I prepared myself for the perfect marriage." For a few moments they exchange vows in verbs of penetration, often neologisms. Then, abruptly, the Devil interrupts their idyll, cynically revealing the sordid aspects of physical love—"below the belt"—and the many temptations to betray love. As the Devil draws to the end of his tirade, war is announced.

The third act dramatizes the effect of war on the Poet. Spurred by the Devil to fight, inspired by the clichés his friend utters, the Poet finds himself on the battlefield, where all races and classes are equal. To the rhythms of modern military percussion, the Poet declaims his potential to destroy. As the Poet fights on stubbornly, a seer keeps chanting: "The goldfinches are obliterated, the goldfinches are obliterated."

The fourth act, "Delirium," shows the Poet seeking peace after devastation. Again the Devil fulfills his traditional evil role. So rebellious is the spirit of the Poet, so indomitable his will to live and love, that the Devil sentences him to be executed by a firing squad. Though the Poet is shot (after one of the longest rhapsodies in the play), poetry soars.

The last act begins with the Devil's outline of a state of system, to which the Poet (again alive and well) is opposed. The two engage in a long wordy debate, the Devil pitting his powers of annihilation against the Poet's powers of imagination. At the last, the Devil falls, fatally wounded. Once he disappears, the Beloved returns for a few lyrical exchanges with the Poet, who concludes the play with an exuberant declaration of his feelings.

In Pichette's play, as opposed to Audiberti's, evil literally runs *out*, and the fantasy resonates idealistically: "It is the book of the world, the wind turns the page, here is the fragment of the singular heart, here the plurals unite, it is the species through all the verbal tenses and the discovery under the immemorial eye."

Even before *Epiphanies* opened, it was sold out for its thirty performances at the 240-seat Noctambules, after which Philipe was committed to a film. For all Vitaly's preperformance boasts of a group theater of rupture, and for all Pichette's accusations against Béteille of the Théâtre Edouard VII, it was Philipe who was acclaimed in the reviews, which were sharply divided on Pichette's text. Philipe performed as Poet without makeup or costume. He dressed like many young men in his postwar audience—in nondescript wrinkled trousers and a heavy dark wool sweater. Blin as the Devil wore a light raincoat, and Casarès as the Beloved wore a simple black dress. ("In black you're always dressed up" is an old French cliché.)

A succinct account was published by the usually verbose Audiberti: "Gérard Philipe in the sweater of a student and Roger Blin in the raincoat of a Central European policeman. No action except gymnastics. Gérard Philipe stood up, sat down, lay down, in the last case on the body of Maria Casarès, who was there only to assume, not without modesty, the dull womanly function in, let us say, our dispute with God. Gérard Philipe, at the pleasure of the woman or the war, stood up, fell down, stood up again. Blin entered, left. . . . The set was limited to a canvas where magnified microbes associated with planets."[63]

In the first act—the birth of the Poet—Philipe was so full of energy that it sometimes seemed as though he would career over the heads of the audience and on to a distant star. The second act—"Love"—almost literally coupled the two name actors in a bed onstage; the simulated intercourse shocked the prurient. The physical beauty of the pair and their rich voices, however, led reviewers to prefer this act to the others. The Devil's long cynical speeches were a triumph for Blin, who stuttered offstage; in defeat, he became a howling dog. The minor characters were sometimes invisible, but their voices were often amplified.

In the third act—"War"—some half dozen actors lay down on the darkened stage, their cigarettes moving like fireflies while explosive sounds signaled the surrounding battle (with which some audience members were all too familiar). But acts 4 and 5 returned to the verbose French tradition, for all the innovative manipulation of words: "[Pichette] tortures and breaks the language, throwing it into chaos; he unties words from their usual functions so as to clash them together in a great shower of sparks; with a kind of self-indulgent presumption in his own virtuosity, he substitutes an improper word for the proper one, an invented word for the usual one, a noun for a verb, by means of which he manages to give his phrases a sumptuousness that is sometimes admirable."[64]

Although the run at the Noctambules was sold out, there was no question of continuing without Philipe. *Epiphanies* was revived in 1948 with the same cast, but without the Matta canvases, too small for the larger theater, the Ambassadeurs; the paintings seem to have disappeared. In 1948, too, Pichette published the text of the play, with symbols designating the characters, and other typographic innovations—a forerunner of concrete poetry. Almost unnoticed was the publication of Pichette's "Apoème 4" in *Transition*, translated by Samuel Beckett.

When Philipe again left *Epiphanies* to fulfill still another commitment, the play closed finally, but the poet and the actor remained friends. In 1952 Philipe not only performed but also directed Pichette's second effort for the stage—*Nucléa*—as a presentation of the newly constituted National Popular Theater. Despite the magnetic presence of Philipe—as well as the considerable talents of Jeanne Moreau and Jean Vilar, mobiles by Calder, and stereophonic sound—the reviews were lukewarm about Pichette's resonant verbiage in the cavernous spaces of the Palais de Chaillot. After *Nucléa* Pichette published several volumes of verse, but he did not write again for the theater.

Years after the production of *Epiphanies* the poet-playwright acknowledged that audiences did not like his play but adored Philipe. An exacting critic, Roger Blin, also admired Philipe:

> I witnessed [at *Epiphanies*] the miracle of the intuitive actor, who had just come from Roussin, Giraudoux, realistic films, yet could instantly throw himself onto a lyrical wave without losing his balance, controlling its eddies and explosions, clarifying it without playing the word, but with great snatches of heartrending joy or with small touches of childish distress. Terribly gifted but also having worked hard, "the young dog" quickly sensed the traps of facility, charm, precocious fame. When I questioned him about [these traps, Philipe] answered me with a smile at the corner of his mouth: "Don't worry about it." Sure enough, there was nothing to worry about.[65]

Blin himself was prodigious, in the opinion of Adrienne Monnier, who saw *Epiphanies* three times at the small Noctambules and twice at the large Ambassadeurs.[66] When Monnier first went backstage to congratulate him, Blin explained that they had done what they could to protect the work. And in spite of full houses, it needed protectors against the charge of being an allegorical poem rather than a play. Even in the mellifluous voice of Gérard Philipe, paroxysmal rhapsodies grew monotonous. Acclaimed as Philipe was in *Epiphanies*, generous as he was to Pichette, flexible as he was under Vilar's direction at the National Popular Theater, he did not after *Nucléa* act in any new plays before he died at age thirty-seven—full of ambitious projects, since he was never told that he had cancer of the liver. In 1961, two years after Philipe's death, Pichette published a volume of poems in mourning for his friend—*The Tomb of Gérard Philipe*.

THE KNACKER'S ABC
(L'EQUARRISSAGE POUR TOUS)
Boris Vian

In 1959, the year Philipe died at age thirty-seven, Boris Vian died at age thirty-nine of a heart attack while discontentedly watching a film adaptation of his controversial novel *I'll Spit on Your Graves* (*J'irai cracher sur vos tombes*). The deaths of these two relatively young men—Philipe and Vian—struck at the generation that came of age during the Occupation, starved for all kinds of freedom. In Vian's jazz they heard the music of which they had been deprived. In Philipe's stage presence they saw the radicalism of the Resistance, in which he had taken part. Except in his earliest roles, Philipe endowed classical stage plays—*The Cid, Lorenzaccio, The Prince of Homburg, The Mandrake, Ruy Blas, Richard II, The Caprices of Mariane*—with the glamour of a movie star. Whether on stage or screen, however, it was as an actor that he magnetized a young public. In contrast, Vian was an engineer, trumpet player, songwriter, novelist, translator, and cabaret sketchwright before he wrote plays; he helped bring a cabaret lightness to legitimate theater. Popularized by other media—Philipe by film and Vian by jazz—both young men were attracted to theater, and they in turn attracted their followings to that venerable art.

Despite the Slavic flavor of the name Boris, Vian was born into a French bourgeois family.[67] Although rheumatic fever weakened his heart while he was an adolescent, he had a happy childhood, with his affluent family indulging the whims of their four children. Indifferent to school, he nevertheless received good grades and was admitted to the highly competitive national school of engineering. Awarded the degree during the Occupation, Vian went to work in the government bureau responsible for setting weights and measures. However, he spent much of his workday writing. In 1946 he changed to a government paper factory because the sympathetic department head there promised him he could spend his *whole* workday writing, but a year later Vian gave up the pretense of an engineering career.

In the rush of welcome for American GIs in Paris in 1944, Vian was one of the first to seek out black jazz musicians, and he was one of the moving spirits in the creation of the postwar myth of St. Germain-des-Prés, where the young listened to jazz between midnight and dawn. From 1946 to his death in 1959 Vian also wrote pell-mell—reviews, essays, sketches, plays, songs, fiction. His brother has described him in a typical moment: "One could often see him making a phone call, telephone wedged into his arm, while his right hand wrote words for a song, and his left—for he wrote easily with his left hand—translated from English, and at the same time he spoke to several people on different subjects."[68]

Vian's first play dates from 1947, when Paris was still suffering food shortages and the memory of World War II was vivid. Vian was nevertheless full of élan, since in 1946 he had completed three novels. Two of them—*Mood Indigo* (literally, The froth of days) and *Autumn in Peking*—retain many devoted readers, but the third—*I'll Spit on Your Graves*—was written in ten days for a publisher friend who wanted a commercially viable "American novel." Under the pseudonym Vernon Sullivan (which combined the names of two black musicians), Vian blended pornography with antiracism, and when he was arraigned for obscenity in 1947 (along with Henry Miller), the book became an underground best-seller.

It was therefore with a certain notoriety that Vian turned his hand to theater in 1947, quickly penning *The Knacker's ABC*, first subtitled "an anarchist vaudeville" and then "a paramilitary vaudeville."[69] The genre of French vaudeville—unrelated to the American form—is a throwback to the nineteenth century when bourgeois audiences laughed merrily through escapades that narrowly avoided scandal; inevitably, sexual affairs terminated, with the help of many doors in the set, on more or less legitimate couplings. But Vian's vaudeville is so anarchic that it ends in the annihilation of almost all the characters.

The place of action is ideal for farce—a horse butcher's (knacker's) foul-smelling house, adjoining a pit for dead horses. The time of the action, however, would seem more suitable to tragedy—June 6, 1944, or D day, when Allied troops of World War II landed in Normandy, with heavy losses. It is a very different D day in the mind of Vian's protagonist, a Norman horse butcher, who wants it to be the wedding day of his daughter Marie. She has spent the Occupation sleeping with a German soldier, Heinz Schnittermach. Marginally irritated by the noise of bombs and shells, the concerned father calls a family council to persuade his daughter to become "an honest woman." Through the cooperation of Radio London, his parachutist son Jacques returns from the American army and his parachutist daughter Catherine from the Soviet front. They both support the convention of marriage for Marie, who, in pre-Ionesco confusion, has the same name as her mother and sister. She is renamed Cyprienne (meaning lewd) despite her four years of fidelity to Heinz.

Since the play is a farce that thrives on confusion, her name is the only confusion to be clarified. American and German soldiers play strip poker for one another's uniforms, but all

6.   *The Knacker's ABC*

speak French. The horse butcher dreams longingly of battles
in the past, when a cavalry charge would have given him profitable carcasses. The sister named Marie lusts for all soldiers,
but she finds her prospective brother-in-law repulsive. An unknown soldier arrives, doubled over like wounded soldiers in
films, but this one merely asks for the toilet and then drops
dead. His is the first of several bodies to be thrown into the
horse pit. When the horse butcher radios for his parachutist
children to come home, a Japanese parachutist arrives, and,
proving he is Japanese, he commits hara-kiri. He too is
dumped into the horse pit.

The involved plot is full of comic detail. Vian's characters mock realistic plays in which parents are horrified by the pregnancy of an unwed daughter: his Norman family want Cyprienne to admit that she is pregnant so that they can celebrate a wedding. Although she denies the accusation even under torture by tickling, wedding preparations proceed, banquet preceding benediction. Commenting on the German retreat in terms that usually refer to working overtime, the family understand why the bridegroom is delayed. When Heinz finally does arrive—with his captain—the captain objects to the wedding: "If I don't have *any* soldiers left under my command, how can I go on being a captain?" But the question proves rhetorical when the Soviet parachutist daughter fells him with a hammer blow and tosses him into the horse pit. Other soldiers appear intermittently, and since there are not enough women for them, the butcher's apprentice dons a dress. It occurs to the family that a wedding requires a clergyman, and since Americans would not take a beachhead without a clergyman, the family assembles one from American supplies; he turns out to be Robert Taylor.

Spurred by the feuding brother and sister, the American soldier Jacques and the Soviet soldier Catherine, the banquet turns into a brawl, and the table collapses. Cyprienne chases the clergyman into the horse pit; Catherine and her mother lose their balance and fall into the pit. Americans and Germans in Salvation Army uniforms serenade the happy Franco-German couple with "I Love You Truly" (in English) and climb upstairs with Cyprienne and Heinz. The horse butcher and his neighbor are peremptorily told by French officers that the house is out of line with reconstruction plans and has to be destroyed. The horse butcher is killed in the explosion of the house, and the French captain shrugs: "Bah! You can't make an omelette without breaking eggs." The horse butcher's neighbor thereupon shoots the captain and is in turn shot by the lieutenant, who leaves the stage in impeccable goose step, to the tune of an off-key "Marseillaise."

Vian spares the sensibilities of no one at a time when war wounds were still raw and the four Allies were at loggerheads about the occupation of Berlin. When Commitment was as much a watchword as Relevance was in the 1960s, *The Knacker's ABC* celebrates the absence of commitment from its opening slang exclamation "C'est dégueulasse." Americans and Germans enjoy drinking *calva* together, and neither side knows the nationality of its enemy. Each soldier admires an item of "enemy" equipment, but everyone scorns the chewing gum or canned goods of the Americans. An American soldier is named Vladimir Krowski; the Jews and the English are disparaged. A fifty-year-old French soldier obeys a fourteen-year-old colonel. A clergyman would rather feast than officiate at a wedding. Neighbors ask each other casually: "Still alive?" All women are lecherous, and the horse butcher's wife breaks into tears at the slightest provocation; her husband comforts her by setting her to pointless tasks. Adults behave like children: the German soldier Heinz needs a note to his captain when he is late for duty; "American" Jacques and "Soviet" Catherine fight at the dinner table. Implicitly, the vaudeville salutes all those who ignore historic occasions. In the words of the paterfamilias: "This landing of theirs! It's beginning to get my goat. . . . my stupid bunch of children fighting in every corner of the earth instead of staying at home and learning the knacker's trade."

Somewhat disingenuously, Vian claimed that *The Knacker's ABC* was not intended to open recent wounds but to arouse laughter at an unlaughable subject—war—but directors were wary of his farce about a subject that inspired such tense dramas as Armand Salacrou's *Nights of Wrath* (*Nuits de la colère*) and Sartre's *Death without Burial* (*Mort sans sépulture*). The cabaret directors Pierre Grenier and Olivier Hussenot flirted for nearly two years with the idea of producing Vian's play, only to decide against it. Jean-Louis Barrault accepted it for production but then did not produce it. In the spring of 1948, over a year after *The Knacker's ABC* was written, the editor Jean Paulhan published an abridged version in *Cahiers de la Pléiade*. (That version also ends in the deaths of all characters, but they are not thrown into the horse pit.) In 1949 Vian's dramatization of his notorious novel *I'll Spit on Your Graves* was per-

formed—for three months—but he could find no theater for
his original play.

By the spring of 1950 Chancellor Konrad Adenauer of Germany was demanding equal rights for his country, and Vian
grew "rather impatient at seeing the diminishing topicality of
the satirical element of this entertainment"—as he phrased it
in his preface to the printed text. He turned to the director
André Reybaz, who had won the 1949 Contest for New Theater Companies with his production of Ghelderode's *Chronicles
of Hell*. Reybaz may have seen in Vian's play a similar grotesque violence. He swiftly committed the main role to memory, enlarged his company to fifteen, and rehearsed virtually
round the clock for two weeks.[70] At first Reybaz wanted a play
by Genet to accompany the hour-and-a-quarter-long *Knacker's
ABC*, but Vian swiftly wrote his own accompaniment—the
anticlerical *Last Profession* (*Le Dernier des métiers*). When this
was refused by the manager of the Noctambules, Reybaz coupled Vian's *Knacker* with Audiberti's *Skin*. (Published in a volume called *Doctors Are Not Plumbers* (*Les Médecins ne sont pas
des plombiers*), *Skin* is a trifle in the long French antimedical
stage tradition.)

Although written in 1947, when it seemed as though the
new French theater would adhere to the old loquacious tradition, *The Knacker's ABC* was not produced until 1950, the
mid-century year that would usher in several premieres of a
different new theater. For the obligatory thirty-performance
minimum after April 11, 1950, the shallow stage of the Noctambules was crowded with a table, a bench, chairs, saw-
horses, a staircase that stopped in midair, and fifteen actors
who doubled several parts. A box at stage right became the
entrance to the horse pit, and into it tumbled—one at a time—
eight bodies, but the actors crawled from the box into the
wing, unseen by the audience. Vian's vaudeville borrowed
from Jarry's *Ubu* the device for clearing the stage; Vian's "Into
the pit" echoed Jarry's "Into the trap." Going into the rehearsal of a farce two weeks before opening, the spirited
young cast invented both physical and verbal gags, but Vian,
whose jazz thrived on improvisation, objected to this early

example of collective creation, and Reybaz straitjacketed his group within Vian's text. The final explosion could not be staged, so the performance ended with the lieutenant's order to dynamite the house.

On the bloodred back flat, in an oval frame, hung an imitation horse's head, although Paris horse butchers used as their insignia gold-painted horses' heads. The stage was littered with nondescript wooden furniture, but the costumes were chosen for variety. Reybaz as the horse butcher wore an ankle-length apron, a work cap, and a fierce mustache. The German and American uniforms were authentic, but the adolescent French colonel wore shorts, the daughter Cyprienne was stripped to bra and panties, and "Soviet" Catherine wore leather boots, a short skirt, and a glittering red star at the nipple of each breast. (Played by Zanie Campan, Catherine may have profited from her farcical experience as Tart in the reading of Picasso's *Desire Caught by the Tail*.) Costumes have disappeared into the horse pit when the French lieutenant finally goose-steps into the wings; he was played by René Lafforgue, who had previously appeared as a Resistance fighter and before that as an American soldier—inauspicious doubling for one who was to have a long active career on the Paris stage. Most remarkable was Reybaz's blocking of the highly physical farce on the tiny stage, which he was rarely to leave in his own role of an ordinary father on an extraordinary day.

Although Reybaz claims that audience laughter on opening night slowed the performance by half an hour (more than a third of the playing time), reviews were mixed, and the show did not continue beyond the thirty-day minimum. An unsolicited testimonial was submitted by Jean Cocteau to the weekly *Opéra*—but was not printed in time to prolong the production. Comparing *The Knacker's ABC* to Apollinaire's *Breasts of Tiresias* (*Les Mamelles de Tirésias*) and his own *Couple on the Eiffel Tower* (*Les Mariés de la Tour Eiffel*) Cocteau conveys the delirium of the Noctambules production:

> And laughter explodes when the bomb explodes, and the bomb explodes with laughter, and the respect one shows toward catastrophes explodes, too, like a soap bubble.
> A group of merry young actors, busy in the wings trans-

forming themselves into Germans, Americans, Resistance Fighters, paratroopers, gallop across the stage, fall from the flies, leap up staircases leading nowhere, bump up against each other, mingle and then detach themselves in a void which is full to the brim.

Nothing could be more serious than this farce which is not a farce and yet is one, reflecting what we are compelled to take seriously and what is really serious in only two respects: the death of our fellow men and the certainty that this somber farce comes to an end only because of physical exhaustion— and then only for the short rest necessary for the participants to get their breath back and start over again as quickly as possible.

("Greetings to Boris Vian from
Jean Cocteau," in Simon Watson
Taylor translation of *The Knacker's ABC*)

When the full text of the play was published as a book, Vian added the daily reviews to Cocteau's account. He allowed the favorable reviews to speak for themselves, but he parried the unfavorable ones—especially that of Elsa Triolet, herself a literary Soviet paratrooper miscast as a theater reviewer.[71] In spite of Vian's efforts to provoke controversy over *The Knacker's ABC*, the play was not revived during his lifetime. By the summer of 1950 Vian was embroiled in the legal action against his novel, *I'll Spit on Your Graves*, and he was sentenced to pay a fine of one hundred thousand francs (some three hundred dollars, which was a heavy burden for him). His money-making schemes came to nought—cabaret collaboration with Reybaz, a guide to St. Germain-des-Prés (published only after his death). His subsequent plays were neither produced nor published during his lifetime, but one of them—*The Empire Builders* (*Les Bâtisseurs d'empire*)—offers evidence of his lingering fondness for his knacker, since the protagonist has practised knackery in Normandy, right after his marriage.

The verve of *The Knacker's ABC* appealed to the College of 'Pataphysics, a miscellaneous group of mainly Paris wits who formed their institute in appreciation and imitation of Jarry's Dr. Faustroll. In 1952 they admitted Vian to their society as a First-class Knacker. To his many other activities, Vian then added the writing of articles for the College's publications, and at his death they honored him: "His literary work is up to the multivalent level of his talents. Never unimportant, often sheer genius. Unequalled for constant invention. No one lived the hic et nunc of the doctrine of imaginary solutions to the extent of Boris Vian."[72]

Although Vian was a local celebrity at the time of his death in 1959, his wider fame is posthumous. His works have been published and republished, and beginning in the 1960s he has been a talismanic figure for young Parisians. The pocket-theater complex Le Lucernaire is centered on the Place Boris Vian. His novels have been adapted for the stage, and his songs are heard on radio and television. *The Knacker's ABC* is rarely revived, although it did play on television. In French accounts of the fortieth anniversary of D day—June 6, 1984— I saw no mention of Vian or his topical farce.

THE BALD SOPRANO
(LA CANTATRICE CHAUVE)
Eugene Ionesco

The weary boards of the Noctambules had no respite when three plays opened close on the heels of *The Knacker's ABC* (and *Skin*). While Vian's vaudeville was in its last week, Ionesco's *Bald Soprano*, another first play, premiered, with Nicolas Bataille directing a new company at the unpopular hour of 6:30. When the Reybaz double bill closed, Jean-Marie Serreau's new company replaced it with a double bill translated from the German—Kafka's *Guardian of the Tomb* and Brecht's *Exception and the Rule* (the first Brecht play to be seen in postwar Paris, and very nearly the first Brecht work ever to play in Paris). Serreau rented the Noctambules for the thirty-day minimum, but the manager of the theater, Pierre Leuris, was so charmed by *The Bald Soprano* that he asked no rent for the undesirable 6:30 slot.

The genesis of *The Bald Soprano* is better known than that of any modern play.[73] A thirty-six-year-old Franco-Romanian proofreader decides to teach himself English by the Assimil

7.   Actors in *The Bald Soprano* surrounding the Ionescos

method, popular after World War II. Absorbing the basic
phrases of his primer, Eugene Ionesco (revealing nothing of
his prewar position in the Romanian literary avant-garde)
suddenly finds that the primer sentences are "fundamental
truths and profound statements." Moving from these fundamental profundities to particulars, Ionesco in the third lesson
meets the Smith couple and then their younger friends, the
Martins. Entranced by their dialogue, Ionesco wishes to communicate his pleasure to the world at large, and the theater
seems the ideal medium, "for drama is dialogue." Ionesco,
whose account I have abridged, claims that at first he es-
chewed originality, merely copying and arranging the phrases
of his primer.

To his surprise, he affirms, these phrases took on a life of
their own, rebelling against the primer. The Martin husband
and wife, struck by amnesia, no longer know one another.

The Smiths are haunted by a whole population of Bobby Watsons. A Fire Chief bursts into shaggy-dog stories and then into an interminable family epic, "The Cold." When he leaves to keep his appointment with a fire, the two couples begin to converse in sentence fragments. Their slender characters collapse, and in an unmotivated quarrel they shout at one another, no longer in phrases but in syllables, consonants, and vowels. "The words had turned into sounding shells devoid of meaning; the characters, too, of course, had been emptied of psychology, and the world appeared to me in an unearthly, perhaps its true, light, beyond understanding and governed by arbitrary laws" (Donald Watson translation). According to Ionesco, his first reaction was nausea. Only afterward was he aware that he had written a satire of a universal bourgeoisie, "the petty bourgeois being a man of fixed ideas and slogans, a ubiquitous conformist: this conformity is, of course, revealed by the mechanical language." A little later than Adamov, who entitled his first play *Parody*, Ionesco wrote more blatant parody.

Ionesco read his untitled and incomplete sketch to friends. He first reports that he was almost surprised at their laughter but soon declares that he himself performed the sketch at home in order to make them laugh. After reading Raymond Queneau's *Exercises of Style*, he recognized a comic similarity with his own sketch. In 1949 Yves Robert, a graduate of Dullin's Atelier, staged *Exercises of Style* at the cabaret Rose Rouge, but Ionesco did not see the performance; still, he may have heard about it.

Monique Saint-Côme, a friend of both the neophyte playwright Ionesco and the neophyte director Bataille, brought the unnamed play from the former to the latter, who burst out laughing when he read it in the subway. Bataille read it aloud to his company, who were immediately enthusiastic about the disjointed dialogue. They wanted to perform what was not yet entitled *The Bald Soprano*, and they invited Ionesco to meet them at the Poche, where they were playing their version of *Till Eulenspiegel*. To Bataille, Ionesco looked like Dickens's Mr. Pickwick. The company began to rehearse scenes even before they had money to rent a theater. By good fortune, one of the company's members read the still-unfinished script to the theater manager Pierre Leuris, who offered them a month's run at the Noctambules. Since Ionesco and his wife were both working, they pieced together money for posters, tickets, utilities, and actors' meals; there was no question of a salary for anyone. In the small Ionesco apartment near the Porte de St. Cloud the now-producible playwright handed the hard-earned sum to the now-producing director, who walked the five miles back to his room in the Latin Quarter so as not to spend a nontheater franc. Without title or conclusion, the play went into rehearsal while the Noctambules stage was still encumbered with the furniture of the Vian-Reybaz Knacker.

Ionesco rejected titles that reduced his play to a satire of England (which he had not yet visited)—"English Without Tears," "An English Hour," "Big Ben Follies." The title *The Bald Soprano* arrived by serendipitous accident. In the Fire Chief's tirade, "The Cold," actor Henri-Jacques Huet inadvertently substituted the phrase *cantatrice chauve*, "bald singer," for *cantatrice blonde*. "There's the title of the play," exclaimed Ionesco, instantly responding to its grotesque and mysterious tone. He thereupon changed *cantatrice* to *institutrice* in the tirade, and he added a leading question to the Fire Chief's farewell sally: "Speaking of that—the bald soprano?" (This account, given me by Ionesco, differs slightly from that in *Notes and Counternotes*.)

The play's ending was more difficult for Ionesco. In the first finale the stage remained empty until angry spectators invaded it, at which point the theater manager with the superintendent of police and his men would fire guns at the audience and then clear the theater. Bataille's company wished a less expensive ending, and Ionesco had one in reserve. In the middle of the Smith-Martin quarrel the maid Mary would announce the arrival of the author; the actors would bow politely to him, but this impolite author would shake his fists at the audience. Since Bataille's actors were cool to this idea, Ionesco had no ending and decided to begin the play again—an exact repetition that is described in the few reviews. Only after some hundred performances (in another theater) was Ionesco inspired to replace the Smith couple by the Martins.

When Nicolas Bataille undertook to direct *The Bald Soprano*, he had had virtually no directing experience. In 1948 he and three young friends who were actors decided to stage Rimbaud's *Season in Hell* as adapted by the movie director Claude Autant-Lara, and a guiding hand seemed necessary, so Bataille's colleagues chose him. The production won a prize in the annual postwar Contest for New Theater Companies, whereupon Autant-Lara gave Bataille some pointers on directing—pointers derived from film experience. Bataille directed the early rehearsals of *The Bald Soprano* as broad farce, with knowing winks to the (absent) audience. When another director, Akakia Viala, watched a rehearsal, she persuaded Bataille to shift his actors to deadpan earnest, and deadpan they remained, although they sometimes dissolved rehearsals in hilarity.

In spite of Ionesco's interdiction of psychology, Bataille distinguished between the bored Smiths and the younger Martins. His maid is patterned on mysterious servants in detective fiction, and his Fire Chief's breezy cheer clashes with the fetid atmosphere of the hermetic English living room. In performance, Bataille also distinguished several levels of language: everyday expressions, false logic, clichés, phrases of boredom, exclamations of solitude, and occasional intrusions of pathos and even anguish. Once the actors acquired a rhythm, Bataille timed the performance at fifty-five minutes, and he requested that Ionesco round out the play to an hour. The author obligingly added five minutes to the love scene between the Maid and the Fire Chief. (At my last viewing in 1983, the duration had shrunk back to fifty-five minutes.)

The Bald Soprano has seduced three decades of amateur actors throughout the world. It has attracted professionals too, but it is almost foolproof in accommodating clumsy acting into its disjunctive farce. By the time Ionesco subtitled it "antiplay," he had developed it beyond a spoof of phrase-book clichés to a parody of traditional drama, and that blend of commonplace phrases and familiar scenes is enhanced by out-

rageous costuming, stylized acting, and pastiche. *The Bald Soprano* has been adorned by fruit on the women's hats, by
men's pocket watches lifted in reply to the aberrantly striking
clock, by suspense patterned after Hitchcock's.

In spite of the subtitle "antiplay," *The Bald Soprano* is a play
with traditional French scenes: that is, a new scene starts
whenever a major character enters or leaves. Since all six characters are major, the short play falls into eleven scenes of un-
equal length. The scenes might easily carry titles: (1) The English Smiths in their English home; (2) The report of their
maid Mary about her day off; (3) The entrance of the Martins,
greeted by Mary's scolding; (4) Circumstantial evidence that
the Martins are married; (5) The error in the evidence; (6) The
Martins' joy at their reunion; (7) The conversation between
the two couples, and an erratic doorbell; (8) The Fire Chief
and his anecdotes; (9) Mary's recognition of the Fire Chief as
a former lover; (10) The departure of the Fire Chief; (11) The
grand finale for the two couples. The twelfth, unnumbered,
scene repeats the opening, with the Martin couple replacing
the Smiths.

Much has been written about Ionesco's mechanical characters who are intentionally unsympathetic. The receptive
spectator, however, perceives that he or she is Ionesco's target
and cringes at the formulaic phrases before they accumulate
anarchically. In the opening scenic directions, often spoken
aloud in performance, the word "English" is repeated sixteen
times. Absurdities follow pell-mell in an avalanche of non-
logic: a clock strikes seventeen times, licorice seasons soup,
an improbable pie contains quince and string beans, yogurt
is excellent for appendicitis and apotheosis, a doctor should
die with his patients, a woman has regular and irregular features, and on to the hammered nonsense of the Bobby Watson
clan, one of whom is a singing teacher, if not a soprano.

In small and larger aspects, however, the surface anarchy
of *The Bald Soprano* is buttressed by pattern. Ionesco himself
is highly aware that a play may arise from the author's unconscious, but he still must shape the material: "A work of art
is not a disordered set of associations. It's a structured series

of associations around a theme. A work of art is primarily a construction."[74] What seemed anarchic at first performance is clearly "a construction." The familiar scene of a talkative wife and a silent husband buried in his newspaper is balanced by a prolonged recognition scene between another husband and wife. The intricate contradictions of the Bobby Watson family are balanced by the intricate family relationships in the Fire Chief's epic "The Cold." (No one asks who has the titular cold!) The Fire Chief's shaggy-dog story is balanced by Mr. Smith's tale. The recognition scene of the married Martins is balanced by the recognition scene of the lovers, Mary and the Fire Chief. Even the capriciously striking clock is balanced by the capricious doorbell. These symmetries are enfolded in shifting alliances after scene 7: Smiths versus Martins, men versus women, two couples versus the Fire Chief, two couples versus the maid, and finally each alienated self versus all the others.

Across these patterns runs the disarticulation of language. At first, sentences tilt in spurious logic, with only an occasional neologism or lapse in sense. The register is ruptured when slang and obscenity rip the smooth courtesies. Scene 2 ends with the Smiths going to change clothes to receive their visitors, but they return in scene 7 wearing the same clothes. So too the Fire Chief's gestures contradict his words. Moreover, he refers to his calling as a business that might yield profit, were it not for taxes. In contrast, Mary the maid associates fire with passion, and she has to be taken offstage to quell her amatory flame. Even before the two couples are finally alone, the surface courtesy has been cracked by innuendos and insults, but these accelerate toward the end. The last scene opens with meaningless aphorisms, including two in English. Sound play soon dictates the dialogue. Mr. Smith's revolutionary call—"Down with polishing!"—triggers a series of rhymes, alliterations, repetitions, spoonerisms, and nonsense syllables before the wild finale in which the half-demented quartet seeks self-assertion: "It's not there, it's over *here*" (my italics).

The impact of *The Bald Soprano* rests on its critique of manners through radical dissection of language. Yet Ionesco did not subtitle his play "antimanners" or "antilanguage" but "antiplay" (without the polysemic resonance of the English word *play*). Ionesco explores and explodes language through a spectrum of linguistic techniques, but he also explores and explodes the drama through a spectrum of dramatic techniques. Like none of his subsequent plays, *The Bald Soprano* in print is divided into French scenes: there are two climactic recognition scenes (such scenes had long before been parodied by Euripides). Other well-worn devices of drama are the realistic living-room setting, the laborious exposition, the maid's asides to the audience, announced entrances and exits, the ominous ringing of a doorbell, an unexpected arrival. Yet Ionesco's first play lacks the sine qua non of the French tradition—a clear plot based on conflict. Instead, the dialogue is characterized by pointless repetition, blatant contradiction, defiance of logic, mesmerizing sound play, and what Richard Coe has called "the apotheosis of the platitude."[75] One can understand the confusion of the first spectators.

The very date of the premiere is today veiled in confusion.[76] Ionesco's published text notes May 11, 1950, but the poster reads May 16 at 18:30. The printed invitation for critics reads May 11 at 18:00, but in a recent exhibition of Ionesco artifacts, the time on the card was inked over to May 18 at 18:30. The first (unfavorable) review appeared in the weekend *Figaro* of May 13–14; in it the second-string reviewer lamented a boring hour after an amusing five minutes. Although he praised the performers, he hoped that they might discover Molière or Vitrac instead of discouraging audiences from attending the theater. In contrast, Renée Saurel in *Combat* was encouraging about the improbable combination of fantastic dialogue and a banal subject. Jean Pouillon of Sartre's *Temps modernes* wrote a sensitive and intelligent review, which concluded:

> What complicates the situation for M. Jonesco [*sic*] is that reality appears to him as nonsense, a ridiculous game. How then express the sense of this nonsense? How express the negative positively? The characters have to speak to say nothing; their remarks have to be as empty as possible; in order that there be

no mistake about the absolute quality of this futility, the play has to end where it arbitrarily began! And the spectator leaves by the same door he entered—as usual, but this time he is aware of it and believes himself mystified. He came to the theater, and nothing happened. He was there, and he is there again; it's stupid. Of course, he can then pull himself together and tell himself that human reality is not only that. But it is that too.[77]

Unfortunately, the review did not appear till mid-June, when the free month at the Noctambules was over.

A few spectators came faithfully to almost every performance—Ionesco and his wife, the successful playwright Armand Salacrou, and the writer-publisher Raymond Queneau, who was more persuasive than the actors at corralling spectators, among them the poet Jean Tardieu and the editor Jean Paulhan. Having no money to advertise, Ionesco and his cast donned sandwich boards an hour before the performance and tried to lure spectators from the cafés. Only once did Ionesco himself snare a spectator, who then stamped out before the end of the performance.

More has been written about the origin of *The Bald Soprano* than about its first performance. Set in a fictional London, the play opened while the North Atlantic Treaty Organization was being established in the actual London, but in Paris the reviewers saw a somewhat different production from the monument later consecrated at Théâtre de la Huchette. Some of Bataille's contributions are preserved in Ionesco's footnotes to the published text, but others are not recorded. The stage of the Noctambules was (relatively) wide and shallow, so to give an illusion of depth Bataille furnished the stage with cheap turn-of-the-century furniture bought at the Flea Market. One armchair was so badly torn that a blanket was draped over it. Since costumes were a gift from Claude Autant-Lara, the director of the movie version of Feydeau's *Take Care of Emily* (*Occupe-toi d'Amélie*), they were willy-nilly turn-of-the-century or, as the French see it, *La Belle Epoque*. The men wore tails and spats, Mr. Smith in black trousers and Mr.

Martin in stripes. Mrs. Smith wore a high-necked at-home gown, and Mrs. Martin wore a striped, long-skirted traveling suit. The actors played deadpan, making mechanical movements. Mary the maid (in a black-and-white uniform) was allowed to complete her poem before being carted offstage.

Other details of the original production have been preserved. In the opening scene Mr. Smith's clucking punctuates his wife's monologue. When the Martins recognize one another, they freeze in an embrace, like characters in a silent film, while the maid Mary addresses the audience directly to explain why the couple is deceived. When both couples are onstage, they cough and fidget before Mrs. Smith utters the first (untranslatable) obscenity: "Il s'emmerde." Mr. Smith's lips move silently through his anecdote, which is unheard, and the Fire Chief is the only one to laugh at his own joke. Both married men turn their backs to the audience when the Fire Chief recites "The Cold"—about a widespread yet petty human affliction, like bourgeois manners, which are mocked throughout this modern comedy of manners.

At the opening of *The Bald Soprano*, whatever the date, Ionesco recalls being so nervous that he locked himself in the theater's toilet, emerging only when he heard laughter. After the opening, the actors nourished their onstage hostility by facing over two hundred empty seats in the small theater. A rainy spring further dampened their spirits as they dodged water that leaked from the roof onto the stage. After the month's run, the cast decided to close the show. On the final evening, June 16, they were further depressed by the outbreak of the Korean War. They nevertheless pooled their resources and went to a nearby restaurant for a polenta dinner. In the way of theater, the actors moved on to their next production. Akakia Viala, one of Bataille's mentors, adapted Dostoyevsky's *Possessed* and gave Ionesco the choice part of Stepan Trofimovitch. He played the role on four successive Tuesday evenings, the dark night at the Théâtre de l'Oeuvre, but he relinquished his acting career to devote his spare time to writing. His next plays, as Martin Esslin has noted, bear informative titles: *The Lesson* (1951) dramatizes a lesson, and the protagonist of *Jacques or the Submission* (1951) is Jacques, who submits to family pressure for conformity.[78]

In 1952 Bataille's company joined forces with the small cast of *The Lesson* on a double bill at the Huchette. One actor, Claude Mansard, acted in both plays—he was Mr. Smith in *The Bald Soprano* and the Maid in *The Lesson*. Since the Pupil of the latter play had to be carried out by the Maid, her part was assigned to a man. That double bill lasted from October 7, 1952, to April 26, 1953—to the surprise of all concerned. Thomas Quinn Curtis of the *Paris Herald* saw *The Bald Soprano* during that run and declared it the strangest play he had ever seen: "It transpires in London and the leading characters are Mr. and Mrs. Smith, but beyond that it is completely unintelligible."[79] The French theater critic Jacques Lemarchand also saw that double bill and became one of Ionesco's main supporters: "When we are very old, we will take pride in having attended performances of *The Bald Soprano* and *The Lesson*."[80] Despite such praise, however, no one grew rich on the long run of the double bill, and Ionesco did not leave his job as proofreader until 1956, six productions later. Mrs. Ionesco continued to work until 1957.

By 1957 Nicolas Bataille's company was no longer so young, and its members were in need of a modest income. They therefore revived the 1952–1953 double bill at the Huchette, and the program continues to this day. Bataille commissioned Jacques Noël, who had designed other Ionesco plays for different directors—Sylvain Dhomme's *Chairs*, Jean-Marie Serreau's *Amédée*, Robert Postec's *Jacques*—to do new sets for *The Bald Soprano*. Noël was instructed not to read the text but to think of *Hedda Gabler* and the Hetzel edition of Jules Verne. This set has been periodically replaced but not changed, with its green-and-black flats and minimal furnishings. Costumes retain their turn-of-the-century look. Of the actors, only Bataille as Mr. Martin and Odette Barrois as Mary continued sporadically in their old parts. In 1975, when the owner of the Huchette died, the cast of *The Bald Soprano*

formed a corporation and bought the legendary pocket theater. Pierre Leuris, the accommodating manager of the Noctambules, had lost his position elsewhere, and the new corporation hired him as manager. Old and new casts, with the
play's author, celebrated the twenty-fifth anniversary of *The
Bald Soprano* in 1975. At a remodeled Huchette, audiences are
larger and wealthier than those of 1952, although they consist
largely of (foreign) students. The play that started with a language primer finally serves as a language primer.

INVASION (L'INVASION) and *THE GREAT AND THE SMALL MANEUVER (LA GRANDE ET LA PETITE MANOEUVRE)*
Arthur Adamov

Like Ionesco, Arthur Adamov was a "foreign" native speaker
of French, but unlike Ionesco, he is virtually unknown in Anglophone countries.[81] Born in 1908 in Russia into a wealthy
Armenian family, Adamov learned French as his first language. World War I surprised Adamov's family in Germany,
where his father indulged in obsessive gambling. The family
fled to Geneva, where young Adamov saw the theater of the
Pitoëffs. The combination of his father's gambling and Soviet
nationalization of the family oil fields reduced the Adamovs
to poverty.

Arthur Adamov later wrote that after his arrival in Paris in
1924 he spent his "days and nights in Montparnasse, mainly
at the Dôme, which is never closed."[82] Attracted to the Surrealists, Adamov was excommunicated by André Breton for
admiring the poetry of Dadaist Tristan Tzara. In 1927 Adamov
joined a demonstration in favor of Sacco and Vanzetti; he was
nearly lynched but was saved by the writer Georges Bataille.
In 1928 Adamov helped found a short-lived theater group,
and in that same year he attended Artaud's production of
Strindberg's *Dream Play*, where the Surrealists rioted against
the official Swedish subsidy of the French production. By 1930

Adamov was a friend of Artaud, Blin, and the sculptor Giacometti. During the 1930s Adamov led a hand-to-mouth Left Bank existence—translating, traveling, experimenting sexually, publishing sporadically, and participating in artistic ferment. In 1933 his father committed suicide. In 1935 he met the French Germanist Marthe Robert—at the Dôme—and together they began to translate the difficult poetry of Rilke. In 1938 Adamov befriended the Surrealist poet and drug addict, Roger Gilbert-Lecomte. In that year, too, he began to write his extraordinarily frank *Confession* (*L'Aveu*). Adamov was surprised by World War II and joined the exodus from Paris, spending over a year in Marseilles before his arrest as an anti-Vichy foreigner. After miserable months in the French concentration camp of Argelès, he was freed through the intercession of the Quakers, and he returned to Paris and his Left Bank life, which included the completion of his *Confession* as well as occasional articles for the weekly *Comoedia*.

Already during the Occupation Adamov felt that literature could never resume its old forms; when Simone de Beauvoir told him she was writing a novel, he queried incredulously: "A novel. —A novel? A real novel? With a beginning, a middle, an end?"[83] In 1943 Adamov nursed his Surrealist friend Gilbert-Lecomte on his deathbed, and in 1944 he traced his friend Artaud to the asylum of Rodez. After World War II Adamov and Marthe Robert helped resettle Artaud in a Paris suburb.

Perhaps it was the reinvigoration of Paris at the Liberation, followed soon afterward by his meeting Jacqueline Autrusseau, who was to be his companion for the rest of his life— Adamov's leisurely Left Bank activities suddenly focused into artistic purpose. With Marthe Robert, he founded a journal whose title was inspired by Rimbaud—*L'Heure nouvelle* from "Oui, l'heure nouvelle est au moins très sévère." It lasted for two issues. After seeing Jean Vilar's 1945 revival of Strindberg's *Dance of Death* at the Théâtre de Poche, Adamov was enthralled by theater, and for two years he worked at his first play, *Parody*, completing it in 1947. (Later he would pay homage to Strindberg by translating *The Father*, *Ghost Sonata*, and

The Pelican—from German; in 1955 he would publish a monograph on Strindberg and later would set his own dream play *Si l'été revenait* in Sweden.) *Parody* is at once a sequel to Strindberg's misogynistic works and a dramatization of the neuroses of Adamov's *Confession*. Self-conscious, it is the first New Theater play to jettison coherent plot, psychological characters, and dialogic sequence and consequence. The critic Bernard Dort distinguished between the playwrights of the New Theater: "Perhaps it might be said that Adamov's theater is against the theater, in contrast to Beckett whose theater is in the theater, and to Genet whose theater is about theater."[84] So revolutionary did the form of *Parody* seem that no theater manager would consider producing it. Even Adamov's friend Blin appreciated it only gradually, but when he did, he started to direct it in 1948 with the hope of playing on the dark night at the Oeuvre—a vain hope. Only in June 1952 did Adamov beg and borrow the small sum needed to rent the Right Bank Lancry for the thirty-day minimum, thus staging *Parody*.

In 1948 *Parody* was unproduced, but Adamov was increasingly magnetized to theater when he attended Jean Vilar's Avignon rehearsals of his translation of *Danton's Death*. By 1949 Adamov completed his second play, *Invasion*—again with an awareness of creating a new kind of drama. While in southern France, he prevailed on André Gide to read *Invasion*, and although Gide reacted enthusiastically, there was still no theater at the impecunious Adamov's disposal. Back in Paris, Jean Vilar suggested that Adamov publish his two disturbing plays, with testimonials from eminent persons of the avant-garde. Adamov acted on Vilar's advice.

Early in 1950, before the performances at the Noctambules of *The Knacker's ABC* and *The Bald Soprano*, Adamov published *Parody* and *Invasion* in a single volume, with an announcement that two other plays would follow—*Disorder* and *The Great and the Small Maneuver*. Paragraphs of praise by seven Left Bank luminaries were intended to lure readers; after the influential words of Gide came those of the actor Roger Blin, the poet René Char, the critic Jacques Lemarchand, the poet and film writer Jacques Prévert, the novelist Henri Thomas, and the director Jean Vilar, who provocatively lashed out at another kind of contemporary theater "that borrows its effects from the alcohols of faith and verbiage. Let us pose the question: Adamov or Claudel? I reply: Adamov." No one but Vilar was posing that question, but it sparked a little flurry in theater circles. Ironically, Vilar himself was drawn to rhetorical flourish rather than to Adamov's ascetic dialogue. A few years later Jacques Lemarchand reassured audiences that they need not face Vilar's choice, and after Adamov's death Lemarchand recalled the striking impact of the playwright's slim volume: "Reading these two works opened my eyes to a theater—several of us thought so—that would best correspond to our time."[85] He does not elaborate.

Vilar's ploy of publication did finally secure production for Adamov; a few philanthropists agreed to finance an 18:30 performance of *Invasion* at the small Right Bank Studio des Champs Elysées. It was directed by Vilar and designed by Maurice Coussoneau, his Avignon assistant. At almost the same time, Adamov and his many friends collected the smaller sum needed to rent the Noctambules at the unpopular early hour so that Jean-Marie Serreau could direct *The Great and the Small Maneuver*. With a month of rehearsals for each, the two Adamov plays opened within three days of each other, after the playwright had run back and forth on the bridges across the Seine, his bare feet in sandals despite the winter weather. Adamov felt more at home at the Left Bank Noctambules, as well as more attached to his latest creation, *Maneuver*. Sometimes, Adamov stayed on after rehearsal to see Serreau's production of Kafka's *Guardian of the Tomb*, but he left at intermission since he had never heard of the other play directed by Serreau—Brecht's *Exception and the Rule*. (He was later to be one of Brecht's most fervent admirers.)

Despite the difficulties in reaching production, the first stagings of Adamov's plays might seem auspicious. The two young directors, Serreau and Vilar, had worked with Dullin, who was venerated after his death in 1949. Vilar had already founded the Avignon Festival, and its success (often in nontraditional structures) would lead to his becoming head of

France's National Popular Theater, a position he held for a decade. In the 1960s Serreau would dedicate himself to Third-World theater, often performed in nontraditional structures. In 1950, however, Serreau and Vilar directed Adamov's plays in conventional small theaters, which charged more rent than he could afford. Adamov was nevertheless ecstatic, and he later wrote nostalgically: "What a great time the fifties were. We were forced to beg for everything; we talked about producing a play without even knowing what theater would accept it and without suspecting that we would be reduced to playing at impossible hours—six in the evening. But all of us—Serreau, Roche, Blin of course, others, myself—shared a similar idea of what the theater should be. We were the playwrights, actors, directors of the active avant-garde, opposed to the old theater of dialogue, which we condemned."[86] It wasn't long before the men he names went their separate ways—Serreau into Third-World theater, the composer Maurice Roche away from the arts, and Adamov into socially committed theater; only Blin, the imperturbable amateur, as he was called at his death in 1984, remained faithful to Paris pocket theaters.

Adamov's life sometimes seems a sequence of contradictions, which Roger Planchon exploited when he staged that life as *A. A.* Adamov's élan at the pocket theater of the 1950s was nourished by the anguish of writing his first two plays; the anguish rather than the élan is reflected in *Invasion*, his second play. The title is ambiguous, since it refers marginally to refugees "invading" an unnamed country, but at the play's center is a manuscript that "invades" the visible stage space. Adamov explained: "By invasion I mean the insidious and simultaneous invasion of a man by his obsessive preoccupations, by the presence of others obsessed by their own preoccupations, and by the external thrust of events that always overlap his interior life very badly."[87] Consistent in all Adamov's plays is a tenuous association between private and public events.

When *Invasion* was published, the manuscript at the center of the drama was compared to the works of Kafka—published in spite of his instructions—or to those of Gilbert-Lecomte, which were left to Adamov to publish. It is possible that Adamov also thought of the recently deceased Artaud, who left reams of manuscript, which were mentioned in a headline of *Figaro littéraire* (March 18–24, 1950): "A poet is dead, and there is a battle over his manuscripts." In a perceptive review of the printed text of *Invasion* Maurice Blanchot evoked Vigny's *Chatterton* and Balzac's *Unknown Masterpiece*, both about a work so powerful that it dominates its creator to the point of destroying him. Blanchot concludes his review with the declaration that the theater is possible only to the degree that "language can become simple and transparent enough to render completely visible this strange absence that is dramatic space."[88] It was too soon, however, for theater reviewers to predict Peter Brook's view of the stage as an empty space.

In Adamov's *Invasion* the author of the manuscript, Jean, is dead, like Kafka, Gilbert-Lecomte, and Artaud, and the manuscript invades the lives of both his friends Pierre and Tradel and his sister Agnes, who is married to Pierre. Adamov grants the individuality of a name only to those who are preoccupied with the manuscript, almost to the point of collaboration with the dead author. Other characters are designated as types, in Expressionist fashion, but the types are unexpressionistically atypical: the Mother is a major character who is selfishly maternal and xenophobic.

In act 1 the manuscript is strewn about the room onstage—on floor, bureau, bookshelves, chairs, tables. Beginning with the early faded drafts, Pierre has tried to decipher every page, and his wife Agnes has then typed Pierre's reconstructions. Pierre criticizes his friend Tradel for minimizing the difficulties and for daring to add so much as a conjunction: "For what proof do we have that so-called carelessness, oversights, omissions, errors are not due to an unknown intention, to a scruple. . . . Or even to a fear?"

By act 2 the room onstage brims with furniture, as in Ionesco's *New Tenant*, still seven years in the future. There are no new tenants in Adamov's room, which is ever more thickly littered with the dead man's pages. Even in act 1 Pierre re-

8.   Agnes and Pierre in *Invasion*

spected the errors of the manuscript, but by act 2 he insists on deciphering each word: "I'll have nothing to do with memories, approximations, perhapses. I need the exact word."

By act 3 the pages are arranged in neat piles on the bureau. To Tradel's dismay, Pierre abruptly announces his retreat from all human society as well as from work on the manuscript, which he calls "flat"—the very word with which critics had damned the dead author. Moreover, Pierre rejects semantics for shape: "What I need isn't the meaning of words but their volume and moving body. (*Pause*) I'll no longer seek anything.

(*Pause*) I will wait motionless in silence." With these words
that foreshadow Beckett's characters, Pierre chooses, despite
the pleas of Agnes and Tradel, to isolate himself from the invading pages. He entrusts the manuscript to his self-centered
mother, whose sense of order visibly dominates the stage.
Inexplicably, she apparently engineers the seduction of Agnes
by The First-One-Who-Comes-Along. Pierre retreats to his
(offstage) den.

In the comfortable, orderly room of act 4, with the Mother's
chair front and center, the manuscript at first appears to be
absent. Pierre reenters the room onstage, apparently free of
his obsession with the writing of the dead man Jean. Going
to the chest where his mother has stored the manuscript,
Pierre starts to tear up the once-cherished pages, but when
he learns of the infidelity of his wife, he returns to his offstage
den. In his absence Agnes enters, ostensibly to borrow a type-
writer, but husband and wife do not meet. Tradel appears
with his wife and child, who stuff the torn pages into sacks.
However, when Tradel discovers Pierre dead in his den, he
departs without the sacks of manuscript. Tradel's little boy has
been playing with the pages, and when his mother drags him
after his distraught father, the child carries a handful of paper
with him. The bulk of the manuscript, torn and disordered,
remains in the untender care of Pierre's increasingly domi-
neering mother. The last words of the play are a cliché as the
Mother's Friend exudes conventional comfort: "I know what
it's like." Adamov's dialogue, far from being a direct invasion,
is oblique; characters speak past one another, yet their speech
lacks the comic subtlety of Chekhov's or Pinter's.

In retrospect, Adamov called *Invasion* a pensum, so painful
did he find its creation, but meager reviews say little of how
the pain was transposed to the stage. The protagonist Pierre
was played by François Chaumette, later a senior member of
the Comédie-Française, who was unwilling to speak of that
early avant-garde venture (at least to me). Vilar, the director,
planning the 1951 Avignon Festival, sometimes left Adamov
in charge of rehearsals, and despite his friendship with Artaud, Adamov was not a director. In a November 14, 1950,

interview in the important daily newspaper *Le Monde* Vilar did not even mention *Invasion*, which opened that very night. The next day, in *Combat*, he admitted: "My own feeling clashes with the spirit emanating from this play. Avignon, in contrast, is lyrical." Scarcely mentioned in the daily press, *Invasion* was reviewed along with *Maneuver* in the weekly *Arts* under the title "Dangerous Intentions."[89] The reviewer Jean-Francis Reille thereby implies that Adamov's intentions exceeded his talent. Summarizing (with errors) the plot of *Invasion*, Reille accuses Vilar of a high-handed attitude toward his audience, and he accuses the production of pointless long silences between flat speeches. Adamov strikes Reille as someone trying to appeal to a Frenchman by speaking Chinese, and indeed in 1950 daily reviewers were as little prepared for new approaches to theater as they would have been for Chinese theater.

Yet Adamov called his theater "literal," that is, the theater consists of what is literally on stage. His everyday objects might resonate most unliterally, however, if the play were directed by someone who could invest them with meaning. Although Adamov did not, like Ionesco, label *Invasion* an antiplay, it is like an antiplay in avoiding big scenes, obvious conflicts, clear resolutions, and psychological portraits. By not quoting from Jean's manuscript, by relating that manuscript to change, indeterminacy, and death, Adamov is a prophet of such later critical concepts as trace, absence, negativity. The author has disappeared into an anonymous text. It is a fate that has cruelly overtaken Adamov himself, in spite of early appreciation by Martin Esslin in his influential *Theatre of the Absurd*. *Invasion* has not been translated into English (at least in print), yet an Anglophone theater hostile to Realism would seem a natural host for this drama of deceptively limpid language and extraordinarily ordinary properties.

Invasion is something of an interruption in the series of Adamov's early plays, whereas *The Great and the Small Maneuver* shows thematic continuity with *Parody*. Based on a dream, the play is nevertheless tailored to pattern. Adamov has offered the following explanation of the title: "The great maneuver, if you like, is destiny or the inevitable; the small one

9.   Fingerless typists in *The Great and the Small Maneuver*

represents the forms that the great one takes in everyday life."⁹⁰ Shifting to the terminology of Artaud, we might equate the great maneuver with cosmic cruelty or, in a Brechtian context, perhaps social cruelty in the capitalist world. The small maneuver is more elusive: personal neurosis? any private life?

Adamov's first play, *Parody*, dramatizes parallel paths to annihilation through the agency of the temptress Lily; the paths parody each other. *Maneuver* dramatizes parallel paths to annihilation through the agency of the temptress Erna. (Adamov's friends called him "Ern.") Through ten scenes of cine-matic rapidity Adamov traces the deterioration of his protagonist, the nameless Mutilated One; in part 1 he loses his hands and in part 2 his legs. After The Mutilated One meets beautiful red-haired Erna, the sequence is implacable and repetitive: at each abuse by Erna, The Mutilated One shivers fearfully and obeys the commands of an invisible voice, and the result is the successive loss of hands, one leg, the other leg, and finally life. In spite of his initial moments of hope that Erna's love will save him, The Mutilated One is basically receptive to these self-destructive orders.

A parallel fate overtakes The Militant One, the brother-in-law of The Mutilated One (linked more clearly in French by the rhythm Mutilé-Militant). Married to the Sister, father of her child, The Militant One obeys the directives of his political cause as absolutely as The Mutilated One obeys his voice. The Militant One therefore deserts his dying child and imperils his wife's safety. Even after the death of his child, The Militant One leaves his wife to deliver—as she remarks ironically—a sermon of hope to all humanity.

Adamov's early plays were labeled Expressionist, but although they, like Expressionist plays, exploit distortion, they are not ecstatic autobiographical pilgrimages. Rather, they dramatize similar patterns in seemingly different lives. Beckett's first plays would theatricalize inseparable couples, but those of Adamov contrast solitary characters who cannot form a couple. In *Parody* and *Maneuver* a public man and a private man are similarly destroyed. Like Sartre's *Dirty Hands* (*Les Mains sales*) and Camus's *Just Assassins* (*Les Justes*), Adamov's *Maneuver* questions the efficacy of political action, but Sartre and Camus have their characters debate the issue, whereas Adamov plunges us into the large maneuvering of a destiny that grinds his characters to almost literal bits. Even the reviewer Reille in *Arts* realized that, but he complained about it: "The theme is persecution, not analyzed but witnessed."

However *Maneuver* might imply a plague on the political houses of both Right and Left, Adamov's milieu was the Left of the Left Bank. His director Serreau and leading actor Blin of *Maneuver* were both associated with left-wing causes, and supporters interpreted Adamov's plays accordingly. Adamov records that Camus congratulated him on the phrase of the Wife of The Militant One: "Go on! Go and carry hope to humanity"—a phrase whose irony about idealism nauseated Adamov himself. On the other hand, a young Communist condemned Adamov's work as right-wing anarchy. Ignoring anarchism and idealism, Roger Blin examined the play as an actor—and summarized much of Adamov's power: "A hunted man and a questing man have the same walk."[91]

At the pocket theater of the Noctambules, some nine months after the Vian-Reybaz production of a farce about the family of a Norman horse butcher, Adamov's play staged a more relentless butchery as the fate of one who dedicates himself to the personal life, as of one who dedicates himself to the political life. Was it the irony of the great maneuver that *Maneuver* opened on November 11, Armistice Day? While politicians uttered pious platitudes about peace, Adamov staged a world of incomprehensible war.

Adamov's self-styled literal theater makes specific demands for ordinary settings. *Maneuver*'s ten scenes take place in five main locales: a city street for scenes 1 and 9; the home of The Militant One for scenes 2, 5, and 8; the room of Erna and Neffer for scenes 4, 7, and 10; a key scene of a typing school for handicapped typists in scene 3; a hospital ward in scene 6. Serreau, the director, was an architect and something of a designer, but he needed help for the variety of scenes on the shallow Noctambules stage.[92] He called on Jacques Noël, who had worked with him in children's theater. At the beginning of his career in 1950, Noël and his family lived in such poverty that they often shared only one meal a day. Later he became one of the leading designers in the French theater, with well over two hundred shows by his hand. (Pocket theaters of the 1950s did not distinguish between scene and technical designers; they were lucky to have a stage manager distinct from the director.) In 1950 at the Noctambules Noël worked with primitive equipment. He created the city street by darkening the stage and recording appropriate sounds. In the first scene he spotlighted The Mutilated One before mutilations, and in scene 9 he spotlighted The Militant One on the shoulders of two partisans. Adroit shifting and lighting of a bed distinguished the home of The Militant One from Erna's room and the hospital. Most difficult was scene 3, the typing school for fingerless typists; with sleeves pulled over their fists, four actors were fitted with wooden hands built by Noël. Facing the audience, the actors displayed these wooden hands which made enough noise on the keys to convey an impression of handicapped typists.

The final vehicle of The Mutilated One—a platform on small wheels—also presented a challenge, but it was Blin rather than Noël who met the challenge. As a man without hands, Blin held his sleeves in his fists through seven of the ten scenes. It was thus hard, without revealing fingers, to manipulate crutches when he was supposed to lose a leg. He later recalled his experience:

> I was supposed to lose my limbs one after another. I began by amputation of the hands. I had cones of wood or iron with a hook at the end. And for my legs, I had a corset that contained my left leg completely folded back on my right hip. Then I put my trousers over the whole and had them trail from the knee to the ground. And I fell like that when Erna kicked me. I had crutches and got up on my own, without arms, with my teeth, I don't know how. . . . I was very supple then; I had quite a bit of dance training. And finally it wasn't my knee that gave way, but my hip and spinal column. Eight discs slipped after all those falls. That's the way it is. That's theater.[93]

Even an unsympathetic reviewer like Reille admired Blin's intensity and the stripped, clean direction, for which he credits Blin rather than Serreau, who goes unmentioned. Nevertheless, the reviewer pronounces the play a failure: "The theater is not an abstract art, and a German style of 1925 cannot pass as an avant-garde in 1950."[94] Paying lip service to the need to break traditions, Reille demands that something replace them but does not suggest what.

Despite the stage cruelty of *Maneuver*, the actors had the usual pocket-theater hope that this unusual play would attract critical appreciation, which in turn would bring audiences. But neither Adamov production found critical favor. *Invasion* was condemned for flat dialogue and incomprehensible characters. *Maneuver* was compared to Grand Guignol by the most influential Paris reviewer, Jean-Jacques Gautier of *Figaro* (November 18, 1950); he declares that the excess of horror provokes hilarity, and he complains about the long silences and the incomprehensibility of the action. In *Le Monde* (November 17, 1950) Robert Kemp is caustic at Adamov's expense: "The text is brief. The silences are long. . . . Leaving, I regained Boule Mich with relief." Regardless of reviews, Adamov remained loyal to both plays, attending performances of *Invasion* at least once a week and almost all performances of *Maneuver*. Neither play was to be blessed with the triumphant revival of Ionesco's *Bald Soprano*.

Adamov's first extended stage run came in 1953, not in Paris but in Lyon, where Roger Planchon directed a double bill of Adamov's *Direction of the March* (*Le Sens de la marche*) and *Professor Taranne*. In 1955 Adamov was back at the Noctambules, where the actor René-Jacques Chauffard (the Valet of *No Exit*) had persuaded Jacques Mauclair to direct Adamov's *Ping-Pong*, which was played about fifty times—his longest Paris run. It was this play that initiated Adamov's involvement with politics—an involvement reflected in his next few plays, before he shifted in his last plays to a dream landscape. After Adamov's death in 1970, the director Planchon wove Adamov's early plays and prose into a biographical tapestry, *A. A.*, which was highly acclaimed. As in the case of his friend Artaud, Adamov's life proved more stageworthy than his plays—at least for a certain period in France.

In 1950 Adamov's two plays attracted few spectators and few reviews, but the New Theater acquired a sympathetic critic in Jacques Lemarchand, who had been recruited by Camus in 1944 for the underground newspaper *Combat*. When Lemarchand moved from *Combat* to *Figaro littéraire* in 1951, his espousal of New Theater began to accumulate adherents. (The astute publisher of the daily *Figaro* and the weekly *Figaro littéraire* employed narrow-minded Jean-Jacques Gautier on the daily and broad-minded Lemarchand on the weekly.) Since Lemarchand admired the plays of Adamov and Ionesco, writing prefaces for their respective first volumes of plays, he decided they should be friends. Admiration for the work of the other was stronger on Adamov's part, and Ionesco has vivid memories of his friend's vociferous defense of the 1952 production of *The Chairs*. When Adamov joined the group of French enthusiasts of Brecht, who became Ionesco's bête noire, the friendship began to dissolve. After Adamov's suicide in 1970, however, Ionesco published his grief: "I hadn't seen him for years. I kept promising myself for years to go see him 'next week.' Alas, I didn't do it, and I feel guilty. His work is the expression of an anguished, absolute quest. It goes far beyond literature."[95]

In a monograph on Strindberg, Adamov wrote a sentence that casts light on his own work: "The constant presence of 'the literal sense' results from another constant presence—humiliation, fear, suffering."[96] In Adamov's early plays everyday objects and places become instruments of cosmic torture—the cleaning apparatus of *Parody*, the miscellaneous furniture of *Invasion*, the bedrooms and streets of *Maneuver*. All the characters in these plays use a simple limpid language; there is no hint of Beckett's quotable lines or Ionesco's sonic madness. Although writing of a later Adamov play, Roland Barthes has accurately assessed Adamov's language: "Woven entirely of fine commonplaces, partial truisms, scarcely noticeable stereotypes. . . . [Adamov's characters] think everything they say! [It is] profound dialogue that underlines this tragic malleability of man by his language, especially when . . . this language isn't even completely his."[97]

Adamov does not devalue dialogue in the way sometimes desired by his friend Artaud. Rather, Adamov's dialogue accumulates cruelties. Ionesco's characters are inadvertently cruel; even the murdering professor of *The Lesson* is caught up in his own momentum, but Adamov's characters seem to collaborate with a cruel destiny: in *Parody* the police state, in *Invasion* anti-immigrant laws, in *Maneuver* mysterious voices.

Most striking are Adamov's palpable unexplained presences that seem to be haunted by absence. Before *Godot*, before Adamov's own first play, he recorded his prescience at the dramatic tension of absence: "The modern artist's preference of absence to presence, of the unnamed to the named, follows the ineluctable direction of the spirit. . . . Let us think of Cézanne's sentence: 'Objects are accidents of light,' of the metaphysics of absence in Mallarmé, and generally of Symbolist poetry that is not stated but suggested."[98]

Adamov is his own prophet, who also predicts the arrival of Beckett on stage. Ionesco's drama strikes through plenitude—too many mushrooms, chairs, clichés—but Adamov (usually) and Beckett (always) denude their stage, highlighting the few objects, resonating the spare dialogue, spiraling around absence. If Cézanne's objects are accidents of light, Adamov's are deliberations of space; "You take up such a small amount of space," says Erna in *Maneuver* to The Mutilated One—literally a haunch on a board. On the one hand, Adamov's dialogue is almost palpable and literally present on the nearly bare stage; on the other hand, it resonates through unfilled space and encroaching silence. Although amateurs can amuse in Ionesco's plays, Beckett and Adamov need meticulous production, as the designer René Allio understood: "How to explain the limited success of [Adamov's] plays? By this contradiction, I think. . . . Although Adamov's theater derives from literature and was first formulated in a written text (Adamov wrote everywhere and always), he nevertheless needed a very rich concretization on the stage. In the acting (down to the last detail), in the use of space, in the treatment of objects and props, in directorial ideas to give reality to all the potential of the text."[99] One might say that this is true for any production, but "poor theater" harms some plays more than others, and the very pocket theaters about which Adamov was enthusiastic—"Joué enfin"—betrayed him.

CAPTAIN BADA
(CAPITAINE BADA)
Jean Vauthier

Like many playwrights of these postwar years, Jean Vauthier was not a native Parisian, having been born in 1910 in Belgium and brought up in Bordeaux.[100] He has claimed that annual trips to Lourdes with his paralyzed brother introduced him to the miracle of theater. At age thirty-nine, after completing

his first play, *Captain Bada*, he left his job as a newspaper car-
toonist, although he was told that his play was unplayable.
Undaunted, Vauthier sent *Captain Bada* to his fellow southerner Gérard Philipe, who replied that with major revision it
might be presented at the Avignon Festival. Vauthier refused
to revise, and his "punishment" was Philipe's request that he
adapt Machiavelli's *Mandrake* for Philipe to direct. In the
meantime a fellow journalist sent *Bada* to the director André
Reybaz in Paris; he not only promised to direct and play the
Captain but also commissioned a play for the Festival of Arras. (That play, in which the fourteenth-century playwright
Adam de la Halle of Arras confronts modern Paris, is lost.) In
the text of *Captain Bada* Reybaz saw an opportunity to create
Dionysian theater, but he nevertheless recognized, after his
company's five years of precarious existence, that his taste
inclined toward neither the Boulevards nor the new verbal
spareness. Having been awarded a subsidy for Aid to a First
Play, Reybaz housed *Bada* in the small Théâtre de Poche.

Despite a cast of five, *Bada* is essentially a two-character
play—Captain Bada and his wife Alice. Since Bada is a captain
(we never learn of what), and his wife's name is Alice, the
imprint of Strindberg's *Dance of Death* is clear, but the war
between Vauthier's husband and wife is at once more gradually developed and less final. It is curious, however, that two
polar playwrights—literal Adamov and baroque Vauthier—
should be indebted to Strindberg.

The day before the premiere of *Captain Bada* the hospitable
daily *Combat* published Vauthier's summary of the play, which
began: "It is the story of a man and a woman, and not determinedly the Man and the Woman. Above all, a drama of
pride, lust, and creative impotence."[101] Vauthier divides *Captain Bada* into three acts, but he traces Bada's passion in five
steps; I mark Vauthier's divisions in Roman, mine in Arabic
numbers.

I (1).   Alice sways Bada from prayer to marriage.
II (2).   Married, Alice flees from Bada, and they duel ver-
          bally about the consummation of their marriage.

10.   *Captain Bada*

(3).   The duel continues, but Alice is finally moved by Bada's plea (on his knees, as for his prayer in the first act), and Vauthier's second act ends in an exchange of epithalamia.

III (4).   They do not live happily ever after, and their duel sharpens into an exchange of insults, which become the subject matter of Bada's writing.

(5).   Married for twenty-seven years, Bada wears a costume to write in his darkened room, against a background of connubial vituperation. When Alice belittles his work, Bada opens the window and throws out his heroic helmet and his manuscript. Summoned by an undertaker, he hears music and climbs high in his room to locate the source of the music. He falls to his death, and the undertaker carries him off in a kind of celestial helicopter. Alice pronounces a eulogy.

This summary links the play to New Theater by its disdain of realism and psychology, minimal plot, few characters, grotesque scenes of pathos through fatuous farce. Thematically, however, *Captain Bada* recalls the nineteenth century: a writer-hero like Chatterton, a Byronic character who both loves and hates women, a religious rebel like Cain, a tragic clown like Pierrot, a pelican-artist who eats his heart out—to create art. What is modern is Vauthier's celebration in Bada of a failed artist who is comically and excruciatingly aware of his failure. Throughout the play Bada the inept writer is juxtaposed ironically against the torrential variety of his own language. Vauthier revels in words that fall pell-mell in what director Reybaz considered a Dionysian tempest. Like the heroes of Audiberti, Claudel, or Pichette, Vauthier's Bada is swathed in words, heedless of incongruity or contradiction. In the first few moments of the play, for example, when Bada is in intimate conversation with God, he prays for the force of the squirrel and the prudence of the lion. No sooner are we startled by these images than Bada cites the force of the squirrel's musculature as it climbs crags and the prudence of the lion as it escapes the tamer's whip to perch on a stool. Thus the seeming incongruity is shown to have its own logic. Frequently evoking animals, Bada's references range from humble kitchen instruments to the sublime stars. His syntax varies from brief declarative sentences to long rhetorical periods. He embraces slang and erudition alike. Vauthier's scenic directions pay attention to rhythm, momentum, and articulation. Moreover, Vauthier is expansive, not only in the words he assigns to Bada but also in his scenic directions, one of which enunciates the very basis of his drama: "Upon the extreme mobility of his mental attitudes depends the conscious and unconscious clownish exteriorization of the character." Thus in the first few minutes of the play, before the entrance of Alice, Bada kneels in prayer, leaps from floor to stool, thunders from a height, bleats like a lamb, tears at his own flesh, shakes his fingers like leaves.

At once magnificent and ridiculous, Bada is diminished by the presence of Alice, for he is terrified of this young woman, barely turned twenty. He recognizes that she is his temptation. Even as he struggles, like Claudel's heroes, with his own desire, his language undercuts pure pain: "And this lewd grace has lovely limbs that are scarcely bourgeois. For she is wholesome as a country girl. There it is, firm as a ham—come on, come on, it's plump, it's buxom. It's made of muscle, it's really stacked. Come on! By thunder! Beat it!"

For no apparent reason, Bada ceases to fear Alice, and when she promises to help him create poetry, he agrees to marry her, slapping his chest like an orangutan. He then bludgeons her with a seven-page monologue, but she affirms her happiness, and he instructs dancers to celebrate the marriage he feared. "The extreme mobility of his mental attitudes" seems self-generated; they are neither psychologically explained nor formally proportioned. They make an impact through their very volatility, submerging Alice, who began by wooing him.

The duel of act 2 is a mating dance based on premodern sexual attitudes: the wedding night of the virile, lusty male and the ignorant, frightened virgin. Vauthier eschews an explicitly sexual vocabulary to speak only of their "dance." His scenic directions try to discourage sympathy for Alice in her wedding gown, but this is difficult to forgo, so egotistically insistent is Bada on his sexual prowess. Even the incidental dancer defends Alice against his onslaught. Instead of joining in a matrimonial dance, Bada and Alice duel round and round. With the outcome in suspense, an intermission is designated in the middle of act 2. The duel then continues, with Alice evoking her childhood. A truce seems to occur when the married couple finally joins the dancers. For all the inventiveness of Bada's imagery, for all the self-regarding ambivalence of his suffering, the two long scenes of act 2 do not build. When Bada kneels to Alice, as he knelt to his God in act 1, she announces: "I believe in your suffering," as though she were not its primary cause.

Only in act 3 does Bada emerge as a writer. He wears a toga for the ceremony of creation in a darkened room. Bada is served by Alice in his material needs—"What would happen to you without your faithful slavey?" She is no longer the frightened bride who nevertheless tortured her husband by withholding her favors. She taunts him with a tongue as sharp, if not as rich, as his. Act 3 most insistently recalls Strindberg's *Dance of Death*, for Vauthier's couple also join in a dance of death. They exchange not only insults but blows, yet the scene ends on the word that Bada has sought in his writing, the word that cements their need for one another—"concupiscence."

In the final scene Alice is shocked that Bada's writing records their duel verbatim, but then she enters into the spirit of their warfare. After they reenact a recorded scene of mutual vituperation, the Undertaker first appears. Once Bada falls, however, Alice cradles her dying husband in a pietà pose. When Bada has been carried away in the Undertaker's chariot, Alice pronounces a eulogy, in which she calls Bada's creations a triumph. She links her husband to God and to poets who will honor him. Without Bada's gift for self-mockery, Alice closes the long play on this humorless praise. Are we to take it seriously?

In rehearsals at the tiny Théâtre de Poche, Reybaz at first welcomed Vauthier's presence while he memorized the long role.[102] Reybaz today belittles the sheer feat of memorizing the mammoth role, but he paced while memorizing it, nuancing Bada's struggle with God from his struggle with Alice, his mockery of self from mockery of Alice. Vauthier was impatient not only if a word was changed or a gesture neglected but also if there was any deviation from a text that was explicit as to nonverbal sounds, lighting, and stage props. Soon Vauthier interrupted rehearsals so obstreperously that Reybaz forbade his disruptive presence. The penitent author apologized and promised to confine his contribution to technical matters. Two hours later the stage manager resigned.

An advance notice of the play called Vauthier "this Dostoyevskian Fratellini clown born in the country of Bordeaux wines of a half-Belgian, half-French father."[103] Almost in spite of Vauthier, *Captain Bada* opened on January 10, 1952, after an unusual four months of rehearsal. Reybaz's booming voice and his accelerated direction filled the tiny Poche with the presence of "René . . . Dédé, diminutive of Dédéboum, or Bada, bada of Badaboum." Not surprisingly, the daily press was deaf to his sonorities, but three favorable reviews appeared in the weeklies. Particularly cogent was Georges Neveux's comparison of Bada to Jarry's Ubu; however, Neveux could not predict that Vauthier, like Jarry, would begin to assimilate his character into himself.

Reviews were not uniform, suggesting cuts but praising Reybaz. Vauthier nevertheless fulminated against what he considered a hostile press. Soon he disturbed the actors at performances, and he was scarcely mollified when the Boulevard playwright André Roussin volunteered a letter of praise in the weekly *Opéra*. Cocteau's recommendation in 1950 could not bring about a revival of Vian's *Knacker's ABC*, but Roussin's recommendation in 1952 did help prolong the run of Vauthier's *Captain Bada*, which played for three months but closed before its hundredth performance.

In 1953, after an illness, Reybaz was invited by Jean-Marie Serreau to revive *Bada* at his Théâtre Babylone. Vauthier, feeling that the demanding role of Bada was the cause of Reybaz's illness, undertook to safeguard the actor's health. This he did by telephoning Reybaz at any hour of the night to ascertain that he was at home and asleep! Reybaz decided reluctantly that he had had enough: "Jean, listen to me. You know how much your work means to me. Nevertheless, and in spite of my present regrets and especially my regrets for the future, I won't act for you any more. Adieu."[104]

But directing was another matter, and when Reybaz was manager of the Noctambules in 1957, he directed *Bada* with a different actor in the title role—to general indifference. During the 1950s, in a German translation by Elmar Tophoven (Beckett's translator), *Captain Bada* was performed in several of the newly built postwar German theaters. In 1965, by request of the manager of a newly designed pocket theater—the Lutèce—Vauthier resuscitated Bada for a few arias, which he entitled *Badadesques*. Fellow southerner Marcel Maréchal based his enactment of Bada on Vauthier himself—large, deep-voiced, passionate. That performance proved to be a warm-up for Maréchal's full *Bada*, sumptuously produced in Lyon in 1966, which subsequently toured through much of Europe. "This time Bada-Vauthier had entered [Maréchal's] guts, his breath, his blood, his depths."[105]

For all his impatience during the original rehearsals of *Bada*, Vauthier continued to write for the theater: *The Struggling Character* (*Le Personnage combattant*), 1955; *The Prodigies* (*Les Prodiges*), 1958; *The Dreamer* (*Le Rêveur*), 1960. At one point in act 3 of *Captain Bada* the writer-protagonist proclaims: "I'd like to solder my century to the Elizabethans." His creator adapted four Elizabethan works (using interlinear translations to compensate for his own lack of English): *Romeo and Juliet*, *Othello*, the anonymous *Arden of Feversham* that also fascinated Artaud, and Marlowe's fragmentary *Massacre at Paris*. After the success of Maréchal's *Bada*, the actor-director asked for a script written especially for him, and the result in 1970 was *Blood* (*Le Sang*), Vauthier's most dense and intricate play. Beginning with *The Revenger's Tragedy*, borrowing characters' names from *Measure for Measure*, Vauthier blends his Bada into his Avenger, poised between his own play and a play within the play. Like Genet in dissolving reality into roles, Vauthier cleaves to his baroque expression of passion. Like Genet, too, in virtually making art sacred, Vauthier is unlike Genet in finally stumbling into respect for morality and religion, as opposed to Genet's consistent inversion. And unlike Genet, too, Vauthier was first played in small pocket theaters.

It is scarcely a coincidence that Vauthier's baroque rhetoric attracts the same directors as that of his fellow southerner Audiberti, but the two men adjusted differently to Paris. Audiberti accommodated happily to the Left Bank life of cafés, hotels, and intellectual ferment. Although Vauthier moved to Paris in 1961, he frequented neither Montparnasse nor St. Germain-des-Prés. Far from the fashionable intelligentsia he pursued his own compulsions. Untranslated into English, unknown in English-speaking countries, he has won the admiration of a few—a very few—of France's most discerning critics, one of whom sums up his career:

> [Vauthier was] lyrical at the moment of the triumph of the absurd, when the power of language was being questioned; he was full-bodied when it was fashionable to be slender; he was faithful to values that everyone around him agreed were discredited; he was prompt to declare his ignorance of schools and his scorn for theories while living among people who take pride in being the most learned and best informed on the earth; he was too modern for conservatives, and yet not shrewd enough to enlist under the banners carried by the wind.[106]

THE CHAIRS
(LES CHAISES)
Eugene Ionesco

In January 1952 when the first production of *Captain Bada* opened, the direction of the New Theater in Paris was not yet clear, and it was not yet evident that Vauthier was sailing against the avant-garde wind. Ionesco, in contrast, nearly two years after his first production, was very much aware of being in the avant-garde. His early characters are straitjacketed into clichés; they cannot communicate what they feel, for they lack a lexicon of expression. In *The Bald Soprano*, *The Lesson*, and *Jack or the Submission* this leads to violence, but in Ionesco's fourth play, *The Chairs*, an old couple engage an orator to deliver to a vast audience the message they cannot verbalize.

The Chairs was seeded by an image of chairs on an empty stage, but unconsciously the playwright may have recalled a paragraph from Artaud's *Theater and Its Double*: "But this conception of theater, which consists of having people sit on a

11.   *The Chairs* at the Lancry

certain number of straight-backed or over-stuffed chairs placed in a row and tell each other stories, however marvelous, is, if not the absolute negation of theater—which does not absolutely require movement in order to be what it should—certainly its perversion" (Mary Caroline Richards translation).[107] Ionesco perversely imaged that very perversion.

Ionesco's chairs multiply in an improbable room—semicircular and lined with doors. It is Ionesco's first nonrealistic room, the home of perhaps his most realistic couple. Although husband and wife lapse into mechanical courtesies (like the Smiths, Martins, Jacques, and Roberts that preceded them in Ionesco's plays), they are at once more bizarre and more poignant; they begin in reciprocal tenderness, and they end in a double suicide. The Old Woman's repeated phrases about the grandeur her husband might have achieved are mechanical clichés, as are his own declarations of his awareness of his mission. What distinguishes them from Ionesco's earlier puppets, however, and points toward the understated heroism of his Bérenger, is their groping toward self-effacement. Only an Orator can mouth the Old Man's message—in the Old Man's opinion. The play's first title was *The Orator*, and of his old couple Ionesco has said: "Who are your two old people? Myself . . . my characters were taken from myself and not from the external world."[108]

Unlike *The Bald Soprano*, *The Chairs* is not patterned on symmetries, oppositions, and repetitions; rather, it moves in a rising tempo. The initial exchanges between husband and wife present a nonrealistic exposition. The action proper begins with chairs for the invisible guests, the first few of whom are individualized—the Colonel, the Lady, her Husband of unknown profession; then the invitees arrive in groups—the tall people followed by small children, triggering comic gestures by the Old Man and Old Woman who address them. In the famous chair frenzy, it is the Old Woman who carries the chairs and the Old Man who welcomes the guests, inverting the more usual division of bourgeois household duties. As the stage fills up with chairs, the couple's phrases grow emptier of meaning. The couple is separated by the crowd of chairs, and there is pathos in this parting. Yet their reunion is undermined by its agency—an outdated Emperor. In the name of this anachronism the old people sacrifice their lives, jumping into the water that is always destructive for Ionesco. After their death cry—"Long live the Emperor!"—what message is possible?

The Orator is effectively mute even before he acts out his muteness, yet he too tries to break his mold, uttering wordless sounds (after the first production). The Old Man had engaged the Orator to deliver his message, and the mute Orator tries to chalk a message on the board. Within nonsense words we can read *Angel* and *God*, with their religious associations. Against a background of nonverbal noise, the "tragic farce" returns to the dim light of the play's opening. *The Chairs* ends without the restored order of traditional farce. Like traditional farce, however, *The Chairs* thrives on a physicality that is abetted by language: social niceties exacerbated to paroxysm, flat contradiction, servile adoration, fragmented series, neologisms, nonce words, untranslatable puns. To counterpoint the long scene in which the Old Couple fill the stage with chairs, Ionesco resorts to his broadest linguistic palette. Ionesco stages the absence at the center of his farcical hurricane.

When Ionesco wrote *The Chairs* in 1951, his *Lesson* was playing at the Poche, and he himself was acting in Bataille's company. He had made the acquaintance of several young actors, would-be directors who admired his plays, but none of them had enough money to rent a theater for the thirty-day minimum. Twenty-three-year-old Sylvain Dhomme and his friend Roger Paschal, however, strayed from the Left Bank to an unused movie house near the Bastille, at 10 Rue de Lancry, which they rented for three months—Paschal to direct Shaw's *You Never Can Tell* and Dhomme to start rehearsals of *The Chairs*.

To accompany the single Ionesco act—still unthinkable as a whole evening's theater—Dhomme chose *The Subway Lovers* (*Les Amants du Métro*) by the poet Jean Tardieu. A decade older than Ionesco, Tardieu had a few unproduced plays in his drawer, but his sketches were being performed in cabaret. *The Subway Lovers* was his first production in "legitimate" theater. Its plot is even thinner than that of *The Chairs*: two lovers in a subway are separated by a crowd of commuters, but the pair are finally reunited. Tardieu described the play as "a popular romance in the form of a comedy. . . . He will succeed in reaching her only by addressing himself to each person in turn, humanly. . . . It's a game. A game between Absence—represented by the anonymity of the unknown travelers—and Presence—imagined by love." Of the double bill, Tardieu added: "We pass from the anonymous crowd to the invisible crowd."[109]

To director Dhomme *The Subway Lovers* must have seemed like the perfect contrast for *The Chairs*: a young couple as opposed to an old one, a visible subway crowd as opposed to an invisible audience for a message, twenty-three cardboard cutouts in the subway as against thirty-two chairs in a room of many doors, and a happy reunion of lovers as opposed to a double suicide. Yet the basic movement is the same in the two plays: a couple separated by a crowd comes together again.

A perfect theoretical match the plays may have been, but only the determination of the young casts was able to bring them to the stage. Afterwards Dhomme recalled the unpromising Lancry ambience: "There was an owner, a lessee, and a sublessee, and we had to pay six thousand francs a night to someone who manufactured corkscrews and paring knives . . . . We had to believe . . . that we were founding a new avant-garde theater."[110]

In rehearsal, Ionesco's play proved more recalcitrant than Tardieu's, but Ionesco firmly resisted cuts suggested by Dhomme:

> The cuts you wanted me to make would remove the very passages whose purpose is, on the one hand, to express meaninglessness and arbitrariness, the vacuity of reality, language and human thought; and, on the other hand (above all), to let this vacuity slowly invade the stage, continually covering up, with words used like clothes, the absence of real people, the gaping holes in reality; for when the old couple speak they must never be allowed to forget "the presence of this absence," which should be their constant point of reference, which they must constantly cultivate and sustain.
> (Donald Watson translation)[111]

It was a tall order for any director—perhaps less so for a neophyte than for one accustomed to the stentorian classical French tradition. Early rehearsals, like those of Bataille's *Bald Soprano*, slipped easily into broad farce, and Ionesco objected. Dhomme then attempted to compromise by imposing a quasi-naturalist acting style on the schematic decors of Jacques Noël. (*The Chairs* was the first of many plays that Noël designed for Ionesco.) Instead of the doors mentioned in the subsequently published text, Noël constructed a series of rudimentary doorways, through which the Old Woman carried thirty-two chairs, built in two days by actor Paul Chevalier, who played the Old Man. Dhomme cautioned his actors: "Let's not show maniacs or crazy people. Let's try to hold a mirror up to the consciousness of each spectator; above all, everyone should recognize in this performance his own reasons for failure, his own reasons for error, his own reasons for alienation."[112]

Dhomme was one of the earliest directors to recognize in what was beginning to be called the Theater of the Absurd the appeal to Everyman, an appeal that did not lend itself to concretization onstage. Paul Chevalier as the Old Man was deliberate and rhetorical, but Tsilla Chelton as the Old Woman (fresh from mime school) was at times a grotesque freak and at other times a comfortable grandmother. An acrobat of chairs, she also railed like the proverbial French concierge. By the time Sylvain Dhomme arrived as the mute Orator, the audience was almost dizzy after the role reversals of the old couple, first one commanding the situation, then the other, with both of them finally forcing it all on the hapless third party, who lacks language.

Despite the remarkable agility and gutterals of Tsilla Chelton, despite the hauntingly skeletal set of Jacques Noël, despite the complementarity of the two plays by Ionesco and Tardieu, reviewers were cool, except for Renée Saurel in the weekly *Lettres françaises*, who recognized that the two playwrights, Ionesco and Tardieu, dramatized opposing visions of the world and that it was Ionesco who had swept away time-honored conventions of the theater. More typical was the confusion of another reviewer (biased in favor of Realism): "Since the guests are represented by chairs, I didn't understand whether this was a symbol of the author, a dream of the Old Man, or a financial economy."[113]

Particularly disappointing to the new company was the adverse review of Jacques Lemarchand, who had been so supportive of other plays of the New Theater. Taking Dhomme to task for program notes that rang with rhetoric against traditional theater, Lemarchand found Tardieu's sketch too long and obvious. He then expressed admiration for Ionesco's text but disapproved wholly of Dhomme's direction:

> The director made the strange choice of following his author's text to the letter. . . . He treats this spontaneous, incongruous

poem realistically, which robs it of all its virtues. . . . The poets who were there the second time I went to see this astonishing production broke into applause at the tour de force of carrying some twenty chairs on to the stage in one minute and thirty-five seconds. I must not be a poet. I had a completely different idea of the art of directing. Experiments like this are dangerous to the extent that they encourage scorn for the young by those of their elders who do not wish them well.[114]

Dhomme thereupon marshaled his troops to fire back at Lemarchand; he collected signatures of support, which were published in the weekly *Arts*, from Jules Supervielle, André Alter, Jean Pouillon, Clara Malraux, Raymond Queneau, Samuel Beckett, and Arthur Adamov. The last of these joined Dhomme in the charge that the critic was afraid of what the play told him about himself, what it made every spectator recognize—"the image of decrepitude that reduces existence to a wail without relief from cradle to grave." (Eschewing the comic in his own "literal" plays, Adamov does not mention the wildly grotesque humor of *The Chairs*.) Jacques Lemarchand did not reply, and the battle of *The Chairs* fizzled.[115] Although Audiberti loyally cried "Bravo," although Adamov paid to attend night after night, and although on one occasion Adamov, Blin, the painter Jean Atlan, and the critic Jean Duvignaud physically forced the conservative critic Robert Kemp to applaud this play he detested, the double bill closed after the minimal thirty-day rental.

Four years later, in 1956, the actor-director Jacques Mauclair revived *The Chairs* at the Studio des Champs-Elysées on a double bill with Ionesco's burlesque of theater critics, *The Impromptu of Alma*. (The Studio of the Champs-Elysées was near the Place d'Alma; as Molière's seventeenth-century *Impromptu de Versailles* was named for the place where it was performed, Ionesco named his impromptu for the location of its performance.) In the program was a note by Sylvain Dhomme recalling the three months' work for his production, with Noël doing five renderings for the intractable Lancry stage, Tsilla Chelton pawning her fur coat to help pay the rent for the theater, Paul Chevalier building the necessary chairs, and Audiberti booming cheers through the nearly empty theater.

   The actor-director Jacques Mauclair had not seen the earlier production, but he moved in the same theater circles as Dhomme and his cast. After training with Louis Jouvet, Mauclair wanted to act and direct in the avant-garde, and it was he who directed Adamov's longest Paris run, *Ping-Pong* in 1955, for some fifty performances. In 1956 Mauclair not only directed Ionesco's *Chairs* but also acted the part of the Old Man, humanizing him in a performance less frenzied than Chevalier's.[116] Although Tsilla Chelton again played the Old Woman grotesquely, she too looked more realistically weary as the evening progressed. Mauclair as director pointed the early lines of the play for laughter, but as the larger and more numerous chairs invaded the stage, nearly burying the old couple, the two characters became increasingly sympathetic. The critic Bernard Dort, ignoring the way Ionesco lampooned him in *The Impromptu*, contrasts the two directors: "Sylvain Dhomme, an intellectual of the theater tempted by a certain symbolism, preoccupied with discovering the point at which words open upon silence, that zero degree of the theater; . . . Jacques Mauclair, above all an actor, who loves flesh, blood, sweat, and tears, possessed by a need for direct corporeal expression."[117]

   Although Jacques Noël was the designer for both productions, he elaborated Ionesco's setting for Mauclair: the Lancry's skeletal doors gave way to real doors; the small nightmarish-red chairs were replaced by sturdy white wooden chairs of familiar size and shape. Lighting emphasized the change from the ordinary concierge's room in the opening scene to a fantastic balcony with transparent walls, then the abrupt return to the tawdry room, emptied of its inhabitants. Noël himself has commented on his work: "In *The Chairs* the most important problem for me was to render the double aspect of the set, which should be simultaneously closed and open. The spectator should have the impression of an egg shape in which an opening is possible. I therefore made an egg-shaped set but situated it in a void. At the entrance of the chairs, the stage became a throne room. . . . Then the set shrank and we again find this dwelling on an island as at the beginning of the play."[118] Although only a few more chairs were added in the Studio production, they seemed more numerous on its deeper stage; they finally spread out fanlike onstage, with the apex furthest from the audience. Immured within the oval of the door-studded surround, confronted with rows of white chairs, dressed in black and standing on white chairs themselves, the old couple are at once enthroned and martyred.

Mauclair was one of the few directors to respond both to Adamov's slow short scenes punctuated by silence and Ionesco's verbal and physical frenzy, and he has commented on the contrast: "What is difficult in Adamov is the division of the play into very short scenes that demand quite arduous technical transitions; in Ionesco it's the constant passing from the real to the unreal in the same place, with the same characters, and a scarcely noticeable shift in the action and language."[119]

In February 1956, three years after the opening of *Waiting for Godot*, almost every newspaper reviewed the revival of *The Chairs*. This "tragic farce" had the good fortune to attract the most successful French playwright of the 1950s, Jean Anouilh. He had not commented on (or seen?) the 1952 production of *The Chairs*, but in 1956 he sent a long letter to the daily *Figaro*:

> It's a fact: recent French theater is named Beckett, Adamov, Ionesco. Nothing very Breton or Perigordin there, and I am their ancestor with my vintage premiere in 1932 . . . not even a respectable ancestor; a sort of shameful, insincere old boulevardier; . . . .
>
> In any case, I thought that these three men who borrowed my language and were performed in my village had one common denominator—let's call it uneasiness—that they would be satisfied with thinking, with rebelling properly (only rebellion is conformist in our time), and with being eternally in the avant-garde. . . .
>
> I just returned from London, where *Waiting for Godot* has been playing for seven months. I consider *Waiting for Godot* one of the three or four key plays of the contemporary theater since the old Sicilian magician burst upon us with his *Six Characters in Search of an Author*. . . . And now Ionesco brings out his *Chairs* I don't know from where. . . . I think that it's better than

Strindberg because it's dark in the fashion of Molière, sometimes madly funny, it's frightful and ridiculous, poignant and
always true. . . . I can't say more, or I will be suspect. However, I conclude on a simple psychologically valid remark. I
know my business, I never laid eyes on Ionesco, I am being
performed in the theater next door, and I have nothing to gain
if people make a mistake as to the entrance.[120]

Anouilh's praise on the front page of the daily *Figaro* made
the fortune of the play—and of the playwright. The actor-
director Mauclair was awarded a prize for his direction, although a Lyon audience left the theater when they thought
Paris had sent them a skeleton cast that couldn't fill the stage
chairs. In 1962 even the astute critic Leonard Pronko, noting
that "the more conservative elements have not accepted Ionesco," predicted that "it is unlikely that they ever will."[121] Yet
by the end of the decade Ionesco was well enough accepted
to be elected to the conservative Académie Française. In 1962,
too, that conservative medium television showed *The Chairs*
with Jacques Mauclair and Tsilla Chelton, who also revived
the play in the theater in 1967 and 1978. In 1965 a larger theater—the Gramont—accommodated a double bill of *No Exit*
and *The Chairs* with Michel Vitold playing in both. In a review,
Jacques Lemarchand praises *No Exit* for not dating at all; he
goes on to explicate the reductive phrase "Hell is other
people": "In whatever circle of hell we live, I think that we
are free to break out of it, and if people don't break out of it,
they remain there of their own free will, so that they place
themselves in hell of their own free will."[122] To the hell of *The
Chairs*, however, Lemarchand impenitently devotes no more
than a tenth of his review, and he comes to a paradoxical conclusion: on the one hand, the play succeeds in its enchant-
ment through a language that denounces the meaninglessness of language; on the other, the characters resemble those
of Dickens. Does he mean that they are caricatures or that—
by 1965—they have become classics?

This public defender of New Theater does not mention the
larger stage and audience that these plays finally attained in
the graduation from pocket theater.

Of the pocket theaters of that decade, only the Huchette, the Poche, and the Studio des Champs-Elysées remain active, but other pocket theaters spring up in the seemingly unlimited supply of underground vaults in Paris. In the post-Occupation years the pocket theaters retained the proscenium arch, but their small size imposed the proximity of actor and audience to which later practitioners aspired. The designers schooled by the Spartan conditions of pocket theater—René Allio, Jacques Noël—learned to be ingenious with new materials, to build quickly, and to cheat space, lessons that stood them in good stead in more lavish theaters. Similarly, pocket-theater directors—Bataille, Blin, Mauclair, Reybaz, Serreau, Vitaly—sometimes expanded into flamboyance in larger theaters but more often followed chance in their very different careers. Bataille, after the 1950s, shuttled between the Huchette and theaters in Japan, where he directed French classics. Blin pursued his "invisible" directing mainly in the small theaters of Paris and in large ones in Germany and Switzerland. Mauclair drafted family and friends to produce his favorite plays in any Paris theater rentable at a given moment. Reybaz, his company dissolved, has divided his time between Paris little theaters, Lyon, and various festivals. Serreau died while he was devoting all his time to Third-World theater. Vitaly lived on an eclectic repertory, often returning to the plays that first enticed him. These were the fortunate directors who were able to exercise their profession, but Sylvain Dhomme wrote a book about directing, tried directing outside Paris and on radio, and retreated finally to educational films. Along with the poet Pichette, he turned away from Paris theater after Paris theater turned from him.

In the spectrum of approaches to theatrical staging in these small theaters, the dominant color was nonrealism. Contrasting playwrights like Adamov and Vauthier—the former with his literal stage and spare dialogue and the latter with his panoplies of verbal fantasy—shared an awareness of the artifice of words spoken on stage. Although the surface distinction between denotation and connotation does not hold in the

theater, there are nevertheless two attitudes toward stage dialogue.

In the famous Saussurian distinction between the signifier
and the signified, the realistic playwright seeks a transparent
signifier, so that the spectator looks through it to the signified.
The linguistically conscious playwright, in contrast, points to
the signifier itself as an object of dramatic validity. Adamov
calls his way "literal," and Vauthier is often called Elizabethan, but they are both highly aware of their respective languages. Ionesco indulges in puns, spoonerisms, alliteration,
repetition with variations. Pichette risks neologisms. Although many critics distinguish between the Theater of the
Absurd and the Poetic Theater born in these pocket theaters
of Paris, both kinds of drama are dedicated to a stage language
that differs, on the one hand, from the classical French tradition and, on the other, from the prose of problem plays. By
1952 it was already evident that language in the avant-garde
theater was bifurcating into the effulgence of *Captain Bada* and
the fragmentation of *The Chairs*. Well over a decade later, comparing Audiberti and Beckett, the critic Gilles Sandier recognized that "these two languages, polar opposites, one seeking
in asceticism what the other seeks in baroque exuberance,
paradoxically arrive at the same result: they both bring man
back to what is distinctive about him, that is to say his language, both playwrights treating it as something almost holy;
both contrive to give us the dizzying impression of touching
with their fingers, of approaching, almost of seizing some unknown essence."[123]

3

Godot Cometh

Behold, the Bridegroom cometh.

Matthew 25:6

> Husband: Has the iceman come yet?
> Wife (*Upstairs*):   No, but he's breathin' hard.

Foreigners belong in France because they have always been here and did what they had to do there and remained foreigners there. Foreigners should be foreigners and it is nice that foreigners are foreigners and that they inevitably are in Paris and in France.

Gertrude Stein, Paris France

After World War II Sartre surveyed the Paris theater scene and declared that its purpose was "to forge myths." None of the dramas he names—by Jean Anouilh, Simone de Beauvoir, Albert Camus—seems today of mythic dimension. Perhaps the only postwar Paris play to achieve such stature is *Waiting for Godot* (*En attendant Godot*), written by that foreigner in France Samuel Beckett and directed by Roger Blin, a Frenchman who told me that he preferred foreigners to *Tout-Paris*.

At mid-century Beckett and Blin, born a year apart (Beckett in 1906 and Blin in 1907), were at comparable points in their respective arts. Blin knew that as actor and director he must reject the rhetoric of the French theater tradition; it was as an actor that he wished to direct fellow actors in poetic plays that imaged human mystery. Beckett knew that he must strip language down to its nearest approach to being; it was as a writer of French that this Irishman wished to delve to human mystery. With hindsight, one might surmise that Blin and Beckett were fated to meet, and in the small avant-garde world of postwar Paris they may have brushed by one another at the painting exhibitions they both frequented. They actually met, however, through *Godot*.

Despite what Gertrude Stein says in the epigraph to this chapter, postwar foreigners in Paris were of interest only to bureaucrats. Postwar recuperation was over by 1951, the Cold War waxed and waned seasonally, and Americans were no longer greeted as liberators. "What they had to do there," along with other foreigners, was contrive some means of financial support, and theater was particularly chary of such support, even though Paris had some fifty performance spaces. Actors—pocket-theater directors were often actors— could usually slip into a film in times of need, but playwrights lacked this resource. And it was the playwrights who tended to be foreigners in postwar Paris. Of the ten whose performances I describe, only two were natives of greater Paris— Sartre and Vian. Adamov, Beckett, and Picasso were not French; Artaud, Pichette, Ionesco, and Vauthier each had a non-French parent; and Audiberti was a southerner with strong Italian attachments. Although the sense of dislocation in their plays must not be ascribed merely to foreign ancestry or passport, it cannot be discounted. As the critic Guy Dumur wrote at mid-century: "Their condition of being exiles merely translates, often inexorably, a pessimism that we natives feel as keenly as they."[1] Paris pocket theaters were marginal to the French cultural tradition, and Paris pocket playwrights were all the more marginal if they were foreigners. At the same time, Latin Quarter cafés and small Left Bank theaters provided foreigners—literal or metaphoric—an opportunity to voice their different solitudes.

I have filtered a dozen performances from the postwar pocket-theater scene, performances that seemed radical to their participants. As I glance back over them, I am astonished at their affinities with Beckett's *Waiting for Godot*, upon which I conclude. It is as though Beckett deployed his silence, exile, and especially cunning to blend earlier ingredients into his *Godot*. But only "as though," for of the predecessors I winnow, only *No Exit* and *The Chairs* were familiar to him. Nevertheless, Audiberti's *Evil Is Running Out* might well be entitled

Waiting for the King. Like *Godot*, too, *Evil Is Running Out* and *The Bald Soprano* dramatize missed meetings. Like Beckett's play, *The Knacker's ABC* has an international cast, and it too theatricalizes a charnel house. *Epiphanies* would seem to contradict the wait for Godot since apparitions *do* appear, but a biblical background joins Pichette's work to that of Beckett, who translated Pichette's "Apoème 4" in *transition 1948*. No such kinship binds Beckett to Vauthier, but the plays of both were early compared to skits by the Fratellini clowns. In Anglophone countries Beckett was paired with Ionesco: not only were they produced at about the same time, but also they both mistrusted language, and that mistrust aroused an uneasy audience laughter. The careful patterning in the "antiplay" *Bald Soprano* parallels the symmetries, oppositions, clichés, and metatheater of *Godot*. Even though Beckett signed the protest against Jacques Lemarchand's hostile review of the 1952 premiere of *The Chairs*, a decade passed before anyone noticed that its basic structure is mirrored in *Godot* (which was written earlier): a couple waits in physical discomfort for the arrival of someone wreathed in metaphysical promise, and the audience perceives the irony of that promise.[2]

Other affinities with *Godot* are more fortuitous. Beckett, active in the French Resistance though an Irish citizen, had fled from Paris by 1944, the year of the festive reading of *Desire Caught by the Tail*, but he had earlier rendered into lyrical English the striking dreamlike imagery of the Surrealist poets André Breton, Paul Eluard, and René Crevel. Although Beckett exercises the control that the Surrealists spurned, he too probed his unconscious for *Godot*, as for all his works. And as Picasso's play obliquely reflected the privations of the Occupation, so do the meager carrots, turnips, and radishes of *Godot*. Picasso sketched and described but did not stage a banquet, whereas Beckett's Pozzo of the jaded appetite dines onstage on chicken and wine. Picasso's characters' feet complain of their chilblains, and Beckett creates an Estragon who blames on his shoes the faults of his feet. Picasso closes his play on a man-sized golden ball labelled "Nobody," and near the end of each act of *Godot* a pale, unlabelled moon rises on a tragicomedy riddled with negatives, from the opening state-ment, "Nothing to be done," to the closing stage direction, "They do not move." Circles and interrogatives proliferate in both plays. Yet these are mere peripheral resemblances be-tween dramas that differ fundamentally, as the carnal taste of Picasso differed from the transcendent yearning of Beckett.

Although the transcendental is considerably attenuated by Sartre in *No Exit*, it nevertheless envelops the very fiction of a self-service hell. Beckett saw *No Exit* soon after his postwar return to Paris, and he was caught up in its claustrophobic grip of punitive repetition. The same two-against-one alli-ances form and re-form, presumably through all eternity. Analogously, repetition becomes a punishment—for charac-ter, actor, and spectator of *Waiting for Godot*; characters are eroded through repetition, actors lose their place in the play, and spectators are hypnotized on the brink of boredom. Ken-neth Tynan's review of Peter Brook's 1946 production of *No Exit* fits *Godot* like a derby: "On this tangled, desolate ques-tion-mark the curtain falls, and we know that the play belongs to the modern group of 'tragedies without finality.'"[3] Sartre himself had ambivalent feelings about *Waiting for Godot*; on the one hand, he implicitly condemns it as bourgeois and Expressionist; on the other, he reiterates that he finds it the best postwar play.[4] At no time did Sartre compare *Godot* to *No Exit*, and yet Estragon exclaims "I'm in hell" as he falls into Vladimir's arms. But the infernal is only one tone of Beckett's palette. Estragon's naive and lovable animality recalls the tails of Picasso's desire, while Vladimir and Estragon's fear of an unknown punitive "they" echoes the no-exit situation of Sartre's characters.

If one view of Beckett places him between Picasso and Sartre, another can perch him between Adamov and Artaud. Several critics have coupled Artaud and Beckett,[5] and it is true that both writers express a tragic vision of man's destiny; it is also true that both writers display remarkable linguistic skill to inveigh against the inadequacy of language. Artaud's performed *Tête-à-tête* virtually illustrates Beckett's trilogy of novels that focus on a man and a manuscript, but the actor's histrionic exhibitionism is utterly foreign to Beckett's temperament, and Artaud's apocalyptic ambition for theater is foreign to Beckett's minimalist aesthetics and metaphysics.

Adamov, the friend of Artaud and Blin, seems to slip away from both toward a prediction of *Godot*. Adamov admired Artaud's poetry more than *The Theater and Its Double*, and however generously he acknowledged a debt to the latter, his own "literality" seems starkly opposed to Artaud's monstrous symbols. In contrast, Adamov's unlocalized, stripped stage resembles that of Beckett, with the focus on a few props that are at once literal and symbolic, with an action delineated through spare pattern, and with dialogue pared to simple limpid sentences whose very simplicity imposes resonant extension. What Bert States writes of Beckett is also true of Adamov: "An ontological parable is pulsating beneath a deceptive crust of actuality."[6]

When Beckett wrote *Godot*, however, he barely knew Adamov. The Irish author had begun to write in French as soon as he returned to his Paris apartment after World War II—first short fiction and then his trilogy of novels. In 1947 Beckett halted between the first two novels, *Molloy* and *Malone Dies*, to write *Eleutheria*, a parody at once of the problem play, of the sensitive antibourgeois protagonist, and of Pirandellian consciousness of the theater as theater. Beckett was rejecting the dramatic styles of the past to empty the space for *Godot*.[7] In 1948, while waiting for *The Unnamable* to take shape, Beckett began a play on October 9, the month of the proclamation of the People's Republic of China. As though oblivious to the world outside his notebook, Beckett finished *En attendant Godot* on January 29, 1949. When asked why he chose to write a play in the midst of fiction, Beckett replied: "I didn't choose to write a play. It just happened like that."[8]

Far from being a commercial venture, *Godot* was a form of play. Like *Eleutheria* of the preceding year, it was Beckett's escape from the increasingly despotic interiority of the fictional trilogy; in Beckett's own phrasing to Colin Duckworth, "I began to write *Godot* as a relaxation, to get away from the awful prose I was writing at that time."[9] And as late as 1985 he told the moviemaker Sean O'Mordha that after writing the trilogy he was not so much bogged down as fogged out, and he wrote *Godot* to come into the light: "I needed a habitable place, and I found it on the stage."[10] So he furnished himself with a cheaply bound graph-paper notebook.

The outer cover of the *Godot* notebook shows, under the play's title, a bird in flight; below the manufacturer's name (Avia!) are the dates of start and termination—"Oct 48 Jan 49." On the inner cover, under miscellaneous French notes, appear eight English words: "storm sudden calm lull / certain wreck brings threat." Although one can easily ascribe the relevance of these words to Beckett's "awful prose," they do not seem to be the seed of the play, which begins on the first graph-paper page. The lines of *Godot* run across the right-hand pages of the notebook and then double back to end on the left-hand pages. The manuscript displays only minor changes and a relatively small number of the doodles to which Beckett resorts when he broods. Some scholar will doubtless be equipped to analyze the number of days Beckett actually spent writing during this four-month period, but the only date in the manuscript is 9.12.48 (December 9) opposite the page in act 2 on which Vladimir reminds Estragon of yesterday's meeting with Pozzo and Lucky. The general impression of the manuscript is one of almost continuous writing—continuity that later amazed Beckett.

The manuscript of *Godot* opens—in French—on the unlocalized but suggestive setting: "A country road. A tree"—horizontal and vertical coordinates committed to graph paper. A scenic direction then describes an old man trying to take off his shoe when another old man enters. The name Vladimir evidently struck Beckett as soon as he wrote that the second old man addresses himself in his opening speech, but when the shoe-preoccupied old man replies, he is designated "Levy," and he remains Levy throughout act 1. By the beginning of act 2 Beckett renames Levy, calling him Estragon (a plant of Arabic origin)—as many Jews during the Occupation took different names to protect themselves from the Occupiers. Only near the end of the play is the name Estragon

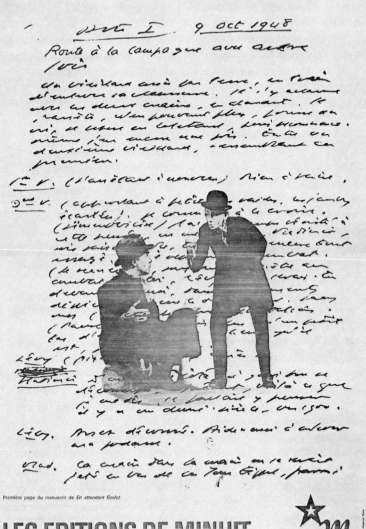

12. Page of Beckett's original manuscript of *En attendant Godot*, with Didi and Gogo superimposed.

uttered in the dialogue, when Vladimir soliloquizes: "That with Estragon my friend, at this place, until the fall of night, I waited for Godot." In act 1 of the manuscript Vladimir calls his friend by what presumably is his family name—Levy—but the latter gives Vladimir the endearing nickname Didi, which is first spoken in the line "Dis, Didi." In act 2 Estragon acquires the nickname Gogo.

When Pozzo and Lucky first appear in act 1, the manuscript designates them as a very large man and a small one; their opposition is immediately visual. Pozzo announces his name almost at once, but Lucky's name is delayed until Pozzo explains that his menial has first refusal of his discarded chicken bones. (In French print, Lucky's name is not mentioned at this point, nor indeed at any point in the dialogue of act 1. Vladimir speaks of Lucky in act 2, but how does he know the name of the menial whom Pozzo has addressed only in terms of abuse? In English this oversight is corrected, for Pozzo mentions Lucky's name as the source of "all these beautiful things" just before designating him as a "knook," a word Beckett invented on analogy with "knout.") When Pozzo and Lucky arrive in act 2 of the manuscript, Lucky is much shorter; he has lost height as well as speech.

The broadly European flavor of the four named characters—Slavic Vladimir, French Estragon, Italian Pozzo, and English Lucky—emerged in the process of writing, as did the alternates for Vladimir (Mr. Albert) and Estragon (Catullus in the French version, Adam in the English, after the deletion of the manuscript's Magrégor, André).

The manuscript provides evidence of Beckett's difficulties with his little plays within the play of *Godot*, when Pozzo and Lucky are "on." However, the bravura monologue of Lucky is scribbled in an unhesitating block of unpunctuated pages, with no indication of the three-part division that Beckett would later point out to actors—indifferent heaven, dwindling man, and earth a wilderness. An initial scenic direction specifies that the monologue should be spoken rapidly, and it is not yet preceded by Lucky's aborted dance. Before the monologue reached print, Beckett made many small revi-

13.   Gogo and Didi in *Waiting for Godot*

sions. As Colin Duckworth has observed, "Repeated, de-
formed, and nonsensical words replace some earlier coherent
expressions."[11] "For reasons unknown" is already the dominant refrain. The manuscript suggests that only after the
monologue was finished to its final "unfinished," did Beckett
imagine the reactions of Lucky's onstage audience—added on
the facing page. (These reactions were modified into a stricter
pattern for Beckett's 1975 Berlin production and further
changed in 1984, when Beckett advised the Anglophone production of *Godot* by the San Quentin Drama Workshop.)

The dog song that opens act 2 is a kind of play within the
play—or what the French call *mise en abyme*. Beckett evidently

14.   The two couples of *Waiting for Godot*

knew by heart the original German of this old round that he quotes to Arland Ussher in a 1937 letter now at the University of Texas Library. An exacting translator, Beckett crosses out his first two attempts at a French version in *Godot*. Similar dissatisfaction is evidenced in his barring of a now-unreadable exchange between Didi and Gogo, which is replaced by the three-hat routine, adapted from the Marx Brothers' *Duck Soup*. Unlike the slow transfers of hats indicated in the printed scenic directions, however, those in the manuscript are rapid.

Of the few characters, Pozzo seems to have troubled Beckett most. In act 1 doodles appear mainly opposite his lines, although his "recitation" proceeds cleanly. In act 2 the doodles reappear after Pozzo is helped to his feet; he is assigned several additional lines, which Beckett inserts on facing pages. Just before the departure of Pozzo and Lucky in act 2, a number of phrases are crossed out, and a few are replaced. Beckett notes parenthetically: "After the Act II departure of Pozzo and Lucky, suggest that the former only pretends to be blind." But he did not develop that idea, which became the province of critics. Another parenthetical note about Pozzo later surprised Beckett when he reread it: "Suggest that Pozzo is perhaps Godot, come to the rendezvous, and that he doesn't know that Vladimir and Estragon are Vladimir and Estragon. But the messenger?" When Colin Duckworth asked Beckett point-blank whether Pozzo was Godot, the author replied: "No. It is implied in the text, but it's not true."[12] The implication is strong enough, however, to arouse expectation of the playwright's more habitual "Perhaps."

If Pozzo proved the most recalcitrant character for Beckett, the endings of each act were the most troublesome scenes. The last page of the manuscript is virtually unreadable (at least by me), so frequent are the changes of Beckett's mind. Although he now recalls *Godot* nostalgically in comparison with the arduous labor of composing *Endgame*, the manuscript reveals that the brilliant economy of *Godot* emerged partly in revision but that the extraordinary shape of the play—the tilting symmetries—is already present in the first draft. The most noteworthy revisions in that draft tend toward what Beckett later (in the manuscript of *Happy Days*) called "vaguening." Through deliberately eliminating specifics of place, time, and identity, Beckett amplified the resonance of his tragicomedy.

The label "tragicomedy" came only with Beckett's translation of *Godot* into English, whereas the elements of farce bounce through the original manuscript. *Godot* opens with a hoary mime's turn: Estragon struggles to take off a tight shoe. During the course of the play, Estragon speaks with a full mouth, uses one lung as a bellows, retrieves a carrot, mimics

Lucky as carrier and dancer, starts to tell a bawdy joke, speaks with an English accent, loses his balance, tries to hide behind the skeletal tree, and finally drops his trousers—all standard pranks of vaudeville. For all Vladimir's superior sophistication, he leaves his fly unbuttoned, laughs painfully, smiles suddenly, spits disgustedly, pulls miscellaneous objects from his pockets, and minces like a model; he too mimics Lucky as carrier and dancer. Together, the two friends juggle three hats, take gorilla postures, huddle in exaggerated fright, examine one another as objects, pose as scouts on the lookout, tug at a rope, and lose their balance. They manipulate their respective props—Vladimir his hat and Estragon his shoe—precisely and identically. Quite differently, however, they take pratfalls, and although Pozzo and Lucky are rarely funny, they too fall to the ground in act 2.

These familiar physical gags testify to Beckett's close study of farce, but he is an original master of verbal dynamics, and his dialogue announces itself as dialogue. Estragon in particular exposes its variants: "Let's make a little conversation." "That's the idea, let's ask each other questions." "That's the idea, let's abuse each other." "That's the idea, let's contradict each other." Vladimir clings more tenaciously to the verb "say" to help fill the long wait for Godot: "You had something to say to me?" "Say something! . . . Say anything at all!" "Say you are, even if it's not true." "What was I saying, we could go on from there." Even "back to back," the two friends patter on. Perhaps Lucky is so obsessed with tennis because that is the game that eludes him; he usually obeys Pozzo's commands (although he starts to dance when ordered to think), but not even once in a way does he return the verbal ball, as Didi and Gogo unbeatably do. In the original manuscript, the two friends already juggle sounds, semantics, syntax, and habits of discourse.

Although Beckett called *Godot* "relaxation," even his first draft reveals his immense erudition. In the graceful sentence of Bert States, "If we were to walk back along the mythic road on which *Godot* takes place, we would encounter numerous shapes from scriptural, historical, and literary memory which might be called ancestors of the scene enacted before us in the play."[13] Perhaps "analogues" is more precise than "ancestors," and history is fainter than literature or scripture.

The Bible washes over the play, not only in the conundrum of the two thieves and a questionable salvation but also in scenic directions that reflect the iconography of Christ crucified between the thieves. There are also echoes of Genesis (Cain and Abel; man in God's image); Kings or Elijah (a little cloud, which also impressed Joyce); Matthew (the wind in the reeds, also heard by Yeats; one brother among sheep and the other among goats; the parable of the wise and foolish virgins); Luke (the parable of the good Samaritan); Revelations (the last moment). Physical falls of the play point to the Christian conception of the Fortunate Fall. Vladimir sententiously assigns every man to his little cross, and Estragon claims to have spent a lifetime comparing himself to Christ. Although Beckett is sometimes irritated by religious readings of *Godot*, the Judeo-Christian tradition is as pervasive as the twilight in his play—and may be that twilight.

Less copious in *Godot* is the classical residue—Atlas, who is the brother (not the son) of Jupiter; Pan; caryatids. Vladimir quotes a Latin phrase—"Memoria praeteritorium bonarum"—but Estragon is also a classicist, claiming his name is Catullus (French text only) and subverting Heracleitus's dictum about not stepping twice into the same stream. Since Estragon is the poet, it is right that he should quote Verlaine—"so blue . . . so calm"—from "Le Ciel," but it is Lucky who invokes Shakespeare's "divine Miranda," and "labors lost," while Vladimir abridges Hamlet's "Words, words, words," and his most celebrated line too: "That is the question." Even though the play was written in French, it concretizes two memorable Shakespeare lines: the set reflects Macbeth's "Stones have been known to move and trees to speak." And the visual impact of Pozzo and Lucky in act 2 is pithily summarized by Gloucester's " 'Tis the times' plague when madmen lead the blind."

Although Beckett has denied knowing philosophy, the Pozzo-Lucky couple tends to be derived not from Shakespeare but from Hegel's master and slave in *The Phenomenol-ogy of Mind*, whereas Vladimir and Estragon are traced to the Cartesian split of mind and body. The "struggle" mentioned in Vladimir's opening speech points back to Hobbes, Leibniz, Hegel, and Marx, and erudite commentators find kernels of *Godot* in the works of Berkeley, Heidegger, and Schopen-hauer. Beckett himself has admired the shape of philosophi-cal ideas:

> Nothing is more real than nothing. (*Democritus*)
> Ubi nihil vales, ibi nihil velis. (Where you are worth noth-ing, there you should desire nothing.) (*Geulincx*)
> Do not despair; one of the thieves was saved. Do not pre-sume; one of the thieves was damned. (*Augustine*, although no one but Beckett has cited it)

Yet Beckett's learning is distributed so deftly in *Godot* that its gravity is felt only in Lucky's monologue.

So familiar is *Godot* today that one can only guess at the reasons for its rejection by Paris theater managers at mid-century—no love interest, no triumphantly suffering protag-onist, no continuous action, and no resolution. Even in the euphoria of postwar Paris theater, performance was a Her-culean problem for an impecunious playwright. In 1949 Suz-anne Beckett carried the manuscripts of *Eleutheria* and *Godot* to several theater managers—and carried them away either refused or unread. As a last resort she brought the two plays to a theater near the small Beckett apartment on Rue des Fa-vorites—the Gaité Montparnasse, managed by Roger Blin. By word of mouth—Blin later thought he might have sent a mes-sage to Suzanne or to Tristan Tzara—Blin communicated his enthusiasm for both plays, but since an empty theater was yawning at his production of Strindberg's *Ghost Sonata*, he did not dare offer Beckett the theater that he supposedly man-aged. Nevertheless, for the sheer pleasure of hearing the rhythms of *Godot*, Blin rehearsed odd scenes in odd places with anyone he could corral for the enterprise.

Born in bourgeois Neuilly in 1907, Roger Blin started on the usual bourgeois path of *baccalauréat* and the Sorbonne.[14]

Instead of attending classes, however, he frequented the Surrealists and shared their enthusiasm for film, poetry, and the visual arts. In 1928, at age twenty-one, Blin met Artaud, and he never swerved from loyal friendship to that irascible prophet. It was not Artaud who lured Blin to theater, however, but Jacques Prévert, the moving spirit of the October Group that performed skits for proletarian audiences. In these skits Blin played small parts, even though he stuttered; and because he stuttered, he decided to become an actor: "If my hands were cut off, I would probably have tried to be a sculptor."[15] Ironically, however, Blin's first professional stage role precluded speech; he played a mute assassin in the 1935 production of Artaud's *Cenci*. He was also the assistant director for his harried friend, and Blin saved Artaud's detailed production plans of the epochal production that was largely unappreciated in its own day. Loyal to Artaud throughout his life, Blin reflected in 1977: "What I owe Artaud is in the field of ethics. What he gave me goes far beyond what can be seen in what I've done. But I don't share his religion of the director."[16] When Artaud left for Mexico in 1936, Blin joined Jean-Louis Barrault in mime lessons—an unusual step for actors in the French theater tradition—and he used his mime work when he played in Barrault's *Numantia* and *Hamlet*.

Unwilling to act in Paris under the Occupation, Blin lived from day to day during World War II, playing bit parts in movies of the so-called Unoccupied Zone and helping Jewish friends escape to Switzerland, but he was never able to trace his good friend, actor-director Sylvain Itkine, who disappeared on August 4, 1944. Blin was more fortunate in locating his friend Artaud, and helped him return to a Paris suburb after the Liberation. Blin was pleased in 1947 when Artaud came to see him act at the Vieux-Colombier in Synge's *In the Shadow of the Glen*, although he could not have known that that was Beckett's favorite Synge play. Blin's performance inspired Artaud to write a poem that contains this prescient line: "Oui, c'est bien Roger Blin qui n'était pas le bon, mais le mauvais larron. . . ." (Yes, it is indeed Roger Blin who wasn't the good but the bad thief.)[17]

When Blin wanted to stage Beckett's "thieves," however, he could afford no theater to house them. It is part of the Beckett legend that the Irish playwright came to the Gaité Montparnasse to see Blin's production of Strindberg's *Ghost Sonata* and that he was reassured by the quality of the production and the emptiness of the theater. This is true, but it is not the whole truth, for Beckett came to see Blin's work only after the latter had expressed enthusiasm for his plays. Then Beckett faced the empty theater that did not reassure Blin, for the Gaité Montparnasse was bankrupt by 1951, with Blin sentenced to pay off its debts.

In 1951, too, after trying for two years to find a theater for *Godot*, Blin suppressed his distaste for government grants and consented to present a request for a subsidy toward production of a first play. Fortunately, the poet-playwright Georges Neveux was on the selection committee. Three years after the completion of *En attendant Godot*, in January 1952, Neveux recorded his admiration for the play: "Dear Roger Blin, you are absolutely right in wanting to perform *Waiting for Godot*. It is an astonishing play; I needn't tell you that I am fiercely for it."[18] Before the award was announced, Blin managed to secure a February 1952 radio broadcast of the patter of Didi and Gogo. Shortly afterward, Blin received five hundred thousand old francs, or a little over fifteen hundred dollars, toward the realization of *Godot*. The sum enabled Blin to rent a small theater for the thirty-day minimum. Modestly, Blin chose the sixty-seat Poche for a premiere in late summer; before then he directed Adamov's *Parody*, which opened in early June 1952 at the Right Bank Lancry. However, Sascha Pitoëff's *Uncle Vanya* was so successful at the Poche that the manager reneged on her contract, and *Godot* was homeless again. Nevertheless Beckett wrote Blin: "Now that we have embarked on this dirty joke (*sale histoire*) together, I think that we can address each other in the familiar form."[19] These two shy, lean men with their striking looks formed a reserved friendship that lasted to Blin's death in 1984. (At that time he was preparing to act in a one-man performance of Beckett.)

Only toward the end of 1952 did Blin persuade Jean-Marie

Serreau to accept *Godot* for his recently opened Théâtre de Babylone, which was already doomed to close. The Babylone, with its 223 seats, was nearly four times the size of the Poche, but the stage was no wider and only a little deeper (six meters by four). To the award money Blin added small sums that he borrowed or begged from friends. The actress Delphine Seyrig recalls that she contributed a small legacy left her by an uncle who had wanted her to travel; an admirer of Blin, she hoped that his work might travel instead. Finally, Blin had enough for a month's rent, a few posters, a roll of tickets, rudimentary lights, bowler hats, and about fifteen dollars a week for each of the actors. Blin drew no salary for directing nor Beckett for writing the play.

In 1982 Blin reminisced:

> [*Waiting for Godot*] struck me as so rich and unique in its nudity that it seemed to me improper to question the author about its meaning. Nor did I ask myself questions about it; during three years of rehearsal [while waiting for money to rent a theater] my major concerns were traps, false trails, allusions. . . . First the trap of the circus. . . . After that farcical trap, the tearful trap, especially for Vladimir. . . . I know that there are different levels in *Godot*, but the desired magic can be attained only by first dealing fully with the most immediately human level. For the characters, I took as springboard their physical defects, real or implied [Vladimir's constant need to urinate, Estragon's drowsiness, Pozzo's heart trouble, Lucky's palsy]. Beckett heard their voices, but he couldn't describe his characters to me. [He said]: "The only thing I'm sure of is that they're wearing bowlers."[20]

What was unsure until two weeks before opening was the identity of the actors under the bowlers. Pierre Latour as childlike, lovable Estragon had previously acted with Blin and remained loyal to him during the long wait for a theater, but there was a succession of temporary Vladimirs until Blin fixed on Lucien Raimbourg from cabaret. His mobile face, agile body, and carefully enunciated slang precluded the tearful trap that worried Blin. Moreover, Raimbourg, accustomed to the disjunctive numbers of cabaret, was unhampered by the trained French actor's inclination to build a character toward a big scene, and this was a decided asset in the performance of *Godot*. Unfailingly good-tempered about a role he did not try to analyze in a play he did not try to analyze, Raimbourg often bicycled across Paris after a Left Bank rehearsal so as to perform in a midnight cabaret near the Bastille. Later he toured several countries in *Godot* and returned to the role as late as 1970, when a reviewer paid him this tribute: "The character [of Vladimir] will be marked forever by his broken, hopping walk, his nasal ruminations of an old clown, and in his eye a question mark, the image of the whole play."[21] Perhaps that image was in Beckett's mind when he attended Raimbourg's funeral in 1973. In 1952, however, Blin delighted in Raimbourg's vivacity. The nimble comedian literally ran circles around the stolid Estragon-Latour. Yet Raimbourg's protectiveness of the larger Latour made comically absurd Vladimir's question whether he is heavier than Estragon. Recalling John Steinbeck's *Of Mice and Men*, Blin found it moving that the smaller man should protect the larger one. Blin was more sensitive to the interdependence of the two friends than to either one alone.

Only after finally casting Vladimir and Estragon and pacing their verbal volleys did Blin turn to Pozzo and Lucky. Again he wanted contrast and relationship in the couple. Yearning for Charles Laughton, whom he knew only on film, Blin chose a heavyset Pozzo to his own Lucky, but two weeks before the opening Pozzo found a more remunerative role. Blin had no choice, knowing the play by heart, but to enact Pozzo himself. He persuaded his friend Jean Martin to play Lucky—what Blin described teasingly as "a one-line part." But Martin has indeed proved lucky as the only adult of the original cast who is still alive.

Waiting for Godot was the fifth play directed by Blin, yet this close friend of the master theoretician Artaud was aggressively antitheoretical in his approach to theater. As early as 1950 he announced: "I have no theory. I try to have no characteristic style."[22] And a quarter century later, in 1976, he declared: "Directing should be invisible. Movements and words should respect the respiration of the play. My pleasure is to go in the direction of the author. That's why I have no theory of theater." Not long before his death Blin looked back at *Godot*: "Beckett is a very shy and solitary man; he was very confused by my method of working. Or I should say by my lack of method of working. I never prepare the next day's work in advance, but I saturate myself in the play and things gradually fall into place through successive approximations, trial and error, alterations. . . . I try to blend words, thought, feeling in a choreography that I never know in advance but that I discover in rehearsal with the actors."[23] Resolutely antirealist, on the fringe of Surrealism, Blin appreciated the concrete unpredictability of Beckett's characters, who would later be labeled abstract.

Blin had an easy rapport with his actors. Unlike his friend Artaud, he made no production notebook, and he welcomed visitors at rehearsals. Since he had lived for nearly three years with the text of *Godot*, Blin would suggest one scene one day and another the next, without advance warning. Rather than explain the play, he might stutter an excuse, then enact a verbal Ping-Pong sequence himself. Or Blin would walk critically with Latour and Raimbourg until each had an individualized stride determined by his malady—Estragon-Latour's aching feet and Vladimir-Raimbourg's prostate trouble. But Jean Martin invented his own palsied tremor and jerky movements, which remained with him for weeks after he relinquished the role of Lucky. Unlike the suffering of Vladimir and Estragon, Lucky-Martin's afflictions were not funny. Pozzo alone was relatively hale in act 1, but Blin as Pozzo groped with large blind gestures in act 2. As in most subsequent rehearsals of Beckett's plays, which are grounded in repetition, actors lost their place in the dialogue. In early runthroughs Raimbourg and Latour sometimes found themselves in the wrong act when they inadvertently seized the wrong cue, and Blin laughed slyly, allowing them to flounder until they reoriented themselves. Without prompting from either Blin or Beckett, Martin divided Lucky's speech into segments to memorize: "Given the existence of a personal God . . . but not so fast and considering what is more . . . and

considering what is more much more grave. . . ." All the actors discovered that Beckett's text made relentless demands
on their skills; with little comment, Blin allowed them to discover it.

Given Beckett's stripped set, Blin did not survey technical
matters until they were actually in the Babylone—the week
of Christmas 1952. A gifted draftsman, Blin designed his own
frail tree to stand only a little higher than Martin, who was
seventy-five inches tall. Brown crepe paper was wound
around wire hangers, and the whole was stabilized in a foam-
rubber base. (For over a year afterward the resilient tree could
be seen in the theater courtyard, awaiting the periodic reviv-
als of *Godot* at the Babylone. After the play began to tour in
the spring of 1953, a similar tree was constructed that could
be dismantled into three parts, to be carried in the suitcases
of three actors.) Blin's friend Sergio Gerstein devised a cheap
back curtain of old sheets, and he covered a moldy footstool
as a mound.

When the cast was finally assembled, the actors rehearsed
in bowlers. Blin stole from his own father (a doctor) a wedding
jacket for Vladimir-Raimbourg, draping it over a loose cellu-
loid white collar and bedraggled black tie. Estragon-Latour's
baggy trousers belted with a rope endowed him with an endearing Chaplinesque quality. Shirtless, he sported a peacoat
and a scarf, once white, jauntily knotted. Blin hid Lucky-
Martin's long thin frame in a stiff scarlet jacket trimmed with
gold braid, such as footmen wore in the eighteenth century,
but his dark tight trousers were too short, disconcertingly bar-
ing his calves. Lucky's mouth was a scarlet gash in a chalk-
white face, with dark circles rendering the eyes stark and pro-
tuberant. Capped by the indispensable bowler, the white hair
of Lucky-Martin's wig fell grotesquely to his shoulders. Martin found a worn valise in a garbage can; by Christmas 1952
wartime privations were far enough in the past that one could
find things in garbage cans.

Blin patterned his own costume for Pozzo, a landed squire,
on pictures of the typical Englishman, John Bull. He wore a
checked macfarlane, with a cape broadening his thin frame

and a pillow amplifying his stomach, over which stretched a velvet vest in a diamond pattern. His bowler was gray, in contrast to the black of the other three. All four actors wore their costumes with style on the Board.

Despite Blin's relative lack of experience—his previous four productions had been box-office failures in pocket theaters, three at the ill-fated Gaité Montparnasse and one at the Lancry—he achieved in that first *Godot* a rare feeling of ensemble. The popularity of café-theater had accustomed audiences to rhythmic sallies but not to long pauses, as though the actors had forgotten their lines. Although such silences had damned Adamov's *Invasion* two years earlier, no review linked the rhythm of the two plays.

Most strange in *Godot* was the eruption of a master-slave couple into cabaret patter. After the friends toss the word "tied" back and forth, Pozzo and Lucky enter, literally tied together. An overburdened Lucky might have strayed from farce, but not when he falls *offstage* after Pozzo jerks the rope. And once Pozzo-Blin asserted his cruel presence, the effect was too grating for cabaret. Why were these two couples in the same play? Later Blin explained that he intended surprise in the entrances of Pozzo and Lucky—one from each wing of the narrow Babylone stage—but what he achieved was dislocation, even while the cast was intensely self-consistent in its own eerily funny world, dominated by an absent presence that was not yet a household word.

Vladimir and Estragon at first resemble unidentical twins, but they gradually diverge, like hat and boot. Active Vladimir is faithful to the rendezvous, whereas inactive Estragon keeps announcing his departure. Pozzo and Lucky at first seem antonymic, but they are finally twinned in picaresque impotence. Like circus clowns or vaudeville comedians, the four men struggle with objects for our entertainment, and each couple tends to treat the other as a recalcitrant object. Concentrated in the small space, Blin's production implied the interdependence of all humanity, especially in act 2 when the four men are sprawled on the ground before rising one by one, more or less helped by one another. Without textual authority for their brotherhood, Blin thus injected his own bias into that scene. And despite the penury of the production, Blin was meticulous about makeup, costumes, and especially the moods of each actor, shifting between comic and pathetic.

In January 1953 Barrault's company was about to return to Paris after an American tour, and the first drama course was about to be inaugurated at the venerable Sorbonne. In its issue for New Year's Day, 1953, the daily newspaper *Combat*, founded in the Resistance, announced the opening of *En attendant Godot*:

> This work is a gamble; imagine a play that is devoid of action, whose heroes have absolutely nothing to say to one another. One might be tempted to describe it as an "antiplay," especially since its theme is boredom. But there lies the miracle: if the characters are bored, the public mustn't be bored for a moment. . . . Samuel Beckett offers us a profoundly poetic work, a desperate work of an author animated by a great epic breath, a man who paradoxically proclaims his love of life.[24]

Thirty reviewers came to the *générale* of *En attendant Godot* before the public opening. January 4, 1953, was cold and rainy, scarcely weather to presage a bright dawn of New Theater. In that year Les Editions de Minuit, Beckett's publisher, would sell 125 copies of *Godot*, yet the performance would play through that year (not continuously) and beyond. People wanted to see, not read, the tragicomedy—nearly three hours of plotless action.

Contrary to later legend, the reviewers were kind. It is noteworthy that thirty people attended the performance, as compared to the handful present at Adamov's *Parody* or Ionesco's *Chairs* just a few months earlier in the Right Bank Lancry. To be sure, the most powerful critic of Paris, Jean-Jacques Gautier of *Figaro* was absent, but "a reasonable percentage" of those present wrote reviews. The earliest is brief but friendly; the experienced critic Marc Beigbeder, who had wanted to back a tour of *No Exit* in unoccupied France, closes his verdict on *Godot*: "But it is hardly sure, despite this brilliant workmanship and . . . an extremely remarkable interpretation . . . that this ideally allusive work can reach much beyond a coterie audience."[25] That coterie audience now numbers some hundred million.

The most mistaken review in this time of Marshall aid for France states: "This unusual work by the American novelist seems to be inspired by the miserable condition of famished tramps hunted down by farmers, who abound in the South of the United States."[26] On the same day another reviewer, recognizing the blend of the light and the learned, entitles his account after two popular clowns: "Alex and Zavatta at the Sorbonne."[27] A discerning reviewer explains that Godot is "happiness, eternal life, the ideal and unattainable quest of all men."[28] Another reviewer, sympathetic to the New Theater, rejoices: "Samuel Beckett is a subversive spirit; you can't imagine how comforting that is."[29] Still another, however, finds such "radical subversion" less comforting: "The general intention gathers all the modish intellectual themes: the absurdity of the human condition, useless freedom (of the vagabonds), humiliating resignation (of the slave, and even the master), and on top of it the delusion of hope."[30] Although Gautier of *Figaro* did not deign to see *Godot* (only in 1956 did he write a favorable review that barely describes the play), that newspaper's second-string reviewer reports favorably, the first to link Beckett to Artaud, Kafka, Joyce, and Flaubert.[31] Of the French daily reviewers, Robert Kemp of the influential *Le Monde* is dependably lukewarm; for him subject and dialogue are not new, and he much prefers a radio skit "On the Bench" about two funny tramps. "If the play shows no genius, however, it is nevertheless full of good will."[32] (By 1981 an account in that same newspaper of a Beckett Festival would be captioned "Welcome to Godot.") Even Thomas Quinn Curtis in the *Paris Herald* was not quite hostile: "Dramatically *En attendant Godot* does not hang together very well and is repetitious and rather clumsy in making its points."[33] Curtis offers no whisper of what those points might be, but he displays his erudition by comparing Beckett's play unfavorably with Lord Dunsany's *Glittering Gate*, Andreyev's *Life of Man*, Thornton Wilder's *Skin of Our Teeth*, and Hofmannsthal's *Everyman*. Curtis recognized *Godot*'s nonrealistic dramatic family, but he was blind to the subversive form. (Nearly three decades later—in its issue of April 18–19, 1981, a headline in the *Paris Herald* would read "Samuel Beckett in the 'Age of Godot.'") Some dozen reviews in daily newspapers range from tolerant to enthusiastic; Raimbourg is singled out for special praise, and Beckett is coupled with both clowns and Kafka.

Reviews in the weeklies are longer and more fervent; moreover, they appeared in time to lure spectators to that first thirty-day run. On January 15 Gabriel Marcel offers measured encouragement: "The performance can be recommended, on condition that one realize that there is almost nothing there that resembles what we usually call theater."[34] But Renée Saurel heaps praises on Beckett: "[*Godot*] might have been a frightfully intellectual play, erudite verbiage about metaphysical anguish and the difficulty of being human. But Samuel Beckett is a poet. He has written intelligible, lively dialogue, made of small, familiar phrases. His very subtle art is full of tenderness, reserve, burning love of life under the surface of a bitter clown show."[35] Claude Jamet is both witty and kind: "Samuel Beckett paints boredom without boring us, sleep without putting us to sleep, despair with merriment, and he mocks theater theatrically."[36] Beckett's fellow playwright Audiberti writes admiringly in the weekly *Arts* that *Godot* is "a perfect work that deserves a triumph. . . . Symbolism is optional, but applause is obligatory."[37]

Jacques Lemarchand, champion of the New Theater (in spite of his resistance to *The Chairs*) situates *Godot* in the drama of its time:

> *Waiting for Godot* is a profoundly original work; as such, it will not fail to disturb. It will charm some and inspire others to scorn and even fury. As for me, I found in it (but well arranged, masterfully accomplished) all those singular, sometimes gauche but always moving actions that I greeted after odd evenings spent with unknown works of the young; I'm thinking of the works of Ionesco, of *Captain Bada* by Jean Vauthier, of the early plays of Adamov. What these works tried to express, to make us understand, I hear much better in *Waiting for Godot*. I understand very well how the efforts I just named could irritate certain spectators, even while knowing that that irritation was unfair, and that it would disappear if the audience would take the trouble to listen carefully. I confess that I would

understand much less well if Samuel Beckett's play produced the same effect of withdrawal and flight. [*Godot*] indicates the true direction of a whole dramatic movement that is still in a period of research.[38]

He was of course prophetic.

Before the end of the first month's run *Godot* even strayed from theater news to actual news when rowdy drunks heckled the cast so crudely that Blin (who attended most performances) ordered the skimpy front curtain drawn before the arrival of the Boy in act 1. The disturbers did not return after the intermission, and act 2 was performed without incident.[39]

No sooner had Blin, taking a deep breath, rented the Babylone for another thirty days than the weekly *Arts* featured *Godot* on its front page, with laudatory words from two of the most successful playwrights of Paris, Jean Anouilh and Armand Salacrou. Anouilh trumpets this premiere, declaring it to be as important as Georges Pitoëff's 1923 Paris production of Pirandello's *Six Characters in Search of an Author*, and he links Beckett's lightness and learning in a phrase that has often been quoted—"the music-hall sketch of Pascal's *Pensées* as played by the Fratellini clowns." Salacrou congratulates the audience on its enthusiasm: "*Waiting for Godot* is not an accident. An author has appeared who has taken us by the hand to lead us into his universe."[40] As the run of *Godot* continued into the spring and then into the summer, *Arts* kept Beckett before the eyes of its readers. After the one hundredth performance—always a landmark achievement in theater—Beckett wrote to a friend that he had "made a good deal of money with [*Godot*] already (more, in a couple of months, than with all my other writings put together)."[41] (This is emphatically different from writing the play *in order to* make money, as Beckett's biographer misunderstood the situation.)

More deliberate and meditative criticism of *Godot* appears in monthly periodicals. As early as February 1953 Alain Robbe-Grillet was not content to echo the daily newspapers; instead, he locates the radical character of the play:

We grasp at once, as we watch them, this major function of theatrical representation: to show of what the fact of being there consists. For it is this, precisely, which we had not yet

seen on a stage, or in any case which we had not seen so
clearly, with so few concessions. . . . [Didi and Gogo] will still
be there the next day, the day after that, and so on . . . tomorrow and tomorrow and tomorrow . . . from day to day . . .
alone on stage, standing there, futile, without past or future,
irremediably present.
                              (Richard Howard translation)[42]

Unlike Camus, who compared the absurd situation of a human being to that of an actor divorced from his setting,
Robbe-Grillet follows Heidegger in defining the human condition as being-there, actualized by the reality of stage presence.

Among the Paris enthusiasts of *Godot* was a German student, Elmar Tophoven, who on his own initiative translated
the play into his native language—in three weeks punctuated
by two afternoons with Beckett. Blin's French production traveled to Germany in spring, 1953; by summer Tophaven's
translation was published, and by fall a German *Godot* was
played at the Berlin Theater Festival. Later that fall the play
opened simultaneously in twelve cities of West Germany,
where theater was flourishing again after the war. Elmar
Tophoven has since translated all of Beckett's works into German, and the second French edition of the play carries six
photographs of German productions.

While the original *Godot* was still (sporadically) playing at
the Babylone but also touring in Germany, Italy, and Switzerland, it attracted the attention of a professional philosopher—Guenther Anders, who published an essay in his phil-
osophic idiom. Disagreeing with those who link Beckett to
Heidegger, Anders calls attention to *Godot* as an inverted
fable, as a farce, as a religious nonexperience: "Whether it
is Rilke, or Kafka, or Beckett—their religious experience
springs, paradoxically, always from religious frustration, from
the fact that they do not experience God, and paradoxically
from an experience they share with unbelief. In Rilke this experience springs from the inaccessibility of God (the first
Duino elegy); in Kafka from inaccessibility in a search (*The
Castle*); in Beckett from inaccessibility in the act of waiting."
Contrasting as "antipodes" a timeless Vladimir and Estragon

and a timebound Pozzo and Lucky, Anders warns against finding "positive or consoling features" in *Godot*. Nevertheless, like many critics after him, the metaphysician Anders closes his essay with a challenge to his own discipline: "Farce seems to have become the last asylum for compassion, the complicity of the sad our last comfort. And although the mere tone of humaneness which springs from this barren soil of meaninglessness may be only a tiny comfort; and although the voice which comforts us does not know why it is comforting and who the Godot is for whom it makes us hope—it shows that warmth means more than meaning; and that it is not the metaphysician who has the last word" (Martin Esslin translation).[43] Perhaps someone in the cast of the Paris *Godot* was attuned to philosophy, for in the summer of 1954, *En attendant Godot* was advertised in *Arts* as "a metaphysical drama unfolding under the tinsel of farce."[44]

During that same summer the American director Alan Schneider saw *Godot* at the Théâtre Babylone in Paris:

> My French is just good enough to get me in and out of the American Express. Yet through the entire performance I sat alternately spellbound and mystified, knowing something terribly moving was taking place on that stage. When the highly stylized "moon" suddenly rose and night "fell" at the end of the first act, I didn't have to understand French in order to react. And when, at the beginning of the second act, the once-bare tree reappeared with little green ribbons for leaves, that simple representation of rebirth affected me beyond all reason. Without knowing exactly what, I knew that I had experienced something unique and significant in modern theater. *Godot* had me in the beginnings of a grip from which I have never escaped.[45]

Inescapably, then, Schneider later directed *Godot* more often than Blin did—in small theaters and large, with amateurs and professionals, and even with an all-female cast in an acting class. Although Blin's first production of *Godot* attained some four hundred performances, with sixteen actors alternating in the roles, the play did not earn enough money to save the Babylone, which succumbed in November 1954 to the usual fate of pocket theaters. *Godot* was absent on tour when the doors finally closed on Brecht's *Man Is Man*, ending a chapter in the history of contemporary theater.

After the success of *Godot* and the inability of its host theater to survive, pocket theaters gradually lost their innocence. Their managers began to seek plays that might transfer to commercial theaters. After the 1950s, experimental theater in Paris no longer focused on new scripts but on collective creation or on a new dynamic between actors and audience. Artaud was vindicated with a vengeance; he was invoked for every theater innovation from drugs to doubling, from nudity to incantation, from literal cruelties to verbal and visual circularities.

Seizing on Artaud's striking image, directors manipulated friendly plagues from Paris to Los Angeles, while *Waiting for Godot* in some two dozen languages staggered away from the avant-garde where it was conceived and produced. (Blin's production came to the commercial Théâtre Hébertot in 1956, without Blin.) Martin Esslin wrote of the play in 1961 that it had been "seen in the first five years after its original production in Paris by more than a million spectators—a truly astonishing reception for a play so enigmatic, so exasperating, so complex, and so uncompromising in its refusal to conform to any of the accepted ideas of dramatic construction." Esslin himself begins his *Theater of the Absurd* with the description of the San Francisco Actor's Workshop performance of *Godot* at San Quentin prison, and Sidney Homan has traveled with his *Godot* to ten Florida prisons.[46] Ironically, money from *Godot* enabled Beckett to buy a Paris apartment with a view of a prison. In 1986 a cast of Swedish prisoners escaped during a production of *Godot*.

If, as Esslin claimed, *Godot* refused conventional dramatic construction, it was nonetheless beautifully constructed from its inception. "The essential doesn't change," to quote Vladimir, yet Beckett made minor changes over a period of thirty-five years. The original manuscript was only slightly revised before being typed (by Beckett) for production and publication. (In 1950 Beckett acquired a publisher in Jérôme Lindon of Les Editions de Minuit; Lindon became a lifelong friend.) Blin was so long in unearthing a host theater for *Godot* that production lagged behind publication, which took place in October 1952. The few rehearsal changes were incorporated into Beckett's English translation—mainly the elimination of specifications about Godot and of a reference to Stalinist comedians Bim and Bom. What with the differences between American and British English, the English censor's demands, and careless American proofreading, there are minor variants in the several English-language editions.[47]

Beckett is fluent in German, and he obligingly offered (mainly sonic) suggestions to Tophoven as he translated the play, but the two men worked too quickly to be careful—given the already insatiable demands for German production. When Beckett came to direct *Godot*, however, in 1974–1975 in Berlin's Schiller Theater, he modified Tophoven's text as well as his own.[48] On the stage he pointed waiting and complementarity. Although waiting was from the first theatricalized through pauses and silences, Beckett introduced into his own production twelve painful freezes. The pain was sharpened by contrast with the comic signs of complementarity—each couple's matching costumes, Vladimir's attraction to the tree and Estragon's to the stone (substituted for the mound), Vladimir and Estragon's duets with hat and shoe, tall Didi's and short Gogo's walking in step as they review their problematic plea to Godot. Pozzo remained Beckett's most troublesome character, and in production the playwright deprived him of pipe, atomizer, and business with the whip as well as cutting the lines that refer to Lucky's refusal to obey him. After Pozzo's mention of Lucky's Net Dance (but elimination of the alternative dance titles suggested by the friends), Beckett cut the three-way conversation up to Estragon's metatheatrical exclamation: "Nothing happens, nobody comes, nobody goes, it's awful!" In act 2 Beckett eliminated the three-way conversation about the time of day. Euphonic phrasing, farcical gestures, and strict rhythm lighten Beckett's German production.

When Beckett returned in 1984 to *Godot* in his native language, as a favor to Rick Cluchey of the San Quentin Drama Workshop, he incorporated his German cuts and introduced a few more into the English text. He suffused the young actors in an atmosphere of weariness. Beckett also has his last Pozzo leave his watch "at the manor on my Steinway," thus pairing him more closely with Lucky, who mentions the tandem of Steinweg and Peterman (literally "stone way" and "stone man"). Visually, however, it is Estragon who is attracted to the stone that has replaced the original mound. And visually, Vladimir and Estragon react as a team against Lucky's verbal barrage.

Through the years, Beckett has imposed his directorial habits on the performance of his texts: by occasionally abridging those texts, by simplifying and "vaguening" the dialogue, by calling for extreme spareness of setting and props, by requiring economy of gesture and emotional expression, by emphasizing symmetries and repetitions—an approach that has been called musical and balletic. With hindsight, we can see how much of this approach is written into the original text of *Waiting for Godot*, however Blin humanized it in performance.

From the first, most reviewers suspected the complexity under the simple surface of *Godot*, and they echoed Pozzo's question: "Who is Godot?" Even the French recognized the "God" in "Godot," but only in 1955 did Suzanne Aron attach the name to an awaited M. Godeau in Balzac's *Faiseur*.[49] Still unpublished is Bernard Dukore's reference (in a personal letter to me) to Jakob Lenz's *Soldiers*, where Godeau is a French actor-manager. It was Beckett who informed Hugh Kenner of a Tour de France bicycle racer named Godeau, and Beckett himself flew from Paris to London in a plane whose pilot was one Captain Godeau.[50] In southern California a professor reads *Godot* backwards as Tod-dog, and in northern California the Godeau Funeral Home is still active. If such details seem trivial, they harmonize with the play's strategy of enfolding the trivial into the profound. "This is becoming really insignificant. Not enough."

The first reviewers, however, sought significance, linking Beckett to Artaud, Joyce, and Kafka and thrusting him, foreigner though he was in France, into the family of French writers preoccupied with death—Ronsard, Bossuet, Pascal, Baudelaire, and Artaud. Poet and fiction writer though he was, Beckett was first celebrated as the playwright of *Godot*, and a virtual history of theater has been read into the play. Beckett strips the setting down to two elements—a road and a tree. The road is usually represented as the stage-board, bared from wing to wing, but in Beckett's Berlin production it was raked foam-rubber; in Alan Schneider's film of *Godot* the road stretches vertically into the distance. The Czech director Otomar Krejca sets the drama on a gigantic white disk.

The tree is more weightily fraught with a literary burden, reaching out not only to the biblical trees of life, knowledge of good and evil, and Judas, but also to Dante's tree at the gate of hell; the pine tree of the Noh stage; Yggdrasil, the tree that spread over the world in Norse mythology; the Buddhist Bo tree; and the tree as cross or as question mark. For a 1961 revival in Paris, Blin prevailed on the sculptor Alberto Giacometti to design a tree, but like the very first wire-and-paper tree, that one also disappeared one day. It is small wonder that Vladimir and Estragon stagger when they "do" the tree.

Beckett has been accused of imitating himself in successive works, and chance details of *Godot* may be strained from his earlier writing. A charnel house is mentioned as early as *More Pricks Than Kicks*. Shoes, ditch, and three announcements of "Nothing to be done" appear in his unpublished "Dream of Fair to Middling Women." Witty conversational volleys bounce through the early fiction and, with a sharper edge, through the 1938 novel *Murphy*. Beckett told Colin Duckworth: "If you want to find the origins of *En attendant Godot*, look at *Murphy*."[51] Characteristically, he gave no hints *how* to look at that novel, which predicts the play in that doubt gradually undermines time, place, language, memory, causality. Beckett used the plural—"origins"—to Duckworth, and if we look below or beyond the novel's scrupulously localized surface, we find the old structure of the quest. Whereas the novel's minor characters go in quest of its protagonist Murphy, that eponymous hero reaches a condition that resembles that of the waiting Vladimir and Estragon. He does so through the mediation of an asylum inmate, Mr. Endon (Greek for "within"). Ever since the premiere of *Waiting for Godot*, intelligent commentators have thrown their weight behind the waiting rather than Godot; yet the French verb has an object—Godot. So too Murphy waits in emulation of Mr. Endon, Beckett's first skew deity. In Beckett's second English novel, the deity figure is more elusive; Mr. Knott seems to be all things to his several servants, most notably Watt. By the time Beckett wrote *Godot*, he exploited the dramatic tension of absence. A mysterious inward-looking character of *Murphy* has evolved into divine but theatrical absence.

In the wake of Duckworth, most Beckett critics find the immediate progenitor of the play in another novel, which Beckett delayed publishing—*Mercier and Camier*.[52] That novel and the play share a double protagonist of two old men—"a pseudocouple"—but Mercier and Camier travel as compulsively and aimlessly as Pozzo and Lucky. While traveling, they converse, often in the cabaret patter of the friends in *Godot*, but no duets literally echo those of the novel. Novel and play also share a tree, a barren setting, and nostalgia about a dimly remembered past. Of Beckett's works, only *Mercier and Camier* and *Waiting for Godot* set vaudeville routines on a metaphysical ground.

Both vaudeville and metaphysics were honed when Beckett translated *En attendant Godot* to *Waiting for Godot*. Although some French wordplay had to be discarded, an English equivalent was sometimes introduced. Specific biblical references are more plentiful in English than in French, and the echoes of Shakespeare and Shelley are new. "Vaguening" increases in the English version, where Godot is a more problematical figure. The play's opening word "Nothing" is more often echoed than the French "Rien." Moreover "rien à faire" is a common French colloquialism, which Beckett refused to translate as a comparable "nothing doing." In English he underlined the play as a performance, since "nothing" has "to be done." But if play is more marked in English, so is the seriousness of the situation. Estragon's neutral repetitions of

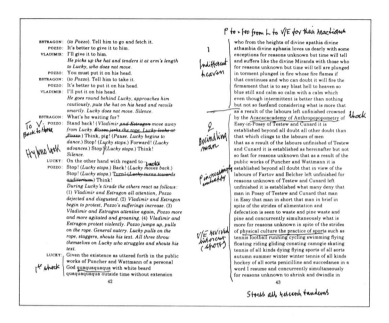

"c'est vrai" become despairing "ah's" in English. The tree in full leaf in the French version of act 2 in the English version bears only four or five leaves. The English text is tightened by omissions, and its vocabulary is less colloquial. Compare for example Estragon's recollection of Lucky in the two languages:

> Je me rappelle un énergumène qui m'a foutu des coups de pied. Ensuite il a fait le con.

> I remember a lunatic who kicked the shins off me. Then he played the fool.

French or English, Beckett has quarried *Godot* for his subsequent writing. Physical misery afflicts most of his characters, both before and after *Godot*. Although there are no sudden mutes after Lucky, Pozzo's blindness seems contagious, caught by Dan Rooney of *All That Fall*, Hamm of *Endgame*, and A of *Theater I*. Complementary couples are the focus of *Endgame, Happy Days, Act without Words 2*, both *Roughs for Theater, Not I*, and *Ohio Impromptu*. A tree reappears in *Act*

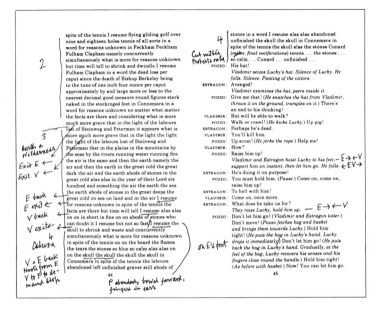

15.   Beckett's stage notations for Lucky's speech in his production of *Waiting for Godot* (*above and left*)

without Words 1, as do carrots in *Act without Words 2*. The ubiquitous bowler of *Godot* is seen again on the protagonist of the BBC production of *. . . but the clouds . . .* ; returned from roaming the roads, he busies himself with the "nothing" that is to be done in *Godot*. But the only *Godot* character's name found in a later work is that of Pozzo, in *Text 5 for Nothing*: "Why did Pozzo leave home, he had a castle and retainer?" Why indeed! Pozzo's toast—"Happy days!"—becomes the title of a major Beckett play, and the word "enough"—often repeated in *Godot*—becomes the title of a 1967 story (translated from the French title "Assez"). The master and servant couple move to center stage in *Endgame*, whereas the landscape of the void nourishes *Happy Days*. Winnie of the latter play inherits Vladimir's sudden and unsatisfying smile. Pozzo's memorable line about birthing astride a grave is differently vivified in *Breath* and *A Piece of Monologue*; the latter moves from "Birth" to "gone." Estragon tries calling Pozzo several names "to hit on the right one sooner or later," and Mouth in *Not I* tries words to "hit on it in the end." Vladimir's sense of being seen—"At me too someone is looking"—splits into two questions in *Play*, where W2 asks: "Is anyone looking at me?" and M asks: "Am I as much as . . . being seen?" The stones of Lucky's oration are picked up by the insidious voice that describes a suicide in *Eh Joe*. Lucky's "unfinished" extends to Hamm's chronicle, Clov's departure, and Mouth's monologue. In *Godot* "nothing" has to be done; in *Ohio Impromptu* "nothing" has to be told, until finally "nothing is left to tell." "Hope deferred" of *Proverbs* is still deferred in *Company*: "Better hope deferred than now." *Godot*'s several references to its audience are the germ of Beckett's later theater-reality (in which fictional and physical situation converge).

These later Beckett works merely glance off *Godot*, but Beckett's best-known play hovers in the shadow of his television play of 1975, *Ghost Trio*, despite its *sole* protagonist who waits for a female presence: "He will now think he hears her." The original title of *Ghost Trio* was *Tryst*, a poetic synonym for *appointment*, and the lone character is no saint, but like Vladimir and Estragon, he too keeps his appointment, and he too is disappointed. Although the setting moves indoors, the man's movements are similarly limited to simple geometric paths. The television protagonist peers not into twilight but into dark night; and like Vladimir and Estragon, he counterpoints gesture against word. As in *Godot* a boy arrives in *Ghost Trio*. Although he does not speak on television, he apparently bears the same message as the boy in *Godot*: "*Boy shakes head faintly*"—twice, as in the two acts of *Godot*.

Vladimir and Estragon grow more inventive as they grow more anxious in act 2 of *Godot*. The converse is true of the solitary man of *Ghost Trio*. In what Beckett calls Pre-Action, words address the television viewer, contouring the room we see—a room resembling that of Beckett's post-*Godot* plays. In the Action proper, the few words no longer address the viewer but the protagonist, instructing him in the matter of movements, but he surprises himself with his reflection in the mirror. In the Reaction, only nonverbal sounds punctuate the repetition of his movements, and it is the Reaction that almost encapsulates *Godot*, with its strict and repetitive pattern. As *Godot* contains a compendium of performance, *Ghost Trio* contains a compendium of the arts—the titular music, the slender narrative, the painterly interior scene, and the television actors focused for the camera.

Beckett's mining of *Godot* is, however, slight in comparison with the ore that critics have carried away. Although academic Beckettians are still far outnumbered by Shakespearians and Joyceans, there is nevertheless a Samuel Beckett Society with an appropriately named newsletter, *The Beckett Circle*. The critic Kenneth Tynan declared himself a "Godotista," but there is as yet no Godot Society, even though the absent Godot is very much present in most of the hundred-odd books devoted to Beckett, a few on that play alone.[53]

More amusing (and sometimes more telling) than the responses of professional critics to *Godot* is the impact of the play on writers. Immediate praise blazed forth from Anouilh, Audiberti, Salacrou, and Robbe-Grillet, but only the last of these took as a model *Godot*'s rejection of psychology, its focus on a few objects, and its incantatory repetition of key phrases.

Godot reached quickly beyond the French frontier. In East Berlin Brecht marked a 1953 edition of Tophoven's translation *Warten auf Godot* with his own notes toward writing a "counterplay."[54] Although the notes stop in the middle of the first act, the direction is clear: Brecht's Estragon will be a proletarian, his Vladimir an intellectual, Pozzo a landowning nobleman (von Pozzo), and Lucky a fool or a policeman (allowing extraordinary latitude of alternatives!). Emending the Beckett-Tophoven dialogue, Brecht rendered Estragon's lines more crisply and colloquially. In keeping with his social designations, Brecht occasionally transferred lines from one friend to the other; thus not Estragon but Vladimir becomes the erstwhile poet, and it is he who wonders whether getting used to the muck as you go along is the opposite of feeling that it gets worse as you eat more. Estragon keeps his words as well as his feet on the ground, and he is not dependent on Vladimir. Brecht mutes Beckett's metaphysical resonance, cutting, for example, Estragon's line about the universe: "This one is enough for you?" It is the intellectual Vladimir who falls asleep so that Estragon alone converses with Pozzo; the proletarian confronts the landowner, but there Brecht's proposed adaptation stops.

Brecht's notes for his own version of *Godot* are undated. He could have seen the original French production in 1953 in Germany (but not in Berlin), or a German production in the fall of 1953 in any one of twelve cities (but not in Berlin). Perhaps he merely read the play he wanted to rewrite. The German critic Hans Mayer guesses that the counterplay was conceived in 1953–1954, when Brecht was revising some of his own early plays for publication. Mayer thinks that Brecht's insertion of the entire round about the unfortunate dog into his *Drums in the Night* implicitly rebuts Beckett, for the song is sung by a German veteran of World War I who refuses to join the Spartacus revolution because life consists of eternal repetition; Brecht's revised play disapproves of the socially negative attitude implied by the song.

By 1954 Beckett's *Waiting for Godot* was a success in theaters throughout Europe. In the summer of 1954 Brecht and the Berliner Ensemble took the Paris theater by storm with their highly theatrical versions of history. Swiftly, two theater camps formed, absurdists versus politicists, their banners unfurled emblematically over Beckett and Brecht respectively. Although neither playwright made a public statement about the other, the two men could not have been unaware of each other. Possibly Brecht's counter-*Godot* notes were ignited by his Paris visit, but he never completed his counterplay. Instead, he began work on a radically estranged *production* plan for Beckett's *Godot*. Rather than tamper with a text, he introduces dialectics by theatrical means: two different, contradictory, worlds are to oppose each other dialectically. Brecht no longer alters the status and dialogue of the characters; he alters the setting, breaks up scenes, and counterpoints the lines with music and film inserts as did Erwin Piscator in his epic theater productions. The tramps are not to be dragged into society. Instead, they are shown as voluntary outsiders, having chosen to isolate themselves from a progressive world.[55] Shortly before his death in 1956 Brecht wanted to show the absurdity of Beckett's Theater of the Absurd by juxtaposing films of revolutionary action in the Soviet Union, China, Asia, and Africa with the inaction of Vladimir and Estragon in a play that his co-worker Kathe Rulicke-Weiler admits is "grossartig geschrieben."

Decidedly not "greatly written" is another rejoinder to Beckett—*Godot Arrived*, which unfortunately *was* completed at loquacious length.[56] Written in Serbo-Croatian in 1966 by Miodrag Bulatovic, the play is dedicated to Beckett, who "took Godot over from Balzac, and Balzac had it from an old French legend." For Bulatovic, Godot may be a god, but he is also human. The Yugoslavian autodidact therefore endows Godot with a trade, baking; through a dreary series of complications the four Beckett characters condemn him to death. Since Godot is indestructible, however, Lucky declares him inexistent. The four characters recall fragments of Beckett's play and then recite in chorus: "For us everything is in order. It ends as it begins. . . ." When the four men disappear, the baker Godot is momentarily alone, but he soon comes to the rescue of the half-dead Boy. Accusing Godot of being the devil, the Boy congeals into a statue while Godot the baker leaves sacks of flour for posterity. On the flyleaf of my edition of the Bulatovic play, Beckett is quoted: "I think that all that has nothing to do with me."[57]

The sentence may be extended to any number of *Godot* epigones, most of which were spared publication, but I cite a few of passing interest. Although Anouilh was generous in his praise of both Beckett and Ionesco, he parodied the former in his 1959 play *The Scatterbrain* (*L'Hurluberlu*). In a play within the play, an antidrama, the entire set consists of a bidet on a bare stage, and two characters intone: "Nothing. There is nothing. There never was anything. Nothing ever happened anywhere, and nothing will ever happen. So what's the use of going on?"[58]

At mid-century, however, quite a lot was happening in the small world of avant-garde Paris theater, where cabaret wit vied with serious drama. Since the appreciation of cabaret sketches had prepared the terrain for Beckett and Ionesco, there is poetic justice in the parody of *Godot* that came back to cabaret. *Waiting for Grouchy* (*En attendant Grouchy*), a sketch by Roland Dubillard, is one of his hilarious two-character "diablogues." In the sketch, which turns on word play between *gare*, "station," and *guerre*, "war," Dubillard's two characters romp colloquially through history, borrowing occasional phrases from Beckett. (Earlier—in 1958—Kenneth Tynan's review of a double bill of *Endgame* and *Krapp's Last Tape* was shaped as a parodic skit entitled *Slamm's Last Knock*, in which Tynan refers to Beckett as the "unrivalled master of the unravelled revels.")[59]

More sustained, or at least more expansive, is *Knock Knock* by Jules Feiffer, the American caricaturist turned playwright.[60] Whether or not he knew that Estragon had started out as Levy, Feiffer's protagonist couple are middle-aged urban Jews, Cohn and Abe, who live interdependently in an isolated and unlocalized house. Although they are waiting for no one, they are confronted by two arrivals—the titular "knock knock." Feiffer splits Beckett's invisible Godot into two visible, and especially audible, characters—a cynical, diabolic Wiseman and an idealistic, voice-hearkening Joan (of Arc). Laced with one-liners and an occasional phrasal echo of Beckett, Feiffer's comedy ends happily with the victory of good (Joan) over evil (Wiseman) in the confused soul of Cohn. The play's disjunctive dialogue and freewheeling fantasy are unimaginable before Beckett's *Godot*, however the sunny ending betrays Beckett's pointed questions.

Godot has occasioned cartoons, musical compositions, and academic scholarship. It has been illustrated (by Dellas Henke), set to music (by Marc Wilkinson and by Roman Haubenstock-Ramati), and translated into two dozen languages. Charles Addams has drawn figures waiting—for Godot, till the sun shines Nellie, for Lefty, for the Robert E. Lee; Tom Johnston's tramp exclaims: "Typical! You wait ages for Godot, then three come at once!"; S. Gross's gagged executive is named Godot. By 1985 Beckett in general and *Godot* in particular are fodder for parody; for example, Vladimir Estragon writes the culinary column of New York's *Village Voice*, and a television serial is mocked: "Vladimir Tubbs and Estragon Crockett are two sexy, funky hobos-turned-narcs."[61]

Imitations proliferate of music-hall duets musing on human destiny while lithe actors take pratfalls on a shifting ground. In a memorable post-*Godot* production of Aristophanes' *Birds*, Herbert Blau topped Peisthetaerus and Euelpides with music-hall derbies. What is inimitable, however, is the intense concentration of Beckett's rhythmic, generic, and linguistic variety. The very first book to be written about Beckett—a Swiss doctoral dissertation—pays tribute to his linguistic kaleidoscope—monologues of Tragedy, misunderstandings of Comedy, approximations and hesitations of Realism, telegraphic spurts of Expressionism, chance associations of Surrealism, catalogues and synonyms of modern lexicons.[62] Behind the humble dialogue of Vladimir and Estragon bristles a panoply of rhetorical techniques—declaration, negation, retraction, interrogation, contradiction, exclamation, repetition, hesitation, modification, qualification, fragmentation, vituperation, implication, circularity, truisms, and even aphorisms. From the opening "Nothing to be done" to the closing, motionless "Let's go," almost every line of *Godot* has served some actor or writer as an aphorism of extensible significance. Unusual if not revolutionary in its original colloquial French, *Godot* accommodates classical parsing and contemporary rules of discourse. In *Endgame* Beckett would underscore traditions of dramatic speech—soliloquy, aside—but he already deploys such forms in *Godot*: not only soliloquy and aside but also stichomythia and even a chorus of adieus.

Beckett remarked in one of his rare commentaries on his drama: "I did not envisage becoming a dramatist, but the work of the novelist is hard; one moves forward in the dark. In the theater one takes part in a game with its own rules, and one cannot not submit to them, even if one seems to flout certain conventions. There are things that one cannot make actors do and that one cannot make an audience accept."[63]

This dramatist who thrives on flouting conventions, on

making actors do what they have never done, and on making audiences accept what they were never before offered—this dramatist has nevertheless wreathed *Godot* around twenty-five hundred years of Western theater. It is less germane to tragedy that Estragon's foot swells visibly (*Oedi-pos*) than that the two friends are at once protagonist and chorus—"all mannd is us"—and that the deus never descends from the machina. Pozzo in act 1 wallows in hubris, but by act 2 he falls—a literal *de casibus* tragic figure. In act 2 Vladimir takes part in four different recognition scenes—first with Estragon's shoes, then with Lucky's hat, later with Pozzo and Lucky, and finally with the Boy—although he himself remains unrecognized: "And then nobody ever recognizes us."

If Beckett nods toward Aristotelian criteria of tragedy, he also teases them. As Vladimir is unrecognized, so peripeteias are repeated or flattened out in the arrivals of Pozzo and Lucky and of the Boy. Pozzo of act 1 may be a hubristic hero, but in act 2 he is a blind prophet, however he may deny it. In both acts a divine messenger arrives with his truncated message. And the problematic catharsis varies with the viewer.

Pervasive in *Godot* is a feeling of tragic vision. The comic resources of such actors as Lucien Raimbourg, Jack Mac-Gowran, Max Wall, and Bert Lahr have elicited chuckles from newspaper reviewers, but the first decade of critics plumbed the tragic depths of *Godot*. Despite Beckett's repertory of farcical devices, and even before Beckett himself directed his own work to display that repertory, the tragic play served as a wedge for serious scholarship on joyous popular arts.

The vaudeville knockabout draws on the commedia tradition.[64] Lucky is a descendant of the pedantic Dottore, but Pozzo has older roots in the Aristophanic alazon; Beckett elaborated their respective *lazzi* to sometimes frightening proportions. Moreover, this residue of farce interlaces with strands of medieval religious drama: Estragon and especially Vladimir are Everyman, seeking their salvation like the protagonists of morality plays. Although the Corpus Christi cycle of plays from Creation to the Last Judgment is considerably curtailed in *Godot*, we can recognize the shards in scriptural analogues.

Neither the gaping mouth of hell nor a stellar heaven is present on the unlocalized stage of *Godot*, but the atmosphere is
haunted by their memory. Lucky summons them both: "Blast
hell to heaven."

Visually, however, the play is of *this* world, with its worn
clothes, meager diet, and unpredictable excretion. Turnips,
carrots, radishes, chicken, and wine are specific and realistic,
as Blin's actors realized when the budget did not provide for
them. But by the time we see food on stage, we have been
warned away from realism by the vaudeville bowlers. Even
though tramps and travelers are staples of realistic drama,
they meet in this play without cause or sustained effect. And
over these characters hover the dreams and ghosts that pre-
cede and supersede realism—in Shakespeare and Strindberg,
for example.

Godot also seems to reach out toward certain modern classics. The tragicomedy confirms the title of Pirandello's *To Each
His Own Truth*, and his *Tonight We Improvise* encapsulates the
evenings of Didi and Gogo. Thornton Wilder was enthusiastic
about *Godot*, which also dramatizes life lived by the skin of
our teeth. A covertly metaphysical *Waiting for Godot* is often
contrasted with Clifford Odets's overtly agitprop *Waiting for
Lefty*, but more revealing is the kinship between Beckett's play
and two earlier dramas of waiting—Chekhov's *Three Sisters*
and Williams's *Glass Menagerie*. One can, of course, arbitrarily
compare any two works, but *Godot* seems imperiously magnetic in attracting comparison with masterpieces of the modern repertoire.

In tracing the dramatic descendants of *Godot*, one can
scarcely limit the lineage. Even today actors occasionally have
their first taste of Beckett when they are cast in one of his
plays, but playwrights cut their teeth on him. Couples as protagonists did not wait for Beckett—witness Shakespeare or
Strindberg—but Beckett introduced surface vaudeville as dramatic tension. After the duets of Didi and Gogo, the verbal
ball could be returned deftly and much more insistently than
"once in a way" in Harold Pinter's *Dumb Waiter* (whose near
tramps also wait), Edward Albee's *Zoo Story*, Tennessee Wil-

liams's *Out-Cry*, David Storey's *Home*, Sam Shepard's *Cowboys #2*, and almost any play by Thomas Bernhard or David Mamet. Even political playwrights who denigrate Beckett—Edward Bond, David Hare, Franz Xaver Kroetz, Jean-Paul Wenzel—strip their dialogue of verbs and connectives, as authorized by *Godot*. J. M. Coetzee, the South African author of *Waiting for the Barbarians*, absorbs more than the titular phrase from Beckett. Most profoundly, the subtly political playwright Heinar Müller arrived at collaboration with the subtly visual artist Robert Wilson only through the pattern of Beckett's minimalist mediation.

The most obstreperous offspring of Beckett is Tom Stoppard, who demurs at the charge that he borrowed "the image of two lost souls waiting for something to happen,"[65] even as he admits that he learned from Beckett a humor of "elaborate structure and sudden—and total—dismantlement."[66] The humor of parody, however, ends *Jumpers* when Archie preaches "Do not despair" and closes his sermon with a twist of Pozzo's birthing at the grave: "At the graveside the undertaker doffs his top hat and impregnates the prettiest mourner. Wham, bam, thank you Sam." But this is one-jump parody in contrast with Stoppard's play-long debt to Beckett in *Rosencrantz and Guildenstern Are Dead*, which nourishes his irrepressible gamesmanship: "With hindsight, we can see that *Godot* was stylistically rather than philosophically seminal for Stoppard—ping-pong dialogue between twinned opposites, rhythmic pauses between beats, lack of answers to many small questions, lack of denouement to the large plot line, metaphysics partially camouflaged by farce."[67] Stoppard plays scintillating variations on Beckett's techniques, but he seems invulnerable to Beckett's pain: "It's the heart. Damnation!"

Someone who lives long with *Waiting for Godot* inevitably falls prey to its tilting symmetries, and with that precarious balance I conclude. When Beckett wrote *Godot* in 1948–1949, he could not have known T. S. Eliot's *Cocktail Party*, completed in 1949. Toward the end of *The Reader's Guide to Samuel Beckett* (after demolishing Esslin and Ionesco in two successive sentences), Hugh Kenner compares and contrasts Eliot, the poet-playwright, with Beckett, the novelist-playwright: "What is accessible and germane is an equal devotion, rigorous and ascetic, to the scrupulously written word."[68] Similar in their primary commitment to another genre—Eliot to poetry and Beckett to fiction—the two dramatists wrote dramas whose differences are instructive.

Beckett and Eliot completed plays in the last year of a half century that witnessed the erosion of realism as an instrument of dramatic exploration. To their credit, both Beckett and Eliot were aware of that erosion, and they both desired to speed it along. Both writers concentrated on depths beneath a comic surface—Eliot's sainthood beneath a comedy of manners, Beckett's hope deferred beneath vaudeville routines. Beckett's shaping imagination moved sure-handedly even in his first draft of *Waiting for Godot*, whereas Eliot revised several elements for over a year—number of acts, relative importance of characters, and events of the plot, as well as many lines of verse dialogue. Eliot's diligence is commendable, but it suggests his lack of ease in the dramatic form after a decade's absence from the stage. His structural crutch was Euripides' *Alcestis*, which served him thematically as well, since his characters, too, learn to accept the human condition.[69] By the end of *The Cocktail Party*, however, Eliot's brittle and amusing Guardians have been upstaged by his Hercules analogue, the priest-psychiatrist Reilly, and conclusive focus rests on the saintly Celia (a seriocomic name in Beckett's *Murphy*). Without Eliot's explicit acknowledgment of his Euripidean debt we might not notice it, as without the dialogue of Vladimir and Estragon about the two thieves we might not notice Beckett's debt to the Bible; however, we could not fail to notice the symmetries of *Godot*, formalizing the human opposition. And therein lies one significant difference between Eliot and Beckett: *The Cocktail Party* grafts branches of drawing-room comedy (a more or less well-made play) onto the trunk of a satyr play and then engineers a mutant protagonist who is alien to both genres; *Waiting for Godot* is formed by its content, even while being nourished by the whole Western theater tradition, classical and popular.

Both plays circle back to their beginnings: the second Eliot cocktail party is mellower than the first, since the married couple is reunited, and the saint has found (I am tempted to write "enjoyed") her martyrdom. Retreating from the corrective satire of the comedy of manners tradition, Eliot's characters snuggle comfortably into Christian community. But the second arrival of Beckett's Boy is bleaker than the first, since we in the audience, with the characters on the stage, have witnessed the lengthening deferral of hope. Modern tragicomedies rarely end happily, and this one doesn't end at all; it just stops. The circular structure is appropriate to events in both plays, but the account of an absent martyr falls like a stone on the brittle crystal of the staged cocktail party, whereas an absent Godot suffuses Beckett's play with longing.

Eliot's third play, *The Cocktail Party* is his most dynamic drama. Except for the scenes involving Reilly the priest-psychiatrist, his characters interact rather than interview one another, as in *The Family Reunion*; he contrived suspense and psychological coherence, as well as the Noël Coward witticisms of his urban professionals. Muting overt symbolism, he stipulated a realistic set and costumes. Nevertheless, Eliot conceived his play as dialogue, however he flattened his lyric gift, however he subdued his three-stress lines. Beckett, in contrast, must have brooded about the vaudeville and silent movies that he had enjoyed in his youth so that he saw his characters in bowlers from the moment of conception, and he did not so much symbolize the Christian Fall in their pratfalls as recognize a lifetime in and as a series of routines performed while waiting.

For all Eliot's religious sincerity and verbal dexterity, he never learned that basic tenet of playwriting: "Don't tell; show." Like so many plays of its time, *The Cocktail Party* is full of talk and lacks memorable image, passionate utterance, or character interaction beyond the cocktail-party surface. It was successful both on Broadway and on Shaftesbury Avenue, fitting snugly into the mode of its day—and ours, as indicated by its acclaimed revival in 1984. Despite Eliot's devotion to "the scrupulously written word," despite his desire "to combine the dramatic and the poetic in a somewhat new way,"[70] he adhered to the major conventions of the well-made play— a French form that was easily naturalized on the English stage. To this day, the form fares well in problem play and farce—in both languages.

The well-made play was spurned, however, in Paris pocket theaters where a new vision was intended to herald a new postwar life. According to their individual talents and temperaments, the pocket-theater visionaries sought to build on or break with traditions. Although some contemporary criticism views them as transmitters of the dialect of the tribe, the young theater enthusiasts acclaimed a new kind of theater. But new visions age swiftly, and those who survive a war soon complain about creature discomforts.

In the pocket theaters of postwar Paris, drama was sometimes submerged beneath lyricism or philosophy, but the funny or the fantastic had more staying power. And then along came *Waiting for Godot*, which wove these strands into a bright banner that was soon unfurled over Western Europe, and a little later over the shrinking globe.

After the acceptance of *Godot* it is hard to imagine any unacceptable form of drama. Worldwide performance of the play, a Nobel Prize for the playwright, a play title that is a household word—this study seems to end in triumph. *Godot* has been welcomed in large subsidized theaters in the Paris where it was born; the Krejca production is playing there as I write, and various eightieth-birthday celebrations honor Beckett. Yet *Waiting for Godot* has succeeded neither on Broadway, on the Boulevards, on Shaftesbury Avenue, nor in the unsubsidized theaters of European countries. (A production of *Godot* with a black cast on Broadway was closed by a stagehands' union that ordered a backstage pinochle table to be manned by seven instead of five people.)[71] Film and television versions of *Godot* have wooed wide audiences, weakening its palpable impact. As long as theaters are expected to pay their own way, they rarely risk this tragicomedy.

Young enthusiasts are doomed to grow less young or less enthusiastic, with one eye trained on subsidy and another on commercial transfer. So perhaps I may be pardoned this nostalgic glance at an age of innocence—when theater mirrored the daily headlines as in a funnyhouse, when stylized performers and stagehands stumbled over one another, when innovative companies outnumbered their audiences, but when sometimes, seldom, players caused the stones to move, the trees to talk, and spectators to behold their humanity.

Notes

Chapter 1

1. Samuel Beckett, "Arènes de Lutèce," *Collected Poems in English and French* (New York: Grove Press, 1977), 50.

2. Jacques Copeau, "Un essai de rénovation dramatique," originally published in *Nouvelle Revue Française* (September 1913); reprinted in Jacques Copeau, *Critiques d'un autre temps* (Paris: NRF, 1923), 239. Unless otherwise designated, all translations are mine. I supply the original French for play titles and, in an appendix, for quotations from the plays themselves.

3. For premodern French theater there is still, alas, no substitute for Eugène Lintilhac, *Histoire générale du théâtre en France* (Paris: Flammarion, n.d.).

4. Figures are taken from *Histoire des Spectacles*, ed. Guy Dumur (Paris: Gallimard, 1965), 766.

5. Héron de Villefosse, *Histoire de Paris* (Paris: Grasset, 1955), 252–60.

6. Quoted in English in Frederick Brown, *Theater and Revolution* (New York: Viking, 1980), 68. For my pocket history I have relied passim on this fascinating work.

7. Marie-Claire Bancquart, *Paris des Surréalistes* (Paris: Seghers, 1972), 9.

8. Léon-Paul Fargue, *Le Piéton de Paris* (Paris: Gallimard, 1980; first published 1932), 149.

9. For the history of the modern French theater to World War II, see Clément Borgal, *Metteurs en scène* (Paris: Lanore, 1963); David Bradby, *Modern French Drama, 1940–1980* (Cambridge: Cambridge University Press, 1984); Germaine Brée and Alexander Y. Kroff, "Vue d'ensemble," *Twentieth-Century French Drama* (New York: Macmillan, 1969); Sylvain Dhomme, *La Mise en scène contemporaine d'André Antoine à Bertolt Brecht* (Paris: Nathan, 1959); Bernard Dort, "Entre la nostalgie et l'utopie," *Cahiers Théâtre Louvain* no. 43 (1980): 7–35; Martin Esslin, *The Theatre of the Absurd* (Harmondsworth: Penguin, 1980); Dorothy Knowles, *French Drama of the Inter-War Years* (London: Harrap, 1967) (she has also offered me access to her fine collection of *dossiers*, for which I am grateful); Geneviève Serreau, *Histoire du*

"nouveau théâtre" (Paris: Gallimard, 1966); Alfred Simon, *Dictionnaire du théâtre français contemporain* (Paris: Larousse, 1970); Paul Surer, *Cinquante ans de théâtre, 1919–1969* (Paris: Seuil, 1969); Georges Versini, *Le Théâtre français depuis 1900* (Paris: Presses universitaires de France, 1970).

10. Mattei Roussou, *André Antoine* (Paris: L'Arche, 1954), 279.
11. Jacques Robichez, *Le Symbolisme au théâtre* (Paris: L'Arche, 1957), 376.
12. Dhomme, 185–86.
13. John Russell, *Paris* (New York: Harry N. Abrams, 1983), 298–99.
14. Dhomme, chapter 4.
15. The literature on Artaud is voluminous. For these few facts I rely on Thomas Maeder, *Antonin Artaud* (Paris: Plon, 1978).
16. Patrick Marsh, "Le Théâtre à Paris sous l'occupation allemande," *Revue de la Société d'histoire du théâtre* 33, no. 3: 197–369; Hervé Le Boterf, *La Vie parisienne sous l'occupation* (Paris: Editions France-Empire) 1974–1975; and the Truffaut movie *Le Dernier Métro*.
17. Pierre-Aimé Touchard, *Les Annales* (March 1968).
18. *Acteurs*, p. 67. My sources of information on Paris pocket theaters are memory, miscellaneous theater programs, *Acteurs* (May 1982), and conversations with Odette Aslan, Simone Benmussa, Bernard Dort, and Geneviève Latour, all of whom I warmly thank. I saw Latour's "Petites scènes—grand théâtre" only after this book was in press.
19. Samuel Beckett, *Disjecta* (New York: Grove Press, 1983), 108.
20. Conversation with Roger Blin, December 5, 1981.
21. George Neveux, review of *Spartacus*, *Arts* (May 29–April 4, 1952).
22. Jacques Audiberti, *La Revue théâtrale* no. 7 (April–May 1948): 25.

CHAPTER 2

1. James Agate, *The Contemporary Theatre* (London: Harrap, 1946), 199.
2. David Pryce-Jones, *Paris in the Third Reich* (London: Collins, 1981), 13.
3. My description is drawn mainly from Patrick Marsh, "Le Théâtre à Paris sous l'occupation allemande," *Revue de la Société d'histoire du théâtre* 33, no. 3: 197–369.
4. Ibid., 369.
5. Colette, *Paris de ma fenêtre* (Paris: Le Livre de poche, 1976), 85.
6. Roland Penrose, *Picasso: His Life and Work* (London: Granada, 1981), 334–38.
7. I use the translation of Bernard Frechtman, *Desire Caught by the Tail* (New York: Rider, 1950).

8. Raymond Queneau, *Bâtons, chiffres, et lettres* (Paris: Gallimard, 1965), 229–37.

9. Michel Leiris, "Picasso and the Human Comedy or the Avatars of Big Foot," originally published in *Verve* nos. 29–30 (Paris, 1934) and reprinted in Leiris's *Brisées* (Paris: Mercure de France, 1966). The English translation by Stuart Gilbert is in Michel Leiris, *Picasso and the Human Comedy* (New York: Random House, n.d.), 20–21.

10. Herbert R. Lottman, *Albert Camus: A Biography* (London: Picador, 1981), 287.

11. My description of the performance blends accounts in a gracious letter to me from Michel Leiris; Simone de Beauvoir, *La Force de l'age* (Paris: Gallimard, 1960), 583–84; and Roland Penrose, foreword to his translation *Desire Caught by the Tail* (London: Calder and Boyars, 1970), 12.

12. Beauvoir, *La Force de l'age*, 583.

13. Pierre Cabanne, *Pablo Picasso: His Life and Times* (New York: Morrow, 1977), 531–32.

14. Gaby Sylvia quoted in *Figaro littéraire* (August 18–24, 1969), 18.

15. Jean-Paul Sartre, *Un Théâtre de situations* (Paris: Gallimard, 1973), 237–38; Frank Jellinek, trans., *Sartre on Theater* (New York: Random House, 1976), 198–99. My translation is closer to the French.

16. Beauvoir, *La Force de l'age*, 597 and passim.

17. Guy Dupré, *Histoire de rire et de pleurer* (Paris: Fayard, 1969).

18. Rhiannon Goldthorpe, *Sartre: Literature and Theory* (Bath: Cambridge University Press, 1984), argues that Sartre is subverting traditional dramatic form: "[*No Exit*] is a parody of a well-made play in exposition, revelation of character, péripétie, climax and dénouement" (90). Although she points out Sartre's misleading exposition, his turning point that does not turn, the anticlimactic climax, and the lack of denouement, these are manipulations of conventions rather than parody, which implies mockery. For exhaustive analysis of *No Exit*, see Ingrid Galster, *Le Théâtre de Jean-Paul Sartre devant ses premiers critiques* (Paris: Jean-Michel Place, 1986).

19. Eric Bentley, *The Playwright as Thinker* (New York: Harcourt Brace, 1946), 197. Like many other Americans, I first heard of Sartre's drama in the ever-challenging criticism of Eric Bentley, who is the theater father of us all—in the United States.

20. Sartre, *Un Théâtre de situations*, 239; *Sartre on Theater*, 200.

21. E. Martin Browne, *The Making of T. S. Eliot's Plays* (Cambridge: Cambridge University Press, 1970), 233.

22. Sartre, *Un Théâtre de situations*, 65; *Sartre on Theater*, 41 (but I use my translation).

23. Patrice Pavis, *Dictionnaire du théâtre* (Paris: Editions sociales, 1980), 298.

24. Sartre, *Un Théâtre de situations*, 239–40; *Sartre on Theater*, 201.

25. My description conflates materials in *R. Supp.* 1600 of the Fonds Rondel of the Bibliothèque de l'Arsenal.

26. André Castelot, review of *No Exit*, *La Gerbe* (June 8, 1944).

27. Alain Laubréaux, review of *No Exit*, *Je suis partout* (June 9, 1944).

28. Henri Lenormand, review of *No Exit*, *Panorama* (June 22, 1944).

29. Robert Brasillach, *Oeuvres complètes* (Paris: Club de l'Honnête Homme, 1963–1966), 12: 712–14; 719.

30. Larry Collins and Dominique Lapierre, *Is Paris Burning?* (New York: Simon & Schuster, 1965), 284.

31. William R. Tucker, *The Fascist Ego* (Berkeley and Los Angeles: University of California Press, 1975), 263.

32. Roger Céré, *La Deuxième Guerre mondiale, 1939–1945* (Paris: Presses universitaires de France, 1964), 497.

33. Quoted in Pol Vandromme, *Jean Anouilh: Un Auteur et ses personnages* (Paris: La Table Ronde, 1965), 115.

34. Herbert R. Lottman, *The Left Bank* (Boston: Houghton Mifflin, 1982), 227.

35. Quoted in Vandromme, 115.

36. Robert Brasillach, *La Reine de Césarée* (Paris: Plon, 1973), 184.

37. Jean-Paul Sartre, "Quand la police frappe les trois coups," *L'Observateur littéraire* (November 27, 1957), 15–16.

38. Lawrence Kitchen, "The Cage and the Scream," *The Listener* (January 24, 1963), 127; Anthony Swerling, *Strindberg's Impact in France, 1920–1960* (Cambridge: Trinity Lane Press, 1971); Vivian Mercier, *Beckett / Beckett* (New York: Oxford University Press, 1977); Thomas R. Whitaker, "Playing Hell," *The Yearbook of English Studies* 9 (1979); and Galster, *Le Théâtre de Jean-Paul Sartre devant ses premiers critiques.*

39. Boris Vian, *Manuel de St. Germain des Prés* (Paris: Chêne, 1974), 244.

40. Jacques Prevel, *En compagnie d'Antonin Artaud* (Paris: Flammarion, 1974), 90–91.

41. My biographical sketch of Artaud is a conflation of Thomas Maeder, *Antonin Artaud* (Paris: Plon, 1978); Paule Thévenin, *Cahiers Renaud-Barrault* (May 1958): 22–23, 42; and Odette Virmaux and Alain Virmaux, "La Séance du Vieux-Colombier," *Obliques* (December 1976): 10–11, 79–88.

42. Paul Gray, "Interview with Roger Blin," *Tulane Drama Review* (Summer 1967): 112.

43. Yves Benot, "Crier sans fin," *Europe* (November–December 1984): 19. My account of Artaud's performance draws on the sources directly quoted and noted and on recordings of Artaud; conversations with Roger Blin and Bernard Dort; accounts in *Magazine litté-*

raire (April 1984); Arthur Adamov, *L'Homme et l'enfant* (Paris: Galli-mard, 1968), 82; Sarane Alexandrian, in *Artaud Vivant*, ed. Alain Virmaux and Odette Virmaux (Paris: Nouvelles Editions Oswald, 1980), 111–12; Jean-Louis Brau, *Antonin Artaud* (Paris: La Table Ronde, 1971), 232–36; descriptions by Jean Follain and Louis Guil-laume in *La Tour de Feu* no. 112 (December 1971); Thomas Maeder, *Antonin Artaud*; Paule Thévenin, *Cahiers Renaud-Barrault*; Odette Vir-maux and Alain Virmaux, "La Séance du Vieux-Colombier."

44. Maurice Saillet, "Le Retour du Mômo," as reprinted in *Magazine littéraire* (April 1984): 49.

45. Susan Sontag, ed., *Antonin Artaud: Selected Writings* (New York: Farrar, Straus, & Giroux, 1976), 656.

46. André Dalmas, "Antonin Artaud," *France-Observateur* (De-cember 21, 1961), 3.

47. *Combat* article, as reprinted in *Magazine littéraire* (April 1984): 49.

48. Sarane Alexandrian, in *Artaud Vivant*, 112, 114.

49. Jacques Baratier, "Le Désordre à vingt ans," *L'Avant-Scène ci-néma* no. 67 (November 1967): 51.

50. Jacques Audiberti, "Artaud," *La Revue théâtrale* no. 7 (April–May 1948): 24.

51. André Gide, *Feuillets d'automne* (Paris: Le Livre de poche, 1971), 145–47.

52. Antonin Artaud, "Lettres à André Breton," *L'Ephémère* (Win-ter 1968): 20.

53. Jacques Robert, *Mon après-guerre* (Paris: Julliard, 1969), 289.

54. Jeanyves Guérin, *Le Théâtre d'Audiberti et le baroque* (Paris: Kleincksieck, 1972), 222–23. My remarks on Audiberti rely on this work as well as on André Reybaz, "Audiberti," *Têtes d'affiche* (Paris: La Table Ronde, 1975); and *Approches: Repertoire* no. 8 (Marseilles: Editions Jeanne Laffitte, 1980). I am grateful to Leonard Pronko for suggesting the translation of *Le Mal court* as *Evil Is Running Out*, preserving a pun.

55. *L'Avant-Scène* no. 137: 32.

56. *Approches: Repertoire* no. 8: 20.

57. Audiberti as quoted in *L'Avant-Scène* no. 137: 132; the critic is Jeanyves Guérin, ed., *Audiberti le trouble-fête* (Paris: Editions Jean-Michel Place, 1979), 153.

58. My account of the performance of *Evil Is Running Out* draws on *R. Supp.* 4874 at the Bibliothèque de l'Arsenal, memories of pro-ductions in 1963 and 1982, and a telephone conversation with Georges Vitaly on June 27, 1983.

59. Information on Henri Pichette draws on *R. Supp.* 2272 at Bib-liothèque de l'Arsenal and on Roger Shattuck, "A Poet's Progress: Henri Pichette," *The French Review* (December 1958): 111–19.

60. Henri Pichette, *Tombeau de Gérard Philipe* (1961; reprint Paris: Gallimard, 1979), 24.

61. *Combat* (November 1, 1947).

62. Georges Vitaly, "Les Epiphanies," in *Gérard Philipe*, ed. Anne Philipe and Claude Roy (Paris: Gallimard, 1960), 99, 100.

63. Jacques Audiberti, "Grands et petits théâtres," *La Revue théâtrale* no. 7 (April–May 1948): 23.

64. Thierry Maulnier, "La Bataille des 'Epiphanies,'" *Figaro littéraire* (July 10–16, 1948), 6.

65. Philipe and Roy, 105.

66. Adrienne Monnier, "Lecture des 'Epiphanies,'" *Mercure de France* (December 1948): 649–65.

67. My account of Vian draws on Geneviève Beauvarlet, *Boris Vian, 1920–1959: Portrait d'un bricoleur* (Paris: Hachette, 1985); Jacques Duchateau, *Boris Vian* (Paris: La Table Ronde, 1969); Françoise Renaudet, *Il était une fois Boris Vian* (Paris: Seghers, 1973); and Michel Rybalka, *Boris Vian* (Paris: Les Lettres Modernes, 1969). By letter and telephone, Professor Rybalka has patiently answered my questions about Sartre and Vian, for which I am most grateful.

68. Alain Vian, quoted in Jacques Baratier, "Le Désordre à vingt ans," 45.

69. Quotations from *The Knacker's ABC* come from Simon Watson Taylor's translation (New York: Grove Press, 1968).

70. Information on the performance of *The Knacker's ABC* draws on personal recollection, telephone conversations with Reybaz, and R. *Supp.* 2975 at the Bibliothèque de l'Arsenal.

71. Elsa Triolet, *Chroniques théâtrales* (Paris: Gallimard, 1981).

72. *Cahiers du Collège de 'Pataphysique* 17.

73. The genesis is well known, thanks to Ionesco's account in *Notes et contre-notes* (Paris: Gallimard, 1962). Other details were graciously offered to me by Messrs. Nicolas Bataille and Ionesco. A comparison of Ionesco's pat phrases and those of *L'Anglais sans peine* appears in *Cahiers du Collège de 'Pataphysique* 8–9 (1952): 87–89. See also Simone Benmussa, *Ionesco* (Paris: Seghers, 1966), and Richard N. Coe, *Eugene Ionesco* (New York: Grove Press, 1961).

74. Damien Pettigrew, "Interview with Ionesco," *Paris Magazine* (Autumn 1984): 26. For aspects of pattern, see Benmussa.

75. Coe, chap. 3.

76. Information on the performance of *The Bald Soprano* draws on personal memory, conversations with Bataille and Ionesco, Benmussa's book, and R. *Supp.* 4368 at the Bibliothèque de l'Arsenal.

77. Jean Pouillon, "La Cantatrice chauve," *Les Temps modernes* (1950): 172–73.

78. Martin Esslin, *The Theatre of the Absurd* (Harmondsworth: Penguin, 1980), 94.

79. Thomas Quinn Curtis, review of *The Bald Soprano, Paris Herald* (October 31, 1953).

80. Jacques Lemarchand, review of *The Bald Soprano, Figaro littéraire* (October 18–24, 1952).

81. Information on Adamov draws on conversations with Jacqueline Adamov and Bernard Dort, to whom I am most grateful; David Bradby's unpublished doctoral dissertation, "Arthur Adamov," Glasgow University, 1971, which he generously placed at my disposal; René Gaudy, *Arthur Adamov* (Paris: Stock, 1971); John McCann, *The Theater of Arthur Adamov* (Chapel Hill: North Carolina Studies in the Romance Languages and Literatures, 1975); Pierre Mélèse, *Adamov* (Paris: Seghers, 1973); and John H. Reilly, *Arthur Adamov* (New York: Twayne, 1974).

82. Arthur Adamov, *L'Homme et l'enfant* (Paris: Gallimard, 1968), 33.

83. Beauvoir, *La Force de l'age*, 488.

84. Bernard Dort, "Sur la singularité de la dramaturgie d'Adamov," in *Lectures d'Adamov*, ed. Robert Abirached, Ernstpeter Ruhe, and Richard Schwaderer (Paris: Jean-Michel Place, 1983), 34.

85. Jacques Lemarchand, *Figaro littéraire* (March 23–29, 1970), 32.

86. Adamov, *L'Homme et l'enfant*, 97.

87. Arthur Adamov, quoted in Jean Vilar, "Avec 'L'Invasion' Adamov nous offre un 'Helzapoppin' tragique," *Combat* (November 15, 1950).

88. Maurice Blanchot, "Le Destin de l'oeuvre," *L'Observateur* (August 17, 1950).

89. Jean-Francis Reille, *Arts* (November 24–30, 1950).

90. Mélèse, 29.

91. For Camus's reaction see Adamov, *L'Homme et l'enfant*, 99; for the Communist's, Gaudy, 77; for Blin's, *La Parodie, L'Invasion* (Paris: Charlot, 1950), 18.

92. Information on the performance comes mainly from a telephone conversation with Jacques Noël, and from dim memories.

93. Roger Blin, interviewed by Elizabeth Auclaire, who graciously made the interview available to me.

94. Reille review of *Maneuver, Arts* (November 24–30, 1950).

95. Eugene Ionesco, *Figaro littéraire* (March 23–29, 1970), 32.

96. Arthur Adamov, *Strindberg* (Paris: L'Arche, 1955), 69.

97. Roland Barthes, *Mythologies* (Paris: Seuil, 1957), 100–101.

98. Arthur Adamov, *L' Heure nouvelle*, first issue (of two).

99. René Allio, quoted in Gaudy, 140.

100. Information on Vauthier draws on Robert Abirached, *Jean Vauthier* (Paris: Seghers, 1973), and André Reybaz, *Têtes d'affiche* (Paris: La Table Ronde, 1975).

101. "Quand l'auteur présente," *Combat* (January 9, 1952).

102. Information on the first production of *Captain Bada* draws on *R. Supp.* 3881 at the Bibliothèque de l'Arsenal, on Reybaz's book, and on a telephone conversation with Reybaz on June 30, 1983.

103. Advance notice of *Captain Bada* in *Opéra* (January 8, 1952).

104. Reybaz, 113.

105. Gilles Sandier, *Théâtre et combat* (Paris: Stock, 1970), 56.

106. Ibid., 53.

107. Antonin Artaud, *The Theater and Its Double* (New York: Grove Press, 1958), 106.

108. Eugene Ionesco, quoted in *Figaro* (April 24, 1952).

109. Jean Tardieu, quoted in *Figaro* (April 24, 1952).

110. Sylvain Dhomme, in program for *The Chairs* at the Studio des Champs-Elysées, 1956. Other information about the first production of *The Chairs* draws on *R. Supp.* 4233 at the Bibliothèque de l'Arsenal, personal recollection, conversations with Ionesco, and telephone conversations with Jacques Noël.

111. Ionesco, *Notes et contre-notes* (Paris: Gallimard, 1962), 167; *Notes and Counter-Notes* (New York: Grove Press, 1964), 195–96.

112. Dhomme, quoted in Raymond Laubréaux, ed., *Ionesco* (Paris: Garnier, 1973), 31.

113. *Arts* (May 1–7, 1952).

114. Jacques Lemarchand, *Figaro littéraire* (May 3–10, 1952); reprinted in *Cahier des Saisons* no. 15 (Winter 1959).

115. Ripostes to Lemarchand's review by Dhomme and others were published in *Arts* (May 17–24, 1952).

116. Information on the Studio performance comes from *R. Supp.* 4845 at the Bibliothèque de l'Arsenal.

117. Bernard Dort, review of *The Chairs*, in *France-Observateur* (February 22, 1956).

118. Jacques Noël, quoted in Benmussa, 133.

119. Jacques Mauclair, quoted in André De Baecque, *Le Théâtre d'aujourd'hui* (Paris: Seghers, 1964), 162.

120. Jean Anouilh, "Du chapitre des chaises," *Figaro* (April 23, 1956), 1.

121. Leonard Pronko, *Avant-Garde* (Berkeley and Los Angeles: University of California Press, 1962), 60.

122. Jacques Lemarchand, *Figaro littéraire* (July 8–14, 1965).

123. Sandier, 36.

Chapter 3

1. Guy Dumur, quoted in Gilles Quéant, ed., *Encyclopédie du théâtre contemporain* (Paris: Olivier Perrin, 1959), 2: 189.

2. Jacques Dubois, "Beckett and Ionesco: The Tragic Awareness of Pascal and the Ironic Awareness of Flaubert," *Modern Drama* (December 1966): 283–91.

3. Kenneth Tynan, *A View of the English Stage* (London: Methuen, 1984), 42.

4. Jean-Paul Sartre, *Un Théâtre de situations* (Paris: Gallimard, 1973), 75, 128; Frank Jellinek, trans., *Sartre on Theater* (New York: Random House, 1976), 51, 99–100.

5. Gérard Durozoi, *Artaud: L'Aliénation et la folie* (Paris: Larousse, 1972), 208, finds Artaud's influence in Beckett's fiction rather than in his "seductive" drama; Ludovic Janvier, *Pour Samuel Beckett* (Paris: Les Editions de Minuit, 1966), 266–67; Franco Tonelli, "Godot ou le temps de la cruauté," *L'Esthétique de la cruauté* (Paris: Nizet, 1972); and Alain Virmaux, *Antonin Artaud et le théâtre* (Paris: Seghers, 1970), 194–95.

6. Bert States, *The Shape of Paradox* (Berkeley and Los Angeles: University of California Press, 1978), 7.

7. Dougald McMillan, "'Eleuthéria': Beckett's Unpublished Discourse on Method," in press.

8. Israel Shenker, "Moody Man of Letters," *New York Times* (May 6, 1956), sec. 2, p. 3.

9. On the composition of *Godot* I supplement my own notes with the exemplary scholarship of Colin Duckworth in the introduction to his edition of *En attendant Godot* (London: George G. Harrap & Co., 1966), xlv.

10. Quoted in Peter Lennon, "Opening Up," *The Listener* (March 28, 1985), 33.

11. Duckworth, lxvii.

12. Ibid., lx.

13. States, 71.

14. Biographical information on Roger Blin comes from Odette Aslan, *Roger Blin and Twentieth-Century Dramatists* (Cambridge University Press), in press, as well as from my conversations with Beckett and Blin.

15. Quoted in Charles-Henri Fevrod, "Roger Blin," *Le Théâtre* (Paris: Le Livre de poche, 1976), 72.

16. Roger Blin, "Artaud l'insoumis," *Nouvelles littéraires* (March 31, 1977), 4.

17. Antonin Artaud, "Un mot à propos de quelque chose," *Théâtre en Europe* (April 1984): 17.

18. Quoted in Roger Blin, "Trente-trois ans après," *Le Nouvel Observateur* (September 26, 1981), 100.

19. Samuel Beckett, letter to Roger Blin, displayed at the Roger Blin Memorial Exhibit at the Odéon, June 12, 1984.

20. Quoted in *Le Nouvel Observateur* (September 26, 1981). My account of the first production of *En attendant Godot* draws on memory; on conversations with Beckett, Blin, and Jean Martin; and on Deirdre Bair, *Samuel Beckett* (New York: Harcourt Brace Jovanovich, 1978), 381–90, whom I sometimes correct.

21. Bernard Poirot-Delpech, review of *Waiting for Godot, Le Monde* (March 18, 1970).

22. Quoted in Cathérine Valogne, "Roger Blin et l'humilité du metteur en scène," *Arts* (February 24, 1950), 7.

23. Quoted in Fevrod, 73. Blin's reminiscence is in Roger Blin, "Conversations avec Lynda Peskine," *Revue d'Esthétique* (Toulouse: Editions Privat, 1986), 163.

24. Marcel Frère, "En attendant Godot," *Combat* (January 1, 1953).

25. Marc Beigbeder, review of *Waiting for Godot, La Revue théâtrale* 22 (January 5, 1953).

26. G. Joly, review of *Godot, L'Aurore* (January 6, 1953).

27. Max Favalelli, review of *Godot, Paris Press* (January 6, 1953).

28. Sylvain Zegel, review of *Godot, Libération* (January 7, 1953).

29. Guy Dumur, review of *Godot, Combat* (January 12, 1953).

30. Luc Estang, *La Croix* (January 9, 1953).

31. J.-B. Jeener, review of *Godot, Figaro* (January 10–11, 1953), 6.

32. Robert Kemp, review of *Godot, Le Monde* (January 14, 1953).

33. Thomas Quinn Curtis, review of *Godot, Paris Herald* (February 13, 1953).

34. Gabriel Marcel, review of *Godot, Nouvelles littéraires* (January 15, 1953).

35. Renée Saurel, review of *Godot, Les Lettres françaises* (January 15, 1953), 6.

36. Claude Jamet, review of *Godot, France réelle* (January 23, 1953).

37. Jacques Audiberti, review of *Godot, Arts* (January 16–22, 1953).

38. Jacques Lemarchand, review of *Godot, Figaro littéraire* (January 17, 1953), 10.

39. *Le Monde* (February 1, 1953).

40. *Arts* (February 27–March 5, 1953), 1.

41. Samuel Beckett, letter, quoted in Carlton Lake, ed., *No Symbols Where None Intended* (Austin, Tex.: Humanities Research Center, 1984), 66.

42. Alain Robbe-Grillet, "Samuel Beckett, Auteur Dramatique," *Critique* (February 1953), translated by Richard Howard in *For a New Novel* (New York: Grove Press, 1965), 120–21.

43. Guenther Anders, "Sein ohne Zeit," *Neue Schweizer Rundschau* (January 1954). I quote from Martin Esslin's translation in *Samuel*

Beckett, ed. Martin Esslin (Englewood Cliffs: Prentice-Hall, 1965), 145, 151.

44. *Arts* (July 28–August 3, 1954).

45. Alan Schneider, "Waiting for Beckett," *Chelsea Review* (September 1958).

46. Martin Esslin, *The Theatre of the Absurd* (Harmondsworth: Penguin, 1980), 10; Sidney Homan, *Beckett's Theaters* (Lewisburg, Pa.: Bucknell University Press, 1984), passim.

47. Hersh Zeifman, "The Alterable Whey of Words: The Texts of *Waiting for Godot*," *Educational Theatre Journal* (March 1977).

48. Ruby Cohn, *Just Play* (Princeton, N.J.: Princeton University Press, 1980), 256–66.

49. Suzanne Aron, "Balzac a-t-il inspiré *En attendant Godot?*" *Figaro littéraire* (September 17, 1955), 12.

50. Hugh Kenner, *Samuel Beckett* (Berkeley and Los Angeles: University of California Press, 1961), 124.

51. Duckworth, introduction to *En attendant Godot*, xlvi.

52. Ibid., xlvi–lxxv. *Mercier and Camier* has been adapted for the stage by the Mabou Mines Company, with Fred Neumann directing, as well as by theater companies in West Berlin, Lyon, Créteil, and Jerusalem.

53. The works on *Godot* include Frederick Busi, *The Transformations of Godot* (Lexington: University of Kentucky Press, 1980); Ramona Cormier and Janis L. Pallister, *Waiting for Death: The Philosophical Significance of Beckett's "En attendant Godot"* (University, Ala.: The University of Alabama Press, 1979); Niklaus Gessner, *Die Unzulänglichkeit der Sprache* (Zurich: Juris-Verlag 1957), draws most of his examples from *Godot*; and States, *The Shape of Paradox*.

54. I have not examined this material in the Berlin Brecht Archive. My description draws on Werner Hecht, *Aufsätze über Brecht* (Berlin: Henschelverlag, 1970), 118–25; Hans Mayer, "Brecht, Beckett, und ein Hund," *Theater Heute* (June 6, 1972), 25–27; Kathe Rulicke-Weiler, *Die Dramaturgie Brechts* (Berlin: Henschelverlag, 1966), 155–56; and Clas Zilliacus, "Three Times Godot: Beckett, Brecht, Bulatovic," *Comparative Drama* (Fall 1970): 3–17, in spite of his errors on the French theater scene.

55. Zilliacus, 8.

56. I have read the Bulatovic play only in the French edition, which mercifully does not include his preface; I quote from Zilliacus, 10.

57. Miodrag Bulatovic, *Il est arrivé* (Paris: Seuil, 1967).

58. Jean Anouilh, *L'Hurluberlu* (Paris: La Table Ronde, 1959), 117.

59. Kenneth Tynan, "Slamm's Last Knock," *The Observer* (November 2, 1958).

60. Jules Feiffer, *Knock Knock* (New York: Hill & Wang, 1976).

61. Alfred Gingold, "Miasma Vice," *The Nation* (November 1985): 46.

62. Gessner, *Die Unzulänglichkeit der Sprache*. I translate Gessner's categories rather freely.

63. Samuel Beckett, *L'Avant-Scène* no. 313: 8.

64. Edith Kern, "Beckett and the Spirit of Commedia dell'Arte," *Modern Drama* (December 1966).

65. "Tom Stoppard," *Translatlantic Review* (Summer 1968): 20. Thomas R. Whitaker, "Wham, Bam, Thank You Sam," in *Beckett at Eighty / Beckett in Context*, ed. Enoch Brater (New York: Oxford University Press, 1986).

66. Tom Stoppard, interview by Kenneth Tynan, "Withdrawing with Style from Chaos," *The New Yorker* (December 19, 1977), 57.

67. Ruby Cohn, "Tom Stoppard: Light Drama and Dirges in Marriage," in *Contemporary English Drama*, ed. C. W. E. Bigsby (Suffolk: Edward Arnold, 1981), 114; and Thomas Whitaker, *Tom Stoppard* (New York: Grove Press, 1981).

68. Hugh Kenner, *A Reader's Guide to Samuel Beckett* (New York: Farrar, Straus & Giroux, 1973), 193.

69. I owe some aspects of this contrast to an unpublished article by Carol Flint.

70. T. S. Eliot, interview in the *Glasgow Herald*, August 27, 1949, as quoted in E. Martin Browne, *The Making of T. S. Eliot's Plays* (Cambridge: Cambridge University Press, 1970), 236.

71. Ethan Mordden, *The American Theatre* (New York: Oxford University Press, 1981), 232.

Chronology of Performances
(with publication data)

1944 (March 19)   *Le Désir attrapé par la queue*
Pablo Picasso. *Le Désir attrapé par la queue*.
Paris: Gallimard, 1945.
————. *Desire Caught by the Tail*. Translated
by Bernard Frechtman. New York: Rider,
1950.
————. *Desire Caught by the Tail*. Translated
by Sir Roland Penrose. London: Calder and
Boyars, 1970.

(May 27?)   *Huis clos*
Jean-Paul Sartre. *Huis clos*. In *Théâtre*. Paris:
Gallimard, 1947.
————. *No Exit*. Translated by Stuart Gilbert.
New York: Random House, 1947.

1947 (January 13)   *Tête-à-tête*
Antonin Artaud. *Tête-à-tête*. Some of the
poems from this performance have been
published and translated.

(June 25)   *Le Mal court*
Jacques Audiberti. *Le Mal court*. In *Théâtre I*.
Paris: Gallimard, 1948.

(December 3)   *Les Epiphanies*
Henri Pichette. *Les Epiphanies*. Paris: Gallimard, 1969.

1950 (April 11)   *L'Equarrissage pour tous*
Boris Vian. *L'Equarrissage pour tous*. In *Théâtre
I*. Paris: Jean-Jacques Pauvert, 1965.
————. *The Knacker's ABC*. Translated by Si-
mon Watson Taylor. New York: Grove
Press, 1969.

———. *Knackery for All*. Translated by Marc Estrin. In *Plays for a New Theater*. New York: New Directions, 1966.

(May 11?)   *La Cantatrice chauve*

Eugene Ionesco. *La Cantatrice chauve*. In *Théâtre I*. Paris: Gallimard, 1954.
———. *The Bald Soprano*. Translated by Donald M. Allen. New York: Grove Press, 1958.

(November 11)   *La Grande et la petite manoeuvre*

Arthur Adamov. *La Grande et la petite manoeuvre*. In *Théâtre I*. Paris: Gallimard, 1953.

(November 14)   *L'Invasion*

Arthur Adamov. *L'Invasion*. In *Théâtre I*. Paris: Gallimard, 1953.

1952 (January 10)   *Capitaine Bada*

Jean Vauthier. *Capitaine Bada*. Paris: L'Arche, 1953.

(April 22)   *Les Chaises*

Eugene Ionesco. *Les Chaises*. In *Théâtre I*. Paris: Gallimard, 1954.
———. *The Chairs*. Translated by Donald M. Allen. New York: Grove Press, 1958.

1953 (January 5)   *En attendant Godot*

Samuel Beckett. *En attendant Godot*. Paris: Les Editions de Minuit, 1952.
———. *Waiting for Godot*. Translated by Samuel Beckett. New York: Grove Press, 1954.

Original French of
Quotations from the Plays

Page	Original Text
29	Je ne vois plus la fin de cet hiver sans qu'une plus grande disette nous accueille.
29	Je m'en vais au bistrot du coin lui arracher de mes griffes le peu de couleur chocolat qui rôde encore dans le noir de son café.
29–30	. . . tes fesses un plat de cassoulet, et tes bras une soupe d'ailerons de requins, et ton . . . et ton nid d'hirondelles encore le feu d'une soupe aux nids d'hirondelles.
30	Ses mains sont de transparentes glaces aux pêches et aux pistaches. Les huîtres de ses yeux renferment les jardins suspendus bouche ouverte aux paroles de ses regards et la couleur d'aioli qui l'encercle.
30	Les tripes que traîne Pégase après la course dessinent son portrait sur la blancheur et la dureté du marbre brillant de sa douleur.
30	Les demoiselles d'Avignon ont déjà trente-trois longues années de rente.
31	Le Gros Pied la prend dans ses bras et ils tombent par terre.
31	Allumons toutes les lanternes. Lançons de toutes nos forces les vols de colombes contre les balles et fermons à double tour les maisons démolies par les bombes.
57	Je parle le totem muré/ car le totem mural est tel/ que les formations visqueuses/ de l'être/ ne peuvent plus l'enfourcher de près.

195

58   Il est ce trou sans cadre/ que la vie voulut encadrer./ Parce qu'il n'est pas un trou/ mais un nez/ qui sut toujours trop bien renifler/ le vent de l'apocalyptique/ tête/ qu'on pompe sur son cu serré,/ et que le cu d'Artaud est bon/ pour les souteneurs en miserere./ Et toi aussi tu as la gencive,/ la gencive droite enterrée/ dieu,/ toi aussi ta gencive est froide/ depuis infiniment d'années/ que tu m'envoyas ton cu inné/ pour voir si j'allais être né/ à la fin/ depuis le temps que tu m'espérais/ en raclant/mon ventre d'absent.

59   C'est par la barbaque,/ la sale barbaque/ que l'on exprime/ le,/ qu'on ne sait pas/ que/ se placer hors/ pour être sans. . . .

59   Je me mets à votre place, et je vois bien que ce que je vous dis n'est pas intéressant du tout. C'est encore du théâtre. Comment faire pour être vraiment sincère.

68   Mais vous, Alarica, vous, chair de ma vie, pensée de ma chair, vous que je sais, vous que je sens qui m'écoutez de toutes vos bouches, qui me saisissez de toutes vos boucles, vous dont le coeur bondit d'amour et de douleur, de quel oeil oserez-vous me regarder quand, aujourd'hui même, ce soir, non loin du fleuve, devant la cathédrale, nous nous rencontrerons dans la présence de nos ministres et de nos tabellions?

68   La faute, la seule faute eût été que Votre Majesté aventurât le lustre de tant de combats et de grands hommes, tout l'Occident romain, les iris et la croix, dans une alliance avec une princesse, moi, dont le père, il n'y a pas si longtemps, donnait des leçons de salade.

68   Mais puisque le roi n'a pas pu, et ses raisons ne sont ni louches ni mesquines, puisqu'il n'a pas pu gravir avec moi toutes les marches de l'autel, je juge équitable de t'avoir donné la joie de mon corps, à toi qui, le premier, non sans courage, vins à moi pour me prendre aux lèvres.

76   C'est le livre du monde, le vent tourne la page, voici le fragment du coeur singulier, voici les pluriels dans leur unissons, c'est l'espèce par tous les temps du verbe et le mise à jour sous l'oeil immémorial.

84   Ils commencent à nous courir avec leur débarque-
      ment. . . . tous ces crétins d'enfants qui se battent dans
      tous les coins au lieu d'apprendre à équarrir proprement.

104   Car, enfin, qu'est-ce qui nous prouve que le soi-disant
      négligences, les oublis, les omissions, les erreurs, ne sont
      pas dus à une intention inconnue, à un scruple . . . [*sic*]
      Ou même à un peur?

105   Je n'ai que faire des souvenirs, des à-peu-près, et des
      peut-être. Il me faut le mot juste.

105–6 Ce qu'il me faut, ce n'est pas le sens des mots, c'est leur
      volume et leur corps mouvant. (*Pause.*) Je ne chercherai
      plus rien. (*Pause.*) J'attendrai dans le silence, immobile.

117–18 De l'extrême mobilité des attitudes mentales dépend l'ex-
      tériorisation bouffonne consciente et inconsciente du per-
      sonnage.

118   Et cette crapuleuse grâce a de beaux membres très peu
      bourgeois. Car elle est saine comme une fille des champs.
      Allez, ouste! c'est ferme comme du jambonneau—allez,
      allez! c'est plein, c'est rebondi. C'est du muscle, c'est bien
      foutu. Allez! tonnerre! décampez!

Index

Adamov, Arthur: and Artaud, 52, 54, 60, 63, 99; *Confession*, 100, 101; *Invasion*, 103–7, 113, 154; *The Great and the Small Maneuver*, 107–12, 113, 114; *Parody*, 90, 100, 108, 113, 149, 155; other works, 44–45, 101, 112, 129; mentioned, 22, 23, 44, 99, 101, 115, 128, 130, 132–35

Agate, James, 23

Albee, Edward, 22–23, 175

Aldebert, Max, 20

Alexandrian, Sarane, 60

Alfred Jarry, Théâtre, 12, 26, 39

Allio, René, 114, 122

Alter, André, 128

Anders, Günther, 159–60

Anouilh, Jean: *Antigone*, 25, 46, 48, 70; and Brasillach, 47–48; *Chairs*, 130–31; *Waiting for Godot*, 158, 169, 171; mentioned, 25, 69, 134

Antoine, André, 1, 6–7, 8, 9

Apollinaire, Guillaume, 35, 86

Aristophanes, 9, 173, 174

Aristotle, 174

Aron, Suzanne, 163

Artaud, Antonin: *Artaud-le-Mômo*, 55, 57–59, 62; and Audiberti, 60–61, 63–64; and Beckett, 135, 137–38, 156, 161, 163; *Tête-à-tête*, 51–63; *Theater and Its Double*, 12, 51, 54, 63–64, 122–23, 138; mentioned, 11–12, 21, 27, 34, 38, 64, 66, 72, 99, 104, 112

Arts, 107, 128, 157, 158, 160

Atelier, 9, 10

Atlan, Jean, 128

Auber, Jean, 33

Audiberti, Jacques: and Artaud, 60–61, 63–64; *Evil Is Running Out*, 66–71; other works, 66, 69, 85; mentioned, 18, 22, 23, 76, 77, 117, 121–22, 128, 133, 157, 169

Autant-Lara, Claude, 92, 96

Autrusseau, Jacqueline, 100

Babylone, Théâtre de, 18–21, 161

Badel, Annet, 37–39, 44, 45, 47, 51, 53

Balachova, Tanya, 10, 13, 39, 43, 44

Balzac, Honoré de, 15, 26, 104, 163

Barba, Eugenio, 8

Barbezat, Marc, 37

Barbezat, Olga, 37

Barrault, Jean-Louis, 6, 10, 13, 27, 33, 46–47, 52, 54, 84, 148, 155

Barrault, Max, 19

Barrois, Odette, 98

Barsacq, André, 14

Barthes, Roland, 113

Bataille, Georges, 33, 99

Bataille, Nicolas: *Bald Soprano*, 90–93, 98, 126; mentioned, 13, 18, 125, 132

Baty, Gaston, 9, 10–11, 12, 14, 24

Baudelaire, Charles, 55, 164

Beauvoir, Simone de, 33–36, 37, 45

Beck, Julian, 17

Beckett, Samuel: *Endgame*, 14, 144, 166, 167, 173; other works, 1, 45, 50, 78, 138, 147, 166–69; *Waiting for Godot*, Beckett's staging of, 162–63; and the Bible, 146, 177; and the classics, 146; derivatives, 169–73; and dramatic traditions, 174–77; first reviews, 156–60; and philosophy, 147;

Compositor:	Wilsted & Taylor
Text:	10/12 Palatino
Display:	Palatino
Printer:	Murray Printing Co.
Binder:	Murray Printing Co.